YOUR MONEY OR YOUR LIFE

Do you want to get your finances on track? Or are you lost in the fiscal maze of baffling and conflicting offers on plastic, policies and pensions? Let Alvin Hall, TV's leading money guru, put you in control of your purse strings. Whether you're daunted by debts, stumped by savings strategies, making plans or moving house, Alvin will help you take charge—for good. He'll show you how to:

- Recognise your personal spending style—and manage it
- Find (practically) painless ways to save money and stick to them
- Understand the real cost of debt and how interest on credit and storecard accounts can be minimised
- Unravel mortgage mysteries and pick the package that's your best option
- Plan your pension and look forward to a rewarding retirement
- Evaluate insurance offers and establish what you really need

Alvin turns complex financial theory into accessible, practical advice. Follow his common-sense solutions today and you'll afford the life you'll love tomorrow.

YOUR MONEY OR YOUR LIFE

A PRACTICAL GUIDE TO SOLVING YOUR
FINANCIAL PROBLEMS AND AFFORDING
A LIFE YOU'LL LOVE

Alvin Hall

with Karl Weber

First published 2002
by
Hodder and Stoughton
This Large Print edition published 2004
by
BBC Audiobooks Ltd
by arrangement with
Transworld Publishers Limited

ISBN 0 7540 5664 3

British Library Cataloguing in Publication Data available

Printed and bound in Great Britain by
Antony Rowe Ltd., Chippenham, Wiltshire

To
Roger Bakeman,
Atlanta, Georgia

Acknowledgements

From my first book for John Wiley & Sons (which he commissioned) to this book (which he helped write), Karl Weber has been encouraging, insightful, and stalwart. As my former editor, former agent, and now my co-author, Karl has always managed me well, helping to keep my compulsive, perfectionist tendencies in check without sacrificing the quality of work. This was a particularly important skill given the relatively short period of time we had to complete this book. As my friend, Karl always tells me the truth, with a gentle smile and grace that I admire. This book is as much a symbol of our friendship as it is a manifestation of our mutual respect for and appreciation of our complementary talents.

Rowena Webb and Emma Heyworth-Dunn, my editors at Hodder, deserve special thanks for giving me frank and useful comments about the original idea and the manuscript. Emma especially must be praised for her patient, diligent, and professional handling of all the little details that had to be pulled together to get this book published on time.

Thanks to Jonathan Drori for recommending Claire Harcup to read and comment on the final manuscript. Claire's comments, insightful questions, and sensitivity to the reader's concerns helped us in refining the manuscript and particularly in making the worksheets clear and useful.

Thanks to Robert McKenzie for his research and comments. Thanks to Paul Killik, Matthew Orr, and Graham Neale of Killik and Co., for the time they gave in responding to questions and for making their research reports, customer account forms, and other information available for use in this book.

Ken Swezey, my lawyer, and Vicki McIvor, my agent, have each brought to my career and life the same attributes as Karl. I cherish their ability to see my career objectively, and at the same time be sensitive to me as a person. I know it is rare to have such good relationships and equally rare to have such a good team.

Finally, thanks to the production team for the television series *Your Money or Your Life* and especially to all of the people who have shared their personal money stories on the programmes. Talking through their financial problems, crunching the numbers, creating the plans, and observing what helps individuals to succeed or fail at getting their personal finances on track, has taught me a great deal about how human nature and money issues connect. That deeper understanding has informed the guidance, the worksheets, and the insights contained in this book.

Alvin Hall
25 January 2002
London

Contents

INTRODUCTION

Magical thinking about money

'I don't know where my money goes!' Said in exasperation. Said in naïve wonderment. Said in resignation. Said in proud acceptance. It's the most frequent statement I hear when people are interviewed for my TV series *Your Money or Your Life*. The individuals and families I counsel speak as if their hands are sieves through which money quickly and uncontrollably drains. Perhaps that's what they want to believe.

Money is magical in many people's minds. And, as a result, they believe that there's no need to apply common sense and control to money. 'Why should I have to worry about money?'—the second most frequent statement made on my show—embodies the belief that one should somehow be exempt from all thinking and decision-making about money. Instead of having to make hard choices, I should simply be able to get anything and everything I want—as if by waving a wand.

But deep inside, we all know that this is a fantasy. For nearly all of us, money is limited, and the hard choices about how to use and preserve it can't be evaded for ever. However, this needn't prevent anyone from creating and enjoying a comfortable, satisfying, and economically sound life.

1

You can do it yourself

This book is designed to help you take control of your finances and make the money you have work best for you, now and in the future. Think of it as a DIY guide for your money: a step-by-step, user-friendly, and practical guide to handling your finances correctly.

Of course, there's more than one way of managing your money wisely. Throughout this book, various methods are discussed, and you're encouraged to use the information presented as a basis for developing strategies that are comfortable for *you*. In short, I want to help you learn how to help yourself.

Many years ago, when I was a student at Bowdoin College in Brunswick, Maine, I met a wonderful and wise woman named Bitsa Wood. A strong, nurturing, earth-mother type, Bitsa once said to me, 'The greatest gift parents can give their children is the ability to cope with life—to think through problems and solve them on their own. This is a gift of strength that stays with them a lifetime.' I have kept Bitsa's words in mind as I developed the strategies in this book.

Many of the ideas I'll present grew out of the questions people ask me most frequently on my TV series, in letters, and during the question-and-answer periods that follow my speeches. Others came from the step-plans that we develop for people on the programme. But the majority come from my common sense, my experiences and those of my friends, and the information I've gathered as I've travelled around the UK and the US, talking to people in many different economic situations.

Regardless of the source, I have tried to make all the information as clear and accessible as possible. You don't have to understand economics or advanced maths to take control of your personal finances. You need only a few basic facts and some uncomplicated procedures that anyone can easily master. If many of the ideas I'll present seem unfamiliar or original, that may be simply because no one has ever mentioned them to you before—or because you were too wilful to listen when they did.

Experience, not genetics

'Have you *always* been frugal with your money?' Almost every interviewer asks me this question. And when I answer 'No,' they seem surprised. Many people want to believe that we are all fundamentally unchangeable; that it's basically impossible to change and improve. That's why people make comments like, 'I've never had a head for finances,' 'I take after my parents—they were bad with money and so am I,' or 'We never learned about savings or investing in school.' All these statements may be true, but the underlying mindset is wrong. There's no need to remain trapped in our limitations, endlessly repeating the mistakes and frustrations of the past. Life is about maturing, growing, and learning, and this applies as much to your personal finances as to any other area of life.

Everything I've said here applies to me—in spades. It's no secret that I've made lots of mistakes about money. Not so long ago, I had too many credit cards and I was spending thoughtlessly, buying too many clothes and dishes, pictures and books, theatre tickets and dinners out. I was sinking deeper and deeper into debt, missing payments and defaulting on loans. I remember what it was like to lie awake at night wondering how I was going to pay my rent.

Eventually, I vowed that I would never get myself into this situation again. I then analysed, with brutal frankness, what I'd done wrong. I had to begin by recognising that the problem was me, not the proverbial 'they' on whom it's so easy and tempting to blame our problems.

The key was gaining control of myself and my financial demons. Easy? No way. Let me tell you, it will *always* be a struggle. I still have to check myself when I see the aphrodisiac-like word 'sale' posted in the window of a shop I love, calling to me as the sirens called to Odysseus. And, like the Greek hero, I have to use all my strength to resist temptation and pass by.

The first exercise in this book—keeping a financial diary—is designed to help you understand your own financial demons. Once you recognise the situations and emotions that cause you to overspend, you can avoid them or prepare to handle them when you know they are coming on.

I now feel I know my own demons and what unleashes them. Recently, while filming a TV programme in Chester, I caught a glimpse of a stunning wristwatch in the window at Boodles and Dunthorpe, a shop that contains beautiful and unusual items. I felt as though an emotional button had been pushed—hard! During a break in filming, I decided to visit the shop, 'just to look', I told myself.

As I walked in the door, I felt myself weakening. The salesman showed me a distinctive pair of cufflinks made only for Boodles. Another button had been pushed! I felt like John Hurt in the movie *Alien*, when after a fierce struggle the monster bursts out of his abdomen. Gut desire—no, all-out material lust—was warring with my financial reason. Worst of all, the salesman was really very nice and attentive. One more button pressed!

Seconds away from pulling out my credit card, I caught myself just in time. 'I need to think about it,' I said, and I fled the shop. Several hours later, I remembered that I already had a pair of cufflinks very similar to those in the shop. My lust evaporated in the cool light of reason. I'd triumphed over my worst tendencies again. And I was pleased with myself for being strong and not wrecking my monthly budget.

I know that if I can learn how to recognise, understand, and control my financial hot buttons, so can you.

Master the basics

When you first get your hands on a little money, knowledge of how to use that money wisely doesn't automatically follow. We've all heard about sports or film or pop music stars who made fortunes and then quickly squandered them. It takes knowledge and a bit of work to manage money intelligently. Ask any rich person who has succeeded in holding on to his or her wealth.

You may want to protest, 'But the rich have professionals to advise them.' True; but anyone who turns his money over to an adviser without controls is likely to find it gone in a shockingly short time. History shows that people who don't know how money works don't manage to hold on to it for very long. This book will help you learn what you need to know through a series of hands-on activities. Make no mistake, these exercises will benefit you only if you really work through them yourself. Put pencil to paper and develop your own financial plan, following the guidance I'll provide in these pages. I promise that you'll emerge a wiser person—and potentially a much richer one as well.

Give yourself choices

Perhaps the most tragic thing about bad money management is this: *it takes away your choices in life*.

Here is a sad—and all too typical—example. I recently interviewed a young woman who had just given birth to a beautiful baby daughter. Understandably, she wanted to stay home with her child. But before the baby was born, straight through the pregnancy, she and her husband had continued to manage their finances as if they were two single people with no responsibilities. They enjoyed deluxe holidays, lived very nicely (although not quite as nicely as they wished), racked up a growing pile of credit card debts, and saved not a penny.

Even after the baby was born, this young mother did not want to reduce her spending. 'I don't think it's right for me to have to do that,' she told me defiantly. The result? Mother had no choice but to keep working. By spending to the maximum of the family income (and beyond), she had destroyed the possibility that she could stay at home and raise her own daughter. She was miserable, but of course it was all her own doing.

Please don't let a similar misfortune happen to you. By making a few small sacrifices today, by saving and investing a certain percentage of your salary, you can guarantee that tomorrow you'll be able to make the choices that will matter the most to you. Few people are wealthy enough to afford everything they want. This book will help you to think about your priorities for the present and the future and create a plan that will let you achieve them.

On my television programme I meet with people who've lost their financial way. In many cases, their future choices have become severely limited as a result. Sometimes it's too late to do much; other times I'm able to help them re-open doors that appeared to be closed for ever.

My fondest dream would be for this book to eliminate the need for shows like *Your Money or Your Life*. That may be overly optimistic. But I hope it will at least help you get a handle on your own financial demons, so that the troubles that afflict so many families will never haunt you again.

MONEY AND YOUR MIND

*Understanding and taking charge
of the ways you spend*

The secret meanings of money

The key to making better choices about your money begins with understanding your own approach to earning, spending, saving, and investing. To do this, you need to uncover the secret meanings that money, risk, and reward have for you. Once you've done this, you can begin developing a more positive and enriching style of financial management that you can really live with.

A crucial step to understanding your own attitudes towards money is to recognise how you *really* handle money. The bad news is that most people are subject to delusions about their spending habits. The good news is that there's a simple process you can use to do away with your money delusions, whatever they are. All that's required is a little effort—and the willingness to face reality, even if it's a bit humbling.

Your Daily Spending Diary

The process begins with keeping a daily diary of income and expenses for a month.

Why a diary? Why not just sit down and list everything you usually spend money on, without the effort of keeping a diary? The answer is simple. No one—and I mean no one—is really capable of remembering accurately everything they spend money on from one day to the next, let alone from one week to the next. As the American poet Robert Frost—who had serious money quarrels with his in-laws—once put it:

> Nobody was ever meant
> To remember or invent
> What he did with every cent.

So if you try to write down your money habits from memory, I promise you that the picture you paint will be inaccurate. And it will probably be flattering—deceptively so.

And why an entire month? Because anything shorter doesn't represent a serious commitment to change. And a spending diary for a week or two isn't long enough to provide a real sample of what you're spending money on.

There's no way around it: the daily diary for a full month is the only way to go. Use a page for each day. In addition to listing *everything* you spend money on, write down your mood and a brief summary of what you did that day. Use the form found on page 11. You can make thirty-one photocopies to use for an entire month. And see the sample form on page 12 for an example of what a filled-in diary page might look like.

Record credit card spending on the day you make the purchase, not the day you pay the bill. Don't overlook online, telephone, or catalogue purchases. Record bills (mortgage, utilities, child care, insurance premiums, and so on) on the day you pay them.

What if you're married or have a financial relationship with a partner, housemate or family member? (In this book, I'll refer to all these situations as 'partnerships'.) In that situation, it's best if you and your partner can do the diary exercise at the same time. Make up two diaries and work through the process together. When it comes to creating the One-Month Spending Summary (as described later in this chapter), combine the information from both diaries into a single form.

Of course, if your partner refuses to take part in the process, so be it. Don't let that become an excuse for your own shirking! Go ahead and create your own diary. You may well find that later, when your partner sees how much more organised (and prosperous) you've become, he or she will be eager to jump on the bandwagon and join you.

If your diary is to be accurate and complete, you'll need to bring it with you wherever you go and record the expense immediately, otherwise you're apt to forget about it—all too conveniently. If carrying the diary around feels awkward, try using a three-by-five-inch notecard, which fits easily in your pocket or purse. Then fill out your diary from the notecard entries at the end of the day. Does this sound like 'too much trouble'? That feeling is your first psychological checkpoint: if you believe you don't have fifteen minutes available to write down your daily expenses, you're building up excuses for remaining disorganised and out of control.

YOUR DAILY SPENDING DIARY

Date: _____

What you did: _____

_____

_____

How you felt: _____

_____

_____

What you spent:	**What it cost:**
_____	_____
_____	_____
_____	_____
_____	_____
_____	_____
_____	_____
_____	_____
_____	_____
_____	_____
_____	_____

TOTAL SPENDING FOR THE DAY: £

YOUR DAILY SPENDING DIARY

Date: 5 January 2002

What you did: Bus to work. Lunch with Susan. After work had a bite at the pub with Geoff. Home at 8. Watched telly and went to bed.

How you felt: Had a little row with boss at work—what a pain!

But felt better after seeing Susan. Great movie on the telly.

Looking forward to date with Rog tomorrow. Life's not so bad after all!

What you spent:	What it cost:
Bus fare to work	0.90
Coffee and biscuit	2.10
Paid Terry back the money she lent me for petrol last week	10.00
Lunch—sandwich, salad	6.95
Dinner at pub—fish and chips, pint	12.55
Magazine	2.95
Bus fare home	0.90
Jacket from dry cleaners	3.50
TOTAL SPENDING FOR THE DAY:	**£ 39.85**

What your Daily Spending Diary will teach you

The diary exercise will show you the reality of where your money is spent—which is likely to provide a number of surprises, some perhaps unpleasant. It will make you keenly aware of the money you're spending daily that tends to 'disappear' with little fanfare. For example, when I went through the exercise, I was stunned to realise how much I spent on magazines and newspapers. Whenever I had fifteen minutes to spare—riding a bus, say, or waiting for an appointment at the doctor or hair salon—it was so easy to buy a glossy or two to pass the time. Do that three or four times a week, and £20 can vanish with little trace.

Eating out is another costly habit that easily gets out of control. The once-a-week dinner out easily escalates in price. One glass of wine becomes two glasses, then half a bottle; the occasional dessert becomes routine. Soon the £15 treat costs £25. And it doesn't stop with a weekly dinner. You're so busy that you find yourself grabbing takeaway meals from the nearest shop rather than cooking at home—first one day a week, then two, then three. The same happens with lunch. And then there are the quick snacks, the tea breaks with pastry, the weekend brunch . . . the damage to your bank account can be enormous. (And it doesn't help your waistline, either.)

THREE RESPONSES

I've found that most people who really pursue the diary exercise react in one of three ways.

1. Sudden surrender

Some are so shocked or disturbed about what they learn that they throw up their hands. Often they abandon the diary after just a few days. This reaction amounts to a refusal to take control of and responsibility for your own life. In fact, it sometimes goes along with an attempt to blame others for your money woes: 'Oh, I'd do better if it weren't for my wife—she's the one who really goes wild with the credit cards.' 'It wouldn't matter how much I spend at the hairdresser if only my husband made a decent salary—he's the real problem.' 'The trouble starts with the kids—they never stop begging for the latest toys they spot on the telly. How am I supposed to say no?' If you fall into this category, don't expect sympathy from anyone. Whatever the causes of your money woes, they are *your* problems, and only you have the power to fix them. The key question is whether you have the will to act.

2. Rapid turnaround

Others find themselves learning about their money personalities and beginning to take control of their habits even during the diary exercise itself. By the end of a month, they discover—almost without trying—that they have a little more money left in their account, that they've cut back on needless or wasteful spending, and that they're beginning to look forward to long-range saving and spending plans. These people were probably psychologically strong and well-disciplined to begin with, and simply unaware of their ways of relating to money.

Knowledge is the key to success for these people.

Something comparable happens among the people I work with on my television series. During the month or so that elapses between the time they're chosen to appear on the show and the time we begin filming their story, their financial problems miraculously start to improve. Simply *paying attention* to where the money goes seems to make a measurable difference. In the production office, we call this the *Your Money or Your Life* Effect.

3. Thoughtful analysis

The third group works through the entire diary exercise without analysing their behaviour or making any changes until the end of the month. For them, the diary process is a purely mechanical one: they jot down their spending each day without reflecting on it and forget about it until the next time. Only after a month do they sit down to add up the totals and compare their impressions with the reality. Then, having seen how bad their spending habits really are (whether in one or two selected areas or across the board), they make a plan for improvement. For this group, change is a matter of reflection and deliberation.

Whichever group you fall into, your reaction to the diary exercise will give you an indication of how you tend to deal with money issues. It's a point we'll be returning to over and over again in this book.

Your One-Month Financial Record

After you've faithfully recorded your spending for a month, it's time to take the next step: to create your One-Month Financial Record. This is a record and analysis of how you're actually spending your money, based on the diary entries. This record will become the basis for a budget by which you can improve your financial habits and money status over the next year.

To perform this analysis, you can use the forms on pages 21–25. Again, you can make a photocopy of the book pages for this purpose. Or, if you prefer, use any of the popular computerised spreadsheet programs. They can easily be adapted to this purpose, and they have the advantage of making calculations instantaneous. A third option is to work with Quicken or Microsoft Money software, either of which can walk you through the budget-making process, providing customised reports and data. (Of course, if you follow the Quicken or Microsoft Money processes, the details of your budget may look different from those we'll examine in the next few pages of this book.) Quicken, Microsoft Money, and spreadsheets such as Excel have been made surprisingly easy to learn, and there are helpful tutorials for all three available online or from books.

If you use the forms we provide, you'll see that the first page is for listing your sources of income. Most people just have a few income items each month. They're usually easy to remember and keep track of. Enter income items for the same month as your spending diary on page 11. Only enter cheques you actually received during the month. And use actual take-home amounts rather than 'gross' or 'pre-tax' amounts. (If you're self-employed, estimate the amount you'll owe in taxes and deduct that. Enter the remainder as your income.)

Then fill in the expenses pages. To do this, go through your monthly diary entries line by line. Sort your expenses into categories as shown in the form on pages 21–25. Read through the whole form before you get started. Notice that the various expense categories are numbered 1 through 60. (Don't be frightened. Not all these categories will apply to your situation.) This is designed to make it easier for you to match up your diary entries with budget categories. You can flip through the pages of your diary and label each entry with a number for the corresponding budget category. For example, when you find a diary entry for mortgage payment or rent, label that with the number 1. Then use a calculator to add up the amounts you spent in each category.

Filling in the spending record form will be a fair amount of work. But most people will get it done in an hour or less. (If your spending diary is orderly, that will make it much easier and faster.) Once the form is complete, you'll be ready to study it to get a better handle on your real money habits.

TWEAKING THE NUMBERS . . . BUT WITH CARE

If you know that this month is not typical in some way, you may want to adjust your figures in particular categories. For example, if you suffered a week at home with the flu (and therefore ate at home all week, spent nothing on entertainment, etc.), take that into account: increase your spending in those categories to represent a typical month. By the same token, if this month's spending includes a few hundred pounds on car repairs (something that may happen only once a year or so), reduce your spending accordingly. As you'll discover later, large one-off expenses will be paid for out of the savings you accumulate as you gain control of your spending. This exercise is designed to capture your *typical* spending patterns. But beware! Don't fall into the trap of convincing yourself that the bad habits uncovered by your diary are just a one-month aberration. We all tend to do this, like the golfer who's convinced that the round of eighty-five he shoots once a year is his 'real' game, while the hundred he shoots nearly every Saturday is due to bad luck. If you fool yourself in this way, you'll miss the chance to really learn something from your diary exercise.

ANALYSING YOUR SPENDING

Your end-of-the-month analysis should focus on these questions:

- What percentage of your total income are you spending on housing, food, transport, clothing, entertainment and each of the other categories?

- What percentage of your total income do you spend on essential things? What percentage do you spend on discretionary or impulse items?

- How well does this breakdown reflect your personal priorities? Are you spending a lot on things that really mean very little to you?

- Can you make the changes (such as reducing your impulse spending and increasing your savings) that will enable you to begin accumulating the money you need to achieve your long-term goals?

Naturally, if you're spending *more* in a month than you take in, red warning flags should be hoisted immediately. But there may be other signs of trouble as well. If you're spending more than you ever realised on categories such as entertainment, drinks, toys, and hobbies; if spending on luxury items is making it hard for you to find the money for necessities; if unplanned spending (what marketers call 'impulse purchases') takes up a significant portion of your monthly income, then it's time to take better command of your money. As it is, the gremlins are in charge, which means that your long-term needs and goals can only suffer.

DAY-TO-DAY PATTERNS

Look for time patterns to your spending, earning and saving. On Fridays, do you have a habit of buying four or five CDs or spending £40 at the pub? When you shop for groceries, do you buy a lot of food that looks good but that ends up sitting in the refrigerator until it goes bad and must be tossed? Do you routinely buy a new piece of clothing on payday because you feel you deserve it (although in truth you've done nothing special during the week)? Do you take your kids shopping or buy them gifts the Saturday after payday to compensate for your being away at work? How does your spending fit your moods? Are you more reckless in the middle of the week? Where are your money vulnerabilities?

MENTAL PATTERNS

Also look for psychological patterns to your spending, especially your excessive spending in particular categories. When do you get out of control? Perhaps it's when you get paid. Perhaps it's when you have an argument with your spouse, your partner, your parents, or your kids. Perhaps it's when you have 'a bad day' at work or school or home (and so feel you 'deserve' a treat). Perhaps it's when you've accomplished something—for example finished a project at work or passed a course at school—and want to 'celebrate' by spending money. By identifying these patterns, you can begin to take steps towards gaining control of them.

YOUR ONE-MONTH FINANCIAL RECORD

For the month of: **in the year:**

Income

1. Salary (take home)   £
2. Government benefits
3. Alimony or child maintenance
4. Investment income
5. Rental income
6. Other (specify)

TOTAL INCOME: £

Spending

A. Fixed costs

HOME

1. Mortgage or rent   £
2. Electricity
3. Gas
4. Water rates
5. Council tax payments
6. Buildings insurance
7. Home contents insurance

    HOME TOTAL (items 1–7):   £

TRANSPORT

8. Car loan payments	£
9. Petrol	
10. Car insurance	
11. Commuting costs	
12. Other transport	
TRANSPORT TOTAL (items 8–12):	£

OTHER MONTHLY BILLS

13. Telephone (fixed line)	£
14. Telephone (mobile)	
15. Child care	
16. Life assurance	
17. Private health insurance	
18. Alimony or child support	
19. Other (specify)	
OTHER MONTHLY BILLS TOTAL (items 13–19):	£

LESS-THAN-MONTHLY EXPENSES

(Estimate your spending for one year in each category. Then divide that figure by twelve. Enter the result in the column at right.)

20. Tax (not covered by PAYE)	£
21. Home repairs	
22. Appliances	
23. Car purchase	
24. Car repairs	

25. Other (specify)

**LESS-THAN-MONTHLY EXPENSES TOTAL
(items 20–25):**   £

OTHER EXPENSES
26. Food (at home)   £

27. Cleaning supplies and toiletries

28. Laundry, dry cleaning, ironing

29. Medicines and medical costs

30. Other (specify)

**OTHER EXPENSES TOTAL
(items 26–30):**   £

**FIXED COSTS TOTAL
(items 1–30):**   £

B. Discretionary spending
FOOD AND DRINK
31. Meals at restaurants   £

32. Pub/Off licence

33. Takeaways

**FOOD AND DRINK TOTAL
(items 31–33):**   £

ENTERTAINMENT
34. TV subscriptions and movie rentals   £

35. Internet connection

36. Magazines, newspapers, books

37. CDs and other music	
38. Tickets for cinemas, concerts, sports, etc.	
39. Other outings	
40. Hobbies	
41. Kids' activities	
42. Gambling	
43. Other (specify)	
ENTERTAINMENT TOTAL (items 34–43):	£

AROUND THE HOME

44. Home decorating	£
45. Gardening	
46. Antiques and collectibles	
47. Pets (including vet)	
48. Other (specify)	
AROUND THE HOME TOTAL (items 44–48):	£

LESS-THAN-MONTHLY EXPENSES
(Estimate your spending for one year in each category. Then divide that figure by twelve. Enter the result in the column at right.)

49. Holiday travel and lodging	£
50. Christmas and other seasonal gifts	
51. Birthday and other non-seasonal gifts	

52. Other (specify)

LESS-THAN-MONTHLY EXPENSES TOTAL (items 49–52):	£

OTHER EXPENSES
53. Clothing   £

54. Toys (for children)

55. Gadgets (for grown-ups)

56. Hairdresser or barber

57. Other beauty (manicures, spa, etc.)

58. Credit card interest

59. Loan repayments

60. Other (specify)

OTHER EXPENSES TOTAL (items 53–60):   £

DISCRETIONARY SPENDING TOTAL (items 31–60):   £

GRAND TOTAL OF SPENDING (FIXED + DISCRETIONARY)   £

Your One-Month Spending Summary

Next, use the form on page 31 to create a One-Month Spending Summary. (A filled-in sample is shown on page 32.) You'll calculate:

- The percentage of your total after-tax income that is spent on fixed costs vs discretionary costs.

- The percentage that is spent on each expense category.

To calculate percentages, divide the amount spent in a particular category by your *grand total* monthly spending. (This is the amount shown in the Grand Total line of your One-Month Financial Record.) Multiply the result by 100 to convert it into a percentage. For example, in the sample summary on page 32, the amount spent on 'Home' is £995, while the grand total monthly spending is £3,164. Using a calculator, you'll find that $995 \div 3{,}164 = 0.3144$. (Actually, the result is a very long decimal, but only the first few decimal places really matter.) Multiply this by 100 and round it off to the nearest whole number, and you get 31 percent.

Naturally, no two people will have spending percentages that are exactly the same in every category, nor should they. There are no absolute 'right' or 'wrong' percentages. But you may spot numbers that are clearly out of line: spending patterns that reflect disordered priorities that are hurting you.

By way of comparison, the Office for National Statistics regularly compiles data concerning what it calls 'Components of household expenditure', which go to make up the Family Spending Report. The most recent such report I've seen reflects typical family spending for the years 1999–2000. Like all statistics, these are subject to their own biases and can't be taken as rules. But it is interesting to notice what the average UK household spends in particular areas. You may find that spending that seems 'normal' to you and your friends is dramatically different from what the typical person in the UK actually spends. I'll mention a few of these stats in the pages that follow.

POTENTIAL DANGER ZONES

Here are some of the typical trouble areas I've encountered with the individuals and families I've worked with. How many of these sound disturbingly familiar to *you*?

- *Clothing*. Since clothes vary so much in style and cost, from the very basic to the highest of high fashion, spending on clothes varies a lot, too. (We all know people who could easily spend half their income on shoes alone!) For comparison, the Family Spending Report says that the average family devotes 4 percent of their annual spending to clothing. If your spending is much greater than this, you may have a problem.

- *Food and drink*. Many people on *Your Money or Your Life* let their spending on food and drink get out of control, especially from takeaways,

27

restaurants and pubs. The Family Spending Report pegs the average spending on these categories of food at around 4 percent. If yours is noticeably higher, why not consider cooking at home more often? It's cheaper, more nutritious, and can even be fun.

- *Entertainment*. This is another category where spending can vary wildly. (One night of 'painting the town red' can cost as much as most families spend on entertainment in a month.) The statistics say that the average family spends 9 percent on leisure activities. Are you far out of line? If so, look for ways to scale back.

- *Toys for children*. Naturally, how much you spend in this area will depend on whether or not you have children, how many you have, and their ages. But it will also depend on the attitudes you want to instil in them. In families where the parents behave as if toys are symbols of acceptance and love, or as if having the latest plaything is the only sure way of having fun, the demand for toys tends to become an ever-growing pressure. Beware: the fun quickly vanishes when the bills can't be paid and the pressure starts to mount.

- *Christmas and other gifts*. Here, too, the attitude and spirit that prevail within the family are crucial. Don't fall into the familiar traps of regarding gifts as evidence of love, or of using gifts as ways of competing for attention and favour, or of trying to make up for eleven months of indifference with one month of lavish generosity. Ironically, many families have been shattered by over-spending on Christmas gifts in a misguided attempt to 'buy' family happiness and harmony.

- *Personal beauty*, including cosmetics and other beauty supplies as well as trips to the salon or spa. The Family Spending Report says that average spending in this category runs at about 1 percent, but I've met individuals who have a powerful and costly weakness for the latest and most lavish lipsticks, nail varnishes, face creams (available only in France or the US, of course) and other beauty treatments. Believe me, a daily walk in the fresh air (or even a weekly tumble in bed) will do far more to put the roses back in your cheeks!

- *DIYs*, especially kitchen makeovers, remodelling lounges, redoing a garden. Home projects are classic 'money pits' that can suck up cash with no apparent limit. (We'll talk more about this trap in a later chapter devoted to finance and your home.)

- *Mobile phone bills*. It's shocking how quickly the cost of a few 'chit-chats and smiles' (paraphrasing Aretha Franklin) can mount up, especially when the phones are used indiscriminately. Watch out!

Just the other day I happened to find myself strolling behind a woman who seemed to be talking on her cellphone with her date from the night before. I couldn't help overhearing her conversation. It consisted of sweet pleasantries intermingled with detailed descriptions of every London block she passed: 'Oh, I had fun with you last night . . . Here's that building with the scaffolding. I wonder when they're finally going to finish redoing the façade . . . Oh, I liked it, too . . . I'm next to that dress store I like; it looks as if there's a sale going on . . . Oh, yes, the dessert was awfully nice . . . This office building seems to be closed, I wonder why . . .' This inconsequential chit-chat went on for a solid seventeen minutes (at least, until our routes diverged). I'd hate to be responsible for *that* month's phone bill!

As I've said, these are some of the most prominent money trouble spots I've encountered on my programme while analysing people's spending habits. But your trouble spots may be different from any of these. Now is the time to look for them and begin dealing with them.

By the way, I *do* practise what I preach. I keep a one-month financial diary periodically just to see how my spending habits have changed over time. During a recent stay in London, my diary revealed that I'd fallen into the habit of spending an alarming amount on taxis. How did it happen? Without realising it, I just stopped using the tube or walking, finding it easier to pop into a cab even for short rides. The problem, of course, is that fares of £5 or £8 or £10 quickly add up, especially on a busy weekday when I have several trips to make.

Thanks to the diary, I recognised the problem before it got out of control. I've gone back to walking instead. Why not? The extra exercise benefits both my wallet and my waistline.

YOUR ONE-MONTH SPENDING SUMMARY

For the month of:		in the year:

TOTAL INCOME: £

A. Fixed costs	Amount (£)	% of total
	£	
HOME		
TRANSPORT		
OTHER MONTHLY BILLS		
LESS-THAN-MONTHLY EXPENSES		
OTHER EXPENSES		
TOTAL FIXED COSTS:	£	

B. Discretionary spending		
FOOD AND DRINK	£	
ENTERTAINMENT		
AROUND THE HOME		
LESS-THAN-MONTHLY EXPENSES		
OTHER EXPENSES		
TOTAL DISCRETIONARY SPENDING:	£	
GRAND TOTAL OF SPENDING	£	**100%**

YOUR ONE-MONTH SPENDING SUMMARY

For the month of: *March* **in the year:** *2002*

TOTAL INCOME:	£3,100	

A. Fixed costs	Amount (£)	% of total
HOME	£995	31
TRANSPORT	85	3
OTHER MONTHLY BILLS	320	10
LESS-THAN-MONTHLY EXPENSES	190	6
OTHER EXPENSES	517	16
TOTAL FIXED COSTS:	£2,107	67

B. Discretionary spending		
FOOD AND DRINK	£250	8
ENTERTAINMENT	292	9
AROUND THE HOME	75	2
LESS-THAN-MONTHLY EXPENSES	90	3
OTHER EXPENSES	350	11
TOTAL DISCRETIONARY SPENDING:	£1,057	33
GRAND TOTAL OF SPENDING	£3,164	**100%**

FINANCIAL FITNESS

For many people, dealing with financial issues feels a lot like struggling with their weight. In fact, many people who work successfully on their finances with me for my television show end up getting their figures under control at the same time—even without trying.

I think this is because both these areas are fraught with emotional baggage. Many of the same anxieties, needs, wishes, fears, tensions, disappointments and dreams we associate with food are also associated with money.

As you study your One-Month Spending Summary, look for psychological 'hot spots': things that make you feel anxious, tense, guilty, angry, or vengeful about money. Money is apt to be a distraction from the real emotional issues that drive your behaviour. You may discover that you've been spending to make yourself feel better, to attract others, to get revenge, to show off your status, or to buy love. Circle the items on the summary that you find yourself feeling strongly about and consider what they mean. If you share your financial (and personal) life with a spouse or other partner, discuss those hot spots with him or her. Simply becoming *aware* of the psychological weight that you attach to financial and material things can often help you begin to master that burden.

Taking control: creating your spending plan

So far, you've been studying your past and present financial behaviour—how you currently make and spend money. In the process, you've learned quite a bit about what makes you tick, and about the personal and financial weaknesses that have got you into trouble in the past. Now it's time to use what you've learned to create a spending plan—a budget—that will help to take control of your financial behaviour in the future. What you want is a budget that is realistic, livable, and responsible, a plan you can really carry out that will give you a chance of reaching *all* your personal goals, both day by day and over your entire lifetime.

You may have tried to create and live by a budget in the past, only to give up in despair. That's a common experience. It happens for many reasons. Sometimes people create budgets that are too rigid, too austere, or too complicated. Sometimes they fail to adjust their budgets as their needs, priorities, and abilities change. Sometimes they try to follow plans that have no connection to their own psychological realities. And sometimes they are simply 'undisciplined', which is usually another way of saying that they have an unexplored inner need to ruin their own financial plans.

I don't want you to repeat past patterns of failure. Instead, I want you to develop a spending plan that makes sense *for you*. And I want you to review it, think about it, adjust it, revise it, and improve it as often as necessary so that you feel comfortable with it. Your budget must be a *living* document, one that you can not only follow but *enjoy* following.

Making adjustments to changing conditions is a continual challenge. As I write, most of the world is living through a business recession. Several months ago, when many people first got an inkling of the coming downturn, I tried to anticipate its effects on me by trimming my spending. For example, I restricted myself to eating out no more than two nights a week. Around the same time, a friend and his wife decided to get rid of one of their two cars for much the same reason.

Adjusting like this *before* disaster strikes gives you a wonderful feeling of being in control of your own destiny rather than feeling helpless. I've noticed that feeling out of control often makes people frustrated and angry, which leads to bad decisions.

Sometimes, a degree of self-denial is essential. If you've developed bad spending habits, there will be a period of adjustment as you break those habits and develop better ones—and that means pain. But the pain should be offset by an increasing sense of pleasure: pleasure that comes from having smaller balances on your credit cards, fewer burdens on your conscience, more money in your pocket or purse, and more savings in the bank. And through it all, you should be able to allow yourself an occasional reward—a special treat, an evening out, a purchase 'just for fun'—without smashing your budget or shattering your growing sense of control.

Secrets of making and keeping a realistic budget

Start with your One-Month Spending Summary. Use this as the basis for a new monthly budget. Your budget will be a spending plan that lays out guidelines you'll follow for how much to spend in each basic category in the months to come.

From all the self-analysis you've already done, you may have some excellent ideas as to how you'd like to alter your past spending practices. If so, now is the time to turn those ideas into concrete plans. Here are some specific recommendations that can help you.

- *Plan for saving*. As we'll discuss in more detail in chapter three, your budget ought to make it possible for you to save about 10 percent of your monthly take-home pay. For most people, this is an amount they won't even miss. As you look through your spending diary, I'm sure you'll be able to find places where you can save this percentage or even more. (It's easy to calculate 10 percent of any number: just move the decimal point one place to the left. For example, 10 percent of £1,900.00 is £190.00.) So *start* your budget with a line labelled 'Saving', where you pencil in 10 percent of your monthly income. Now work on filling in the rest of your budget with appropriate reductions in your least-essential spending categories so as to keep that line intact! (We'll talk about what do with your savings in a later chapter.)

- *Trim your fixed costs.* Write down the items you listed in this category on your Spending Summary. You may not be able to change many of these, but look for opportunities to save. To take one example, is it possible to reduce your spending on transport? Maybe you can get by with one car rather than two. Or perhaps you can cut down the amount you spend on petrol by combining two or more chores into a single trip; by walking short distances rather than driving; or even by trading in your old car for a more efficient model. Scrutinise each line in the same way.

- *Get control of your discretionary spending.* Here is where the greatest opportunities for reductions are likely. Study each spending category carefully. Look for instances where you are spending money without receiving much physical, psychological, or emotional benefit in return. Do you accumulate magazines with little chance to read them? Cancel the subscriptions and save a few pounds a month. Do you own shirts or blouses you've scarcely worn? Only buy clothes when you really need them and save a few more pounds. Are three nights out at the pub per week getting a little stale? Cut back to one night and you may enjoy it more, while saving even more. And as for that smoking habit—try adding up all the pounds you'll save if you can break it once and for all.

After jotting down preliminary spending figures for each category, add them up. Have you managed to arrive at a total at or below your monthly take-home salary? If so, congratulations: you have a spending plan that should work, at least on paper. If not, study the numbers again, looking for the additional cutbacks needed to balance the budget.

Being real

I just used the word 'balance', and indeed that's the key word. If your budget isn't truly balanced—not only fiscally but also psychologically and emotionally—it probably won't work. Your budget should reflect your personality, your priorities, your interests and your dreams. When spending cuts are needed, trim the things that don't matter to you, while preserving as much as possible from the things you really care about.

You may have a consuming passion few people share. If so, your budget ought to accommodate it. I know an American named Nancy who collects 'snowdomes', those glass bubble-shaped souvenir items that make a little snowstorm when you shake them. She finds them at jumble sales, auctions, curiosity shops—you name it. Nancy could never really live with a family budget that didn't allow her to buy a snowdome or two from time to time. Of course, it would be irresponsible for her to budget £100 a month for her hobby—she and her husband have relatively modest incomes and two strapping children outgrowing their clothes almost monthly—but £20 a month is affordable, and essential for Nancy's mental health.

In the same vein, don't try to live by a budget that allows you no room for self-indulgence. Sometimes a little 'luxury' makes all the difference between happiness and depression. It can even save a relationship. My co-author Karl and his wife Mary-Jo lived through a number of financially painful years when their three children were small and their jobs weren't very lucrative. But they made a special point of finding the money to go out for dinner alone together once a week. Some weeks it was all they could do to pay a local teenager to sit with their kids for an hour while they went out for a hamburger or a pizza. Yet having the opportunity to treat themselves in this small way—and, more important, to have a little private time for a relaxing chat—made a crucial difference in their marriage and family life.

So the art of improving your spending habits is a kind of balancing act. You need to balance:

- Consistency . . . with flexibility.

- Self-discipline . . . with realism.

- A sense of control . . . with occasional self-indulgence.

One step that will do a lot to help you trim needless spending is to reduce the amount of credit card interest you have to pay every month. That means cutting the burden of debt that may well be dragging you down financially. In the next chapter, we'll look at how you can accomplish that goal.

2

CONSUMER DEBT

*How you (probably) got into it,
and how to get out*

The awful truth about credit cards

Credit is simply another word for the right to borrow money. The word *credit* comes from the Latin for 'I believe', which makes sense: when a banker gives you credit, he is saying, in effect, 'I believe you'll repay me.' To this day, the way a person handles credit is considered a mark of his or her personal integrity. What's equally important, the way you manage credit can make or break your financial future. That's why I've chosen to speak about it so early in this book: it's one of the most crucial keys to getting your money life in order.

In the UK today, credit is rather widely and easily available, especially in comparison to the old tight-money days of a generation ago. For this change you can thank former Prime Minister Margaret Thatcher. A staunch believer in free markets, the Iron Lady pushed British banks to ease up on credit and make loans available to more people. As a result, home mortgages are more widely accessible, which is (mainly) a good thing. But the same trend has also created the temptation of easy credit card debt, and with it the danger of excessive debt, which has damaged the financial situation of thousands of people in the UK.

The statistics about mushrooming debt are

pretty scary. I'll cite just one: in 1991 the total outstanding debt owed by individuals in the UK stood at around £2,000 million. Just ten years later the figure had more than *trebled*, to over £7,000 million. No wonder we all know people who have maxed out on their credit cards . . . and have applied for a couple more to pay next month's bills!

But if you think I'm about to launch into a tirade about the evils of credit and the bad faith of the credit card companies, think again. The awful truth about credit cards is that in themselves they're neither bad nor good. In fact, they're a very convenient way to make purchases and manage one's monthly expenses. And for a few things (like renting a car or arranging a holiday) they're practically impossible to do without. So it would be unfair to demonise credit cards. No, if too many people have got themselves too deeply into debt— and they have—the blame must be placed squarely where it belongs: on the people themselves, or at least on those who misuse and abuse their credit cards.

If it makes you feel any better, the truth is that I've been guilty of credit abuse myself. In this chapter, I'll explain how I climbed out of the deep hole I dug for myself, one purchase and cash advance at a time. Saving myself from debt didn't require magic, just a bit of determination and hard work and, above all, the adoption of a new attitude towards money and debt.

The Sally Field syndrome:
the psychology of the credit card

A major part of our debt problem is the psychology of the credit card. Many people who receive solicitations from credit card companies in the mail misunderstand what they mean. They think of them, consciously or unconsciously, the way actress Sally Field viewed her Oscar: as proof that 'You like me—you really like me!'

Perhaps it is flattering to receive a credit card offer in the mail—and the direct-mail experts who write the letters and design the brochures are clever enough to make them highly appealing. But remember that these are advertisements, and as such they are only sent out to benefit the *advertisers* (that is, the banks and credit card companies), not you. They want to give you a credit card not as a service to you or as a validation of your worth as a human being but because they view you as an easy mark, someone from whom they can make a lot of money. Why should you help them do so?

Of course, modern marketing methods are designed to capitalise on our credit card psychology. Once you receive the solicitation in the mail, it's temptingly easy to sign your name and return the prepaid form. Many people I work with on their finances try to justify their woeful balance sheets by explaining, 'I got into debt because they offered me the card.' The innocence and naïveté of this statement would be touching if it weren't so horrifying. It assumes that the burden of responsibility lies with the credit card company— not with you.

Maybe it's true that the credit card hucksters

deserve some blame for their indiscriminate blanketing of the population with credit. But the real responsibility for controlling your debt lies with you. After all, when the bills come due, *you* will have to find the money to pay them—no one else!

HOW THE DEBT MOUNTAIN GROWS

Of course, the problem only begins with the credit card solicitation. Once you get the card, it's all too easy to use it, and to do so without keeping track of how much you're spending on what. The card company logos seem to be in every shop window, inviting you in to sample the glittering wares, whether or not you have any cash in your pocket or purse. And because there's a lag of up to four weeks between the time when you do your shopping and the moment the bill arrives in the mail, it's easy to pretend that the debt isn't 'real'. After all, who knows what may happen between now and when the bill comes? 'Maybe a rich uncle (of whom I've never heard) will die and leave me his diamond mine in South Africa or his oil wells in Dallas! It could happen!'

Of course, it *doesn't* happen. (I know it doesn't—I've been waiting in vain for the same letter myself!) But the credit card bill arrives without fail. (Have you ever noticed how very punctually your bills arrive every month, while payments due to you seem to take forever to show up? How irksome.) And the bill always seems to be half again as large as you expected. You scan the list of purchases and discover all kinds of items you'd forgotten about: the fancy lunch you splurged on, the blouse or CD or shoes you plumped for, the weekend getaway you took at the last moment. There's just no way to pay the full bill—at least not this month.

That's when the real debt crisis begins to build. Once they get into debt, many people make only the minimum required payment each month. (I'm told that 50 percent of all credit card holders in the UK fall into this pattern. The figure is even higher in the US.) They may even feel virtuous about it: 'After all, I paid the requested amount, right on time. Doesn't that make me a responsible credit card holder?' Indeed it does—from the point of view of the credit card company. They *love* customers who pay only the minimum amount each month. Why? Because the balance that is carried over to the next month accrues interest. Making the minimum payment will keep your debt alive virtually *for ever*.

(How is that possible? Most cards set the minimum payment at 10 percent of your balance, which means that, at least in theory, there'll *always* be something additional due, even if you *never* make another purchase. In practice, of course, when the balance is finally whittled down to £1— after many, many years of payments—most people will finally pay up.)

For every month you carry a credit card balance, you are paying a little more interest on the money due, which jacks up the price of what you've purchased. Think about that: if you splurge at the shop during your lunch break today, you may still be paying for that handbag or that camera attachment two to four years from now. And when the interest payments are added in, a £20 item may end up costing £40 or more. Some bargain!

A simple example illustrates how an item charged on a credit card can cost you much more than the actual purchase price. Let's imagine you use a credit card to buy a £100 Christmas gift for your beloved. The card's annual percentage interest rate is 18 percent, or 1.5 percent per month, on the outstanding balance. Let's assume that you leave the £100 balance outstanding for a full year. As the chart below shows, by the end of 12 months the interest added to your balance would *not* be just £18 (even though this represents 18 percent of £100). The actual interest would be higher because each month the interest is calculated on the original charge *plus* the accumulated interest.

Month	Starting balance	Monthly interest rate	End-of-month balance
January	£100	1.5%	£101.50
February	£101.50	1.5%	£103.02
March	£103.02	1.5%	£104.57
April	£104.57	1.5%	£106.14
May	£106.14	1.5%	£107.73
June	£107.73	1.5%	£109.35
July	£109.35	1.5%	£110.99
August	£110.99	1.5%	£112.65
September	£112.65	1.5%	£114.34
October	£114.34	1.5%	£116.06
November	£116.06	1.5%	£117.80
December	£117.80	1.5%	£119.57

By leaving the balance outstanding, you are in effect adding almost 20 percent to the purchase price.

Reflect for a moment. Have you ever bought something—for example, a television that cost £600—on a credit card and let the balance remain outstanding for a few years, making only the minimum payments before you paid it off? How much did that television *really* cost you when you add in the interest? When you finally take off those blinders, what you see won't be pretty.

The ultimate danger, of course, is that, as the months pass, your balance due continues to grow. (Do you really believe that you'll stop making credit card purchases altogether?) Eventually, the bill becomes too great ever to be repaid. The result can be a complete financial collapse: a ruined credit rating, bankruptcy and, at its worst, a shattered life.

The secret workings of credit and store cards

I'm telling you all this not to frighten you. No, I take that back. I *do* want to frighten you. But that's simply to get your attention. Now that you see how very serious credit card debt can be, it's time to get a grip on it.

To begin, let's review how credit and store cards work, since this has a major impact on your financial well-being. Their interest rate rules are not actually 'secret', but so few people take the trouble to understand them that they might just as well be secret.

STALKING THE ELUSIVE APR

Every time you use a credit card or store card, there is the potential that interest will be charged. Interest, of course, is a fee for borrowing money—and when you don't pay a credit or store card bill immediately, you are in fact taking out a loan for the amount owed. The amount of interest you are charged is called the *annual percentage rate (APR)* and is usually charged on your average daily balance during the billing period. The APR varies from one card to another. When you sign up for a card, you receive a 'Terms and Conditions' sheet, generally covered in fine print, that spells out the rules of the card in excruciating detail. One of these provisions is the APR.

If you've never done so, look up the APR on each of your credit and store cards right now. Finding it may take some doing. (On page 50 we've reprinted a portion of a Terms and Conditions sheet from Barclaycard, which is currently the most widely held card in Britain. But even if you have a Barclaycard, don't assume that the excerpt reprinted here applies to you, since company terms and policies do change from time to time.) You'll notice that several rates may be offered, depending on the precise kind of card you hold. For example, Barclaycard charges lower APRs on its Platinum card than any other card they offer; but then the Platinum people pay a higher annual fee for the privilege. You'll also notice that, in place of or in addition to the APR, a monthly interest rate may be listed, which is *less* than one-twelfth of the APR. This is so because compounding—the charging of interest on interest—multiplies the cost of credit over time. Finally, you'll notice that the interest charged on cash advances is *higher* than on purchases.

You may be a bit shocked at the interest rates charged on your credit card purchases. These rates are higher than most people realise. It may be that when you signed up for the card originally you were charged a much lower 'teaser' rate. Of course, this was simply a marketing ploy by the card company. They gave you fair warning that the teaser rate would give way to their usual higher rates within a few months. But many people forget about this and fail to notice when the shift kicks in.

Interest rates on store card purchases are even higher than on credit cards, ranging up to 31 percent. (The other main difference between store cards and credit cards is that store cards don't offer cash advances. Otherwise, the two kinds of cards work almost the same.)

HOW TIMING AFFECTS YOUR CHARGES

Other factors affect how much interest you'll have to pay. One factor is timing. For cash advances, interest charges generally kick in immediately, the moment you walk away from the ATM or the bank teller with the cash in hand. This means that even if you pay your bill in full the week it arrives, you'll have paid some interest for the privilege of using the company's money. In addition, you may be charged a fee of up to 1.5 percent of the amount of the cash advance. Although this isn't called 'interest', it has the same effect: it increases the cost of borrowing.

The system is a little different when it comes to

purchases. Here, the interest charges begin after a so-called *grace period*, which ends when your next month's credit card payment is due. Thus, if you buy a pair of shoes on 15 September, for example, get the bill for them on 1 October, and pay the bill in full by the due date of 7 October, then you'll pay no interest on the purchase. But if you pay your October bill only in part and carry over the rest until November (and perhaps beyond), interest on the shoes (as well as other purchases you make) will be tacked on to the bills and will continue to mount, month by month.

UNEXPECTED FEES

It may get worse. If you have a card issued by a US bank (Providian and MBNA are two US card issuers that are active in Britain), you will also be charged a late payment fee, in addition to the interest, if your payment is not received on time. In effect, this increases your interest charges beyond the official APR. Another fee may be assessed if you carelessly charge beyond your credit limit. And of course if you continue to carry a balance from month to month after the fees are added to your account, you will end up paying interest on these fees as well!

Don't feel smug if all your credit cards are issued by British banks. More and more credit card issuers in the UK are shifting over to the fee practices pioneered by US banks. So these unpleasant surprises are probably heading your way in time.

Terms & Conditions

BARCLAYCARD CONDITIONS
Credit Agreement regulated by the Consumer Credit Act 1974.

**This is a copy of your agreement for you to keep.
It includes a notice about cancellation rights which you should read.**

1. **Definitions**
   In this document, the words and phrases below have the meanings shown next to them. **Account** - the account we keep to record transactions. **Additional cardholder** - any person you have asked us to give a **Card** to so that they can use your account. **APR** - the cost of credit calculated on an annual basis. **Balance transfer** - any amount which you ask us to pay to another lender on your behalf including interest, but not including any use you make of a **Barclaycard Cheque**. **Barclaycard Cheque** - a cheque you can use with the account. **Barclays Group** - us, our parent company and any companies we or our parent company totally or partly own at any time. **Card** - any Barclaycard we give you or an **additional cardholder** to use with the account. **Cash advance** - cash or travellers' cheques obtained using the **Card** or card number and any use of a **Barclaycard Cheque**. **Cash advance balance** - the amount you owe us on the account in respect of **cash advances** (including any handling charges and interest on that amount). **Credit limit** - the most we allow you to owe us on the account at any time. **Minimum payment** - the smallest amount you must pay us each month, which we work out as explained in Condition 5.1. **Payment date** - the date given on your statement by which you must make a payment. **Payment holiday** - the month or months when we allow you to miss a **minimum payment** under Condition 5.6. **Payment** - amounts you pay us to reduce the amount you owe us. **PIN** - your personal identification number. This will either be the number we give you or the number you choose. **Promotional balance** - the amount you owe us on the account for **transactions** made under a **special promotion**. **Special promotion** - a promotion we may make available to all or some cardholders from time to time. **Standard balance** - the amount, including interest, you owe us on the account which is not a transfer balance, promotional balance, cash advance balance. **Statement balance** - the total you owe us on the statement date. **Subscription date** - each anniversary of the date we open your account and each anniversary of that date or, if different, of the date on which a membership fee or account servicing fee was last charged or due to be charged. **This agreement** - the credit agreement you have signed, the **Barclaycard Conditions** and any changes made to those Conditions from time to time. **Transaction** - any purchase made or **cash advance** obtained by you or an **additional cardholder** using the Card, a **Barclaycard Cheque** or the **Card** number, including a **balance transfer**. **Transfer balance** - the amount you owe us, including interest, on the account for any balance transfer. **United Kingdom or UK** - this includes the Channel Islands and the Isle of Man. **We, us, our** - Barclays Bank PLC and any business or other person we transfer any or all of our rights and responsibilities to under this agreement. **You, your** - the person who signed **this agreement**. **Your information** - personal and financial information we (a) obtain from you or from any third parties such as credit reference agencies or other organisations when you apply for a **Card** or any other product or service or which you or they give us from time to time or (b) learn from the way you use and manage your account and from the transactions you make such as the date, amount, currency and the name and type of supplier (e.g. supermarket services, medical services, retail services).

2. **Using the Card and Barclaycard Cheques**
2.1 **You** must sign your Card as soon as you receive it and follow any reasonable instructions that we give about using **Cards** and keeping them safe. You must also make sure that any **additional cardholder** follows the same instructions.
2.2 **You** and any **additional cardholder** can use **Cards** and you can use **Barclaycard Cheques** for transactions up to the **credit limit** (and for any other use that we allow). When deciding whether you have gone over the **credit limit** we can include the amount of any **transaction** we have approved but have not yet put on the account.
2.3 **We** will convert all **transactions** on the account into sterling using the exchange rate and a percentage commission on the amount of the **transaction**. Please note that the exchange rate we use may not be the same as the rate on the date of the **transaction** as conversion may take place at a later date.
2.4 When **we** open your **account** we may ask if you want to make a **balance transfer**. After the **account** is opened you may take advantage of any additional **balance transfer** offer or **special promotion** we tell you about. If you ask us to make a **balance transfer**, you will still have to pay any amounts you owe to the lender before and after we add the **balance transfer** to your account.

Terms and Conditions

2.5 **You** must only use **Barclaycard Cheques** for spending in sterling. **You** cannot use them to make **payments** to **us**.

2.6 **We** will give **you** replacement **Cards** from time to time. A replacement **Card** will either be the same as **your** existing **Card** or another **Card** that **you** are then eligible for and which is covered by **this agreement**.

2.7 **Cards** and **Barclaycard Cheques** belong to **us**. **We** can ask **you** to return them to **us** and **we** can ask others to hold on to them for **us** at any time.

3. Credit limit

From time to time **we** will work out **your credit limit** and tell **you** what it is.

4. Charges

4.1 **We** do not normally charge for servicing the **account**. However, if in the 12 months before a **subscription date** the total value of **transactions** on **your account** is less than £200 and if no interest has been charged, **we** will charge **you** an **account** servicing charge of £10 in advance for the following 12 months. This charge does not count as a **transaction** or interest when **we** calculate whether the account servicing charge is payable.

4.2 **We** will charge a handling fee each time **you** or any **additional cardholder** make a **cash advance**. For Barclaycard First Classic, Classic or Gold Barclaycard and Barclaycard Platinum the handling fee is 1.5% of the amount of the **cash advance** with a minimum fee of £2.00. For initial Visa the handling fee is 2.5% with a minimum fee of £2.50.

4.3 Except as set out in clause 4.5, **we** will charge the following monthly interest rates:

(a) If **you** apply for a **Card** and a **balance transfer** on an application form contained in promotional material offering an **APR** of 6.9%, **we** will charge 0.561% (**6.9% APR**) fixed until the **transfer balance** is fully repaid although **we** will charge the rate applicable to the **standard balance** on each statement date if **you** have not made a purchase or **cash advance** using **your Card** or a **Barclaycard Cheque** since **your** last statement.

(b) For the **standard balance** and **cash advance balance** we will charge the rates **we** work out as follows:

	Purchases		Cash	
	Monthly Interest Rate	**Standard Balance**	**Monthly Interest Rate**	**Cash Advance Balance (the APR includes the handling fee)**
Platinum	1.240%	15.9% APR	1.349%	19.2% APR
Gold	1.456%	18.9% APR	1.492%	21.3% APR
Classic	1.456%	18.9% APR	1.492%	21.3% APR
First Classic	1.667%	21.9% APR	1.667%	23.8% APR
initial Visa	1.873%	24.9% APR	1.873%	28.1% APR

In working out the **APRs** we have ignored any changes **we** may make to the account servicing fee, the interest rates and handling fees at any time by giving **you** notice under Condition 12.

4.4 The interest rates **we** charge on **your** F.A. Premiership Barclaycard will depend on **our** assessment of **your** application and the conduct of **your** account, but in any event will be one of the rates set out above. The **minimum payment** percentage under Condition 5.1 will relate to the interest rate. For example, if the interest rate is the same as the rate for Gold Barclaycard the **minimum payment** percentage will be 2%. **Your** F.A. Premiership Barclaycard will also have the other features of Barclaycards with the same interest rates. If **you** use **your** F.A. Premiership Barclaycard to purchase a season ticket from a sports club, promoter, or stadium, **we** will charge interest on that purchase at the rate of 0.639% (**7.9% APR**) until it is fully repaid. The purchase will be treated as part of **your standard balance** for the purposes of Condition 5.2 and as a **promotional balance** for an open-ended period for the purposes of Condition 5.7.

4.5 The rates set out in clause 4.3(a) are **our** current **balance transfer** rates for new cardholders. If the interest rates **you** pay for **your** **promotional balances** or for additional **transfer balances** are different to the rates on the **standard balance**, **we** will tell **you** what the rates will be when **we** give **you** details of the **special promotion** or **balance transfer** offer. **You** can always check the rate which applies to any **transfer balance** or **promotional balance**, by looking at the statements **we** give **you** on the **account**.

4.6 If **we** charge **you** interest on **your account** in any statement, this will be a minimum of 50 pence.

5. Repayments

5.1 Each month **you** must make a **minimum payment**. This will be:

(a) 3% of the **statement balance** for initial Visa, First Classic and Classic and 2% of the **statement balance** for Gold Barclaycard and Barclaycard Platinum or £5 whichever is more; or if the **statement balance** is less than £5, the **statement balance**; or

(b) if a **special promotion** allows **you** to put off making repayments for a period, the amount worked out under (a) but with the relevant **promotional balance** taken away from the **statement balance**.

The **minimum payment** must be received by **us** and paid into **your account** on or before the **payment date**.

5.2 **We** will always charge interest on the **cash advance balance** and **transfer balances** up to the statement date even if **you** repay them in full on or before the **payment date**. **We** will not charge interest on any other items shown in that statement as part of the **standard balance** if **you** pay the **standard balance** in full on or before the **payment date**. If **you** do not pay the **standard balance** in full on or before the **payment date**, **we** will charge interest on the **standard balance** and add it to **your account** on the next statement date. **We** will charge this interest at the relevant **standard balance** rate.

5.3 **We** may charge interest on **promotional balances** for a period which **we** will tell **you** when **we** give **you** details of a **special promotion** (the **"promotion period"**):

(a) at a lower rate than the rate **we** are then charging for **standard balances**. If **we** do this, **we** will add the **promotional balance** which is left at the end of the **promotion period** to the **standard balance**; or

(b) **we** may give **you** an interest-free option. If **we** do this, **we** will not charge **you** any interest if **you** pay off the whole of the **promotional balance** before the end of the **promotion period**. If **you** do not do so, **we** will work out the interest on the **promotional balance** either at a rate which **we** will tell **you** when **we** give **you** details of a **special promotion** or at the rate which applied during the **promotion period** to **standard balances** and add that interest, and the **promotional balance** which is left at the end of the **promotion period**, to **your standard balance**.

If **you** pay any **promotional balance** in full on or before the **payment date** **we** will not charge interest on any items shown in that statement as part of the **promotional balance**.

5.4 **We** may charge interest on **transfer balances** at a lower rate than the rate **we** are then charging for **standard balances**. **We** may charge interest at this rate for a period which **we** tell **you** when **we** give **you** details of the **balance transfer** offer. If **we** do this, **we** will add the **transfer balance** which is left at the end of the period to the **standard balance**.

5.5 **We** charge interest on a daily basis from the date of the **transaction** except for **transactions** using **Barclaycard Cheques** when **we** will charge interest from the date the item is put on the **account**.

5.6 **We** may give **you** the opportunity from time to time to take a **payment holiday**. During **payment holidays** we will continue to work out and charge interest under Conditions 5.3, 5.4 and 5.5.

RETHINKING CREDIT CARD DEBT

Unfortunately, most people don't realise these facts about the high cost of carrying debt from month to month. The average credit card debt carried by people in the UK is £2,300, which is more than 10 percent of the average gross income. This costs people countless thousands in interest payments, enriching the banks needlessly.

When evaluating their use of credit, people tend to look at the 'credit available' line rather than the 'debt outstanding' line on their monthly bills. They seem to feel comforted by the fact that there is still money available to them, as if it represents some sort of gift motivated by the generosity of the credit card company. Others regard it as a kind of safety net, like a bank balance, that they can draw upon without consequences in time of need.

Of course, this is not so. Your credit available line simply indicates the amount of money you can borrow (and pay interest on). To think of it as a gift or an asset of any kind reflects an unfortunately deluded sense of entitlement. It's one of the greatest causes of financial problems among people I've met on my television show.

Fighting back against the menace of debt

Here are some tips for keeping your credit card debt under control.

OVERCOME YOUR CREDIT CARD DEPENDENCY

Limit the cards you have. First, consider how many credit cards you actually need. My answer is: one or two. I *do* recommend having a card. They're useful in various situations, such as international travel. A major credit card makes it easier and faster to rent a car or buy a plane ticket. And in an emergency, you wouldn't want to be stranded in Istanbul or Buenos Aires without a credit card. But one or two cards will suffice; there's no need to sport the array of five or ten cards I see many people carrying. Having fewer cards makes it much easier to track the amounts you owe, the payment due dates, and other details of your debt.

Avoid store cards. I urge you *not* to use store cards at all unless you pay the full balance every month on time. As I've noted, they charge the highest interest rates of any credit cards. In fact, the credit department is the most profitable business segment in many retailing companies! This means that the stores are making profits not so much from selling coats or lamps or television sets but from charging their customers interest on their debts. Why contribute to that?

Actually, there is one useful benefit to holding a store credit card. It often entitles you to receive special sale announcements and offers for 'preferred customers'. I like getting those myself—

in fact, I got a card for Bergdorf Goodman's, a posh US department store, specifically for the announcements. But when I shop at Bergdorf's, I only use their card during special promotions when substantial additional discounts are offered on store card purchases. Bergdorf's happens to be my favourite store, and this is the one and only store card I have.

When you do use any credit card, pay off the full balance every month. This means spending each month only what you can afford to pay for that month. If you're in doubt as to how much you've spent, you can call the phone number provided by the credit card company to get your balance. (I'm always stunned to discover how many people don't realise they can do this.) If necessary, postpone purchases.

Cut your own limit. Another way of curbing your spending is to call the credit or store card company and ask them to reduce your credit limit to an amount you can afford to pay off in full each month. For some people, this will be a very difficult call to make. In essence, it's an admission that you can't control yourself. You may even feel that you are rejecting the sense of approval or validation that the company has provided by extending credit to you. Don't let these misgivings dissuade you. Be strong about it: lower the limit to what you can afford.

If you are not willing to take these kinds of steps to reduce your credit card dependency, then perhaps you really don't want to be in control of your finances.

MINIMISE THE INTEREST YOU PAY

Take advantage of your credit card's interest-free grace period. This period exists only on purchases, not cash advances. The grace period may range in length from zero to fifty-five days, depending on when your next month's bill comes due. At the end of the grace period, interest charges kick in. So the best money-saving strategy is to buy at the beginning of the grace period and pay off your purchase in full just before the end of the grace period. Payment must be posted at the credit card company's offices by the end of the grace period, and it usually takes two to three days for the money to be credited to your account. Jot down in your personal diary or calendar the date on which you must mail your payment to the company to take full advantage of the grace period.

This is one of the advantages of cutting back on the number of cards you hold. It's easy to keep track of the grace periods on one or two cards. When you have several cards, this strategy is likely to become too complicated to follow.

I've used this technique myself for years. I always knew in advance when the big seasonal sales were scheduled. I would buy a few items with my credit card and keep the money to pay the bill in the bank, where it would be earning interest for me. Then just before the end of the grace period I would send in a cheque for the full purchase amount.

There *are* times when you may have to use your credit card for purchases you can't pay off in full immediately. If the roof develops a leak or the cooker goes, you may need to overspend. For some people, Christmas is also such a time. If this happens to you, minimise the damage to your finances by giving yourself a fixed deadline to pay off the larger-than-normal bill—no more than six months. If necessary, cut your other spending to make this possible. Your main objective must be to pay off the debt as quickly as you can.

Some people practise what I call 'serial monogamy' with their credit cards. This means that they use just one credit card at a time, but they switch from one card to another frequently. Often they switch in order to take advantage of low advertised teaser rates. They jump from one card to another, moving their debt balances as they go. Use this technique *only* if you've established—and are adhering to—a clear limit as to when you're going to pay off the debt. It's *not* wise to use this method as an excuse for letting your debt hang on indefinitely. And if you do jump from one card to another, don't forget to cancel the old card! Having too many outstanding lines of credit will generally hurt your credit rating, even if you've paid off the money you owed.

In any case, you should realise that the serial monogamy game can only go on for so long. In time, the credit card companies will catch on and stop offering you fresh cards, just as, if you insist on making pick-ups in the same bar every night, you're bound to eventually run out of fresh faces to approach.

PRACTISE TOUGH SELF-LOVE

Some people find it overwhelmingly hard to follow the kinds of credit card rules I've laid out in the last couple of pages. They get such a thrill of empowerment out of opening up a wallet full of cards and saying, 'Charge it, please!' that the idea of cutting back to one or two cards, of paying off their bills in full, of strictly limiting the times they shop—these ideas are almost unbearably painful and seemingly impossible to follow.

If this psychology applies to you, go further than I've suggested so far: *get rid of your credit cards completely*. Yes, cut them up! Torch them! If the thought reduces you to tears, think how pathetic it is that a piece of plastic should mean so much to you. (And it's not even plastic by Prada!) Please do it—for your own happiness' sake. Believe me, you'll be glad you did.

I wouldn't feel right about giving this advice if I hadn't lived through the experience myself. Growing up in a poor farming family in the 'panhandle' area of northern Florida, I was raised in the Southern Baptist tradition of discipline, self-denial and shame. In reaction, when I moved to Miami as a young man, launched a successful career, and began to have a little money running through my fingers, I went a bit mad. No matter how much I bought, there were always more beautiful things worth buying, from cashmere coats to Wedgwood china to fancy dinners with my new posh friends.

Unfortunately, I couldn't really afford all the things I was enjoying. So the debt rolled over and expanded, month to month. Within a few years, I was suffering a full-blown case of Sally Field Syndrome. The credit card companies 'liked me—they really liked me!' And I returned their affection by charging the maximum on each card and paying the minimum each month. When you consider that I had no fewer than *twenty-nine* cards, you can see the trouble I was in!

In the end, only a course of tough self-love saved me from a real financial crack-up. I took the shears to all but one of my credit cards. (To this day I limit myself to two.) I painfully paid off my debt, and as my income gradually grew, I managed *not* to revert to my old free-spending ways. Instead, I learned to control my behaviour using what I'd learned about my own money psychology. I figured out how to reward myself for a month of frugality with a single small treat: an art book I'd coveted, a glass of champagne at the King Cole Bar at the St Regis Hotel, or a slice of apple pie at the bar of one of my favourite restaurants. And I learned to enjoy the fun of tending my growing bank balance—and eventually my stock portfolio.

Beyond the credit card

Credit card debt is the biggest bugbear haunting most people in the UK. But there are other kinds of debt that need managing as well. Let's take a moment to consider them.

- *Mortgages* are loans used for buying property— a house, or a flat. We'll save our discussion of mortgages for chapter four, which is devoted to property ownership.

- *Unsecured loans* are bank loans given without security—that is, against which property or other assets are *not* pledged. They are very expensive and should generally be avoided, although they are easy to get. I'd steer clear of such loans unless they are the only way to manage some unexpected, unavoidable problem, such as a legal judgement against you.

- *Bank overdrafts* are actually a kind of unsecured loan. Sometimes the interest rates charged on overdrafts are relatively attractive compared to other types of borrowing—credit cards, for example. However, the overdraft limits are generally low, and a fee is charged whenever you exceed the limit. And since interest is charged from day one, using your overdraft privilege is *not* a smart way of managing your monthly expenses.

- *Second secured loans* (or *second mortgages*) are bank loans against which your home is pledged as security. These are popularly used as a means of getting access to the equity that has built up in property due to price appreciation and using cash to pay off credit card and other debts (in which case they are sometimes referred to as 'consolidation loans'). Because the interest charged on second secured loans is lower than credit card interest, such a loan is preferable to carrying a huge credit card balance. But be careful: if you fall behind on your loan payments, you could lose your home! So be very conservative about this form of borrowing.

- *Car loans* are secured loans for the purpose of buying an automobile. They're quite common, and since the monthly payments are usually manageable, most people don't run into problems with them. But do shop around among various lenders: the interest rates on car loans vary greatly, and you shouldn't assume that the arrangement your dealer offers is the best available.

- *Hire purchase* (also called *rent-to-buy*) is less popular today than in the past, but some people still use this as a means of buying appliances, furniture, and other expensive items. If you can possibly avoid hire purchase plans, do so. Interest rates are high and pre-payment is generally forbidden. So even if you receive a windfall and want to pay off your debt early, you won't be able to get out from under the steep interest costs. And if, for some reason, you're unable to make the sixtieth payment, for example, you may lose your furniture and all the money you've sunk into it, even though you were never a day late with any of the first fifty-nine payments. If you must go this route, reading the fine print is essential. Never rely on the salesperson's description of the deal: read every word with your own eyes before signing anything.

Another type of consumer debt is those tempting nought percent financing offers for furniture and appliances in the newspapers, magazines, and on television. 'Buy your dreams now and pay no interest for six months or a year!' At least, that is what the ads want you to infer. But is it really that easy or that cheap? Not quite.

In most of the 'nought percent' financing deals, the payment schedule you receive is calculated on a longer period than the period of no interest. For example, suppose you sign a contract to buy a set of furniture with no interest for the first six months. Your payments are calculated on a 12-month repayment schedule instead of the six-month nought percent interest period. When the six months are up, if you pay the outstanding balance immediately, then you indeed will pay no interest. But if you do not, the interest on your remaining

> **Alvin says . . .**
>
> If you *must* borrow from a friend or relation, handle it as a business transaction. Write a note that mentions the amount borrowed, the repayment scheme, the interest to be charged, and what happens if you fail to repay. Then live up to those terms—religiously—if you ever want to have a happy Christmas dinner or a civil family holiday again!

payments will be exceedingly high.

The trouble doesn't stop there. Some contracts allow the interest on your balance to be recalculated over the entire time of the contract, not just the period of the remaining balance. In other cases, pre-payment is forbidden. So even if you receive a windfall and want to pay off your debt early, you won't be able to get from under the steep interest costs.

I've heard many horror stories from people who sign these nought percent agreements. If you must go this route, reading and understanding the fine print in your contract is essential. I can't emphasise this enough.

Finally, a word about borrowing from friends and family: Don't! Sorry to be a bit flip, but I do want to emphasise the risks involved in mixing affection with business. It takes a very strong relationship to survive when money changes hands. There are just too many opportunities for awkwardness, resentment, guilt, and anger. What happens if you need to make a late payment? Will your mum or cousin Sheila charge you a late fee, as the bank would, or will she simply smile and say, 'Never mind,' all the while seething with annoyance whenever the subject comes to mind? What if there's a disagreement about the borrowing terms? It's very easy for two honest, well-intentioned people to remember the same conversation in radically different ways. Who can arbitrate such a dispute without being bloodied in the emotional crossfire?

Yes, it's tempting to take advantage of the generosity of loved ones. A loan between relatives or friends involves no application forms or credit checks. And there *are* some rare relationships in which all involved are honest, secure, and forthright enough to deal with the inevitable stresses of finance without suffering hurt feelings or embarrassment. But please avoid becoming indebted to family and friends if you possibly can. It's bad enough having money difficulties—why screw up your personal life in the bargain?

Getting out from under: a step-by-step approach

If you're deeply in debt, first step back from the problem and get a handle on it. Here's a three-step guide to organising your debts properly and developing a get-out-of-debt plan. Use it in conjunction with the form Your Credit Card Debt Reduction Plan on pages 67–69.

Step 1. *List your cards.* Gather the most recent bills for all your outstanding credit or store cards. Don't forget any! Check with your spouse or partner—he or she may have a card you rarely or never use. And don't forget the card you may have left in your other wallet or purse or in a desk drawer. List the cards on the form provided. In the second column, list the annual interest rate on each one. You may be able to find this figure on your monthly bill. If not, look on the Terms and Conditions sheet you received when you first accepted the card. (Call the company for a copy if necessary.)

Step 2. *Sort your debt.* Now rewrite the list of credit cards from Step 1, arranging them in order from the *highest* to the *lowest* annual interest rate. (If two cards happen to have the same interest rate, list the one with the larger outstanding balance first.) Fill in the other information requested on the form: your total outstanding balance on each card, and the minimum monthly payment required.

Step 3. *Create your pay-off plan.* Start by deciding how much of your debt you can afford to pay off each month. Push yourself a bit! If you're in serious debt, you won't be able to get out unless the amount you repay each month *hurts* a little. So if you think (for example) that you'd be comfortable repaying £500 every month, try for £600 or even £700. The philosophy is the same as with physical training: no pain, no gain. Write in the amount you decide at the top and bottom of the form as shown in the example.

Now it gets just a little complicated. Copy the list of credit cards from Step 2 in the form provided in Step 3. (If you find it tricky to fill out the form, see the sample we've provided, all filled in. It appears on pages 70–71.) Then allocate your monthly repayment amount as follows:

- Starting with the second card on the list, write in the minimum payment required. Then do the same with the third card, the fourth card, and so on, to the bottom of your list.

- Add these minimum payment amounts together. Then subtract this sum from the total monthly repayment you've committed to.

- Allocate the remaining balance to the first card on the list. (If this amount is more than you owe on the first card, then allocate the difference to the second card.)

Do you see what we're doing? We're setting up a plan so that you'll pay off the *maximum* possible amount on the card with the *highest* interest *first*. This is the card that is costing you the most in needless interest expense every month. The sooner you get that monkey off your back, the more you'll benefit. Yes, it's important to pay off all your debts, and you shouldn't be satisfied until every card has been paid off in full. But you have to start somewhere—and the best place to start is with the card that hurts you the most.

Follow the monthly repayment plan we've just created until the first card on your list is completely paid off. When that happens, celebrate by cutting up that card and cancelling the account. Then make a new plan, with the next worst-offending card at the top of your list. Continue the process for as many months as it takes to clear out your list altogether, from top to bottom.

YOUR CREDIT CARD DEBT REDUCTION PLAN

Date _____

STEP 1. LIST YOUR CARDS. On the form below, list all your outstanding credit cards. In the second column, list the annual percentage rate (APR) on each one.

Credit card   **Interest rate (%)**

_____

_____

_____

_____

_____

_____

_____

STEP 2. SORT YOUR DEBT. Rewrite the list, arranging your credit cards in order from the *highest* to the *lowest* annual interest rate. If two or more cards have the same interest rate, then arrange them beginning with the largest outstanding balance. Fill in the other columns indicated.

Credit card	Balance due (£)	Mimimum payment rate	Interest rate (%)

STEP 3. YOUR PAY-OFF PLAN. Decide how much of your debt you can afford to pay off each month. Write that figure here: £   .
Also write it at the bottom of the second column in the form below under Total Monthly Payment.

Copy the list of credit cards from Step 2 in the form below. Then allocate your monthly repayment amount as follows:

- For the second, third and later cards on the list, write in the minimum payment required (as shown in Step 2).

- Add these figures, and subtract that amount from the total monthly repayment.

- Write the balance next to the first card on the list. (If this amount is more than you owe on the first card, then allocate the difference to the second card.)

Credit card	Monthly payment (£)
TOTAL	

YOUR CREDIT CARD DEBT REDUCTION PLAN

SAMPLE

Date *13 March 2002*

STEP 1. LIST YOUR CARDS. On the form below, list all your outstanding credit cards. In the second column, list the annual interest rate on each one.

Credit card	Interest rate (%)
ABC Bank	17.5
Northern Bank	15
XYZ Company	23.5
Jones Store	27
Harringtons	20.5

STEP 2. SORT YOUR DEBT. List your credit cards in order from the *highest* to the *lowest* annual interest rate. Fill in the other columns indicated.

Credit card	Balance due (£)	Mimimum payment rate	Interest rate (%)
Jones Store	790	16.49	27
XYZ Company	240	6.67	23.5
Harringtons	1,720	35.83	20.5

70

ABC Bank	4,350	72.50	17.5
Northern Bank	2,175	60.42	15

STEP 3. YOUR PAY-OFF PLAN. Decide how much of your debt you can afford to pay off each month. Write that figure here: £ *450.00* Also write it at the bottom of the second column in the form below.

Copy the list of credit cards from Step 2 in the form below. Then allocate your monthly repayment amount as follows: for the second, third and later cards on the list, write in the minimum payment required (as shown in Step 2). Add these figures, and subtract that amount from the total monthly repayment. Write the balance next to the first card on the list. (If this amount is more than you owe on the first card, then allocate the difference to the second card.)

Credit card	Monthly payment (£)
Jones Store	274.58
XYZ Company	6.67
Harringtons	35.83
ABC Bank	72.50
Northern Bank	60.42
TOTAL	450.00

NOW THE GOOD NEWS

As you move down the list, you will actually begin paying off your debts at a faster rate. Your new total payment on the next debt down the list will now include the minimum payments you were making before. Also, because interest rates are lower on the later cards, more of the money will be going to pay off the principal (as opposed to interest, and interest on interest). In short, the longer you stick with the plan, the easier it works and the faster your progress. But remember: *don't* add any more debts during this period. As you pay down each item, be sure to cancel the credit or store card so that, as we said in the first section, the weapon is no longer in your hands.

WHAT ABOUT BORROWING TO PAY OFF YOUR DEBTS?

If your debts are large, it could take years—and a lot of discipline—to get out of debt. With this long, winding and narrow road stretching out in front of you, you might be tempted to get some relief by borrowing enough money (perhaps secured by your house) to pay off all your credit and store cards at one time. You would then have a single monthly repayment cheque to write each month that would, most likely, be for a smaller amount than the total you are currently paying by making only the minimum payment on all of the cards. Of course, it usually takes longer to pay off the consolidation loan. The result is that you can end up still paying quite a substantial amount of interest.

But the interest isn't the most significant

problem with consolidating your debts into a single loan. The biggest danger comes from the sense of relief that you feel when your monthly payment decreases. All too often this leads to further spending (which I call 'relief retail therapy') and a spiral into an even worse debt problem. So consider consolidating your debt *only* if you're very self-disciplined and if you've made a strong personal commitment to steering clear of the shopping centres, the online sites, and the travel agencies until you have paid off the loan.

WHAT ABOUT HELP FROM A THIRD PARTY?

No, I am not referring to your parents and their bank account! While having a martini at Duke's Hotel in London, I began chatting with the young couple sitting at a table next to mine. The lady confessed that she had had a huge amount of credit and store card debt, but her father had paid all of it off. She had promised him that she would not get another credit card. But guess what? She had got one anyway and was keeping it a secret from her father. When I gently questioned her further, she said she was sure if she got into trouble with the new credit card, she would confess and he would bail her out again. As for repaying the money he had used to pay off her past debts, she responded only with a beguiling smile and fluttering eyelashes. I wondered how she would respond if I said: 'You got yourself into this mess of debt and it is your responsibility to get yourself out.'

For those who are truly overwhelmed by debt, third-party help is available from two quite different sources: 1) charitable or government-funded organisations, or 2) debt management companies (also called debt consolidation companies). The Citizens Advice Bureau (CAB) is the most widely known of the publicly funded organisations that help people with debt problems. Its services are free. The CAB serves as a disinterested third party that will help you work with your creditors to get debt under control. For example, the people at CAB may be able to help you negotiate a gradual repayment plan with your creditors. Thus, you can reduce your debt while keeping your home and avoiding bankruptcy. Importantly, with the CAB you have to take charge of your finances, rather than hand them over to someone else. In order for you to benefit most from their services, you must be honest with yourself and them about the extent of your debt problem.

Debt management companies, in contrast, are for-profit companies that advertise enticingly about relieving the burden and stress of too much debt. Can you watch TV without seeing their ads? To me, this is as much a sign of their marketing savvy as it is of the increasing problem of personal indebtedness in the UK. These companies work in two ways. First, debt management companies put you on a budget that requires you to make one payment to the company each month. It then allocates this money to your creditors according to a plan it has worked out with them. Second, the debt consolidators arrange a long-term loan that you use to consolidate your debts. You must then make prompt, monthly payments to the company.

Sounds easy? For many people who want a low-sacrifice and somewhat parental-like solution to their financial and psychological debt problems (i.e., let someone else handle this for me), the debt management companies can be a somewhat Faustian pact. These for-profit organisations have a less-than-stellar reputation. Some of their clients have complained of excessively high fees, poor administration, and sometimes high-handed attitudes. I recommend you avoid this type of 'helper' altogether and arrange to pay off the debts yourself.

Understanding your credit status

You've probably heard about *credit reporting agencies*. If you've ever been turned down for a credit card or a loan, you may have blamed 'the agencies' for putting a 'black mark' on your credit report. If so, you may have a backlog of resentment against these organisations without really understanding their role.

Contrary to what many people believe, credit reporting agencies are not 'credit police'. The agency does not give you black marks on your credit rating or offer any evaluation of your credit. It simply reports information it receives from credit card companies, stores and banks as to your history of borrowing and repaying debts. Those who are considering offering you future credit use this information in making their own, independent decision as to whether they want to lend to you.

Experian and Equifax are the two leading UK credit agencies. The chances are excellent that both companies already have files about you. Most of the information they have on record is undoubtedly correct—but some of it may be wrong, and here is where trouble lurks.

Errors in credit histories are unfortunately fairly common. Since there are no national ID numbers in the UK (unlike in the US, where Social Security numbers are used for this purpose), your identity is tracked based on your name and address. And, of course, it's quite common for two people—or several people—to have the same name, or names that are confusingly similar. As a result, cases of mistaken identity are pretty frequent. Correcting such errors can be very time-consuming, but it's very important.

Therefore don't assume your credit rating is correct, even though you may be regularly receiving credit offers in the mail. It's quite possible that your history, as tracked by Equifax and Experian, may contain one or more errors that will affect you when you apply for a mortgage or other loan. Negative data about you—an indication that you missed a payment or defaulted on a past loan, for example—may cause you to be rejected by a bank or, perhaps, accepted but charged a higher-than-normal interest rate.

To start the process of cleaning up your credit record, order a copy of your report from each of the two agencies. (You can see a sample of such a report on page 78.) You can request your Equifax report online at www.equifax.co.uk, or by writing to Equifax PLC, P.O. Box 3001, Glasgow G81 2DT. For your Experian report, write to Experian Ltd, Consumer Help Service, P.O. Box 8000, Nottingham NG1 5GX. With both requests, you'll need to indicate your full name, your date of birth, your current address, and any addresses you've lived at during the past six years. For each report, there's a fee set by statute at £2.

Once you've received your reports, study them carefully. If you find any mistakes, contact both the reporting agency (Equifax or Experian) and the company involved in the error: for example, the bank that has mistakenly claimed you never repaid a loan. I strongly suggest you communicate in writing (rather than by phone) and keep copies of your correspondence.

Over:
A sample credit report from Experian displaying the different categories of information provided. Please note that this is an example only and that the names, addresses, and other details presented are fictitious.

Reproduced by permission of Experian International Ltd

Names and Addresses Searched

These are the names and addresses you provided when making your application for a file and the addresses we have searched

Main Applicant:
Name: MR EDWIN SMITH
Date of Birth: 17/07/1947

Present: FLAT 2, 186, HIGH STREET, BIRMINGHAM, WEST MIDLANDS, B429HY

Other: 1, MANOR ROAD, SOUTHPORT, MERSEYSIDE

Electoral Roll Information

Further information about the electoral roll is given on page 2 of the explanatory leaflet. The following names are confirmed on the electoral roll at the addresses quoted from and until the dates shown:

Present Address

Local authority BIRMINGHAM LA
186, HIGH STREET, BIRMINGHAM, WEST MIDLANDS, B429HY

Flat 2
SMITH EDWIN   From 1996   to
present

Flat 1
PRICE JUDITH   From 1995   to
present

Association/Alias

Details of any individuals with whom you have a financial connection are shown below. A financial connection can be due to a joint account, a joint application, a joint judgment, or from information you have provided to us. If you have been known by another name (for example, a maiden name), this information may also be recorded below. For further information please refer to pages 4 and 5 of the explanatory leaflet.

MR EDWIN SMITH, 1, MANOR ROAD, CHURCHTOWN, SOUTHPORT, MERSEYSIDE
Associated with MR SIMON R CASTLE
Date of Birth 02/05/52
Associated type JOINT ACCOUNT
Association created by BARCLAYS BANK PLC Date 23/12/96

Other Public Record Information

This section includes details of court judgments, bankruptcies, and individual voluntary arrangements. For further information please refer to pages 2 and 3 of the explanatory leaflet.

EDWIN SMITH, 186, HIGH STREET, BIRMINGHAM, WEST MIDLANDS, B42 9HY

Information type **SATISFIED JUDGMENT**

Date 05/97 Amount £481

Satisfied 07/00

Court name **SOUTHPORT** Case number DC701043

Source REGISTRY TRUST LTD

Unless a County Court Judgment was paid within one calendar month, it will continue to be retained on file for six years from the date of the judgment. Please see page 1 of the leaflet for further information.

Credit Account Information

If you have any queries regarding the credit account information recorded below and would like to contact the company concerned yourself, a list of useful addresses is included at the end of your file. An explanation of the status history is provided on page 3 of the explanatory leaflet.

MR EDWIN SMITH, 186, HIGH STREET, BIRMINGHAM, WEST MIDLANDS, B42 9HY

Date of birth 17/07/47

FIRST NATIONAL TRICITY FINANCE LIMITED BUDGET ACCOUNT

Started 19/05/00 Balance £344 Credit Limit £360

Status history 00000UU
In last 7 months, number of status 1–2 is 0;
number of status 3+ is 0
File updated for the period to 15/10/01

**MR SIMON CASTLE, 1, MANOR ROAD,
SOUTHPORT, MERSEYSIDE, PR10 5LE
FIRST NATIONAL TRICITY FINANCE
LIMITED** BUDGET ACCOUNT
Started 16/05/97 Balance £344 Credit Limit
£360 Settled 01/05/00
Status history 000U
In last 4 months, number of status 1–2 is 0; no
of status 3+ is 0
File updated for the period to 14/10/00

*Settled accounts are kept on file for six
years from the settlement date. The status
history in respect of a settled account relates
to the period of time prior to the date of
settlement.*

Previous Searches

*The details shown below are those input by
the company when they made the search.
This information does not imply that an
account is held with the company which
made the search. Details of companies which
have searched are kept on file for 12 months.
Further information about Previous Searches
is shown on page 4 of the leaflet.*

**MR EDWIN SMITH, 186, HIGH
STREET, BIRMINGHAM, B42 9HY**

Searched on 15/07/01 Time At Address 00
Years 09 months
Searched by **BRADFORD & BINGLEY**
Application type UNRECORDED ENQUIRY

Linked Addresses

Linked addresses are created from information provided either by the lender(s) shown below or by you. For further information please see page 4 of the explanatory leaflet.

MR EDWIN SMITH
Moved from: **1, MANOR ROAD,
CHURCHTOWN,
SOUTHPORT,
MERSEYSIDE**
    to: **186, HIGH STREET,
BIRMINGHAM, WEST
MIDLANDS**
Source **CAPITAL BANK**
Date of information 03/02/01

MR SIMON R CASTLE
Moved from: **1, MANOR ROAD,
CHURCHTOWN,
SOUTHPORT,
MERSEYSIDE**
    to: **13, MARRIOT DRIVE,
SOUTHPORT,
MERSEYSIDE**
Source **FIRST NATIONAL TRICITY
FINANCE LIMITED**
Date of information 04/03/01

Credit Industry Fraud Avoidance System (CIFAS)

An explanation of CIFAS details can be found on page 4 of the leaflet. For further clarification about CIFAS details, please contact the lender at the address provided below. This information exists to help prevent fraud.

Name Used **MRS MARY JONES**
Date of Birth Used
12/09/1967
Address Used **1, MANOR ROAD, CHURCHTOWN, SOUTHPORT, MERSEYSIDE, PR10 5LE**
Date information
was recorded 08/07/01
Lenders name **GRANADA TV RENTAL**

Lenders address Granada House, Ampthill Road, Bedford, Beds MK42 9QQ
Case reference 14AY2400
Product Type PERSONAL CREDIT CARD
Type of case USE OF A FALSE NAME WITH AN ADDRESS
Reason for entry DATE OF BIRTH

Gone Away Information Network (GAIN)

GAIN is explained on Page 4 of the explanatory leaflet. If you have any queries about this information contact the company who provided us with the information.

Mr Edwin Smith
Date of birth 17/07/1947

Last known at	**1, MANOR ROAD, CHURCHTOWN, SOUTHPORT, MERSEYSIDE, PR10 5LE**
Located at	**186, HIGH STREET, BIRMINGHAM, WEST MIDLANDS**

By: **FIRST NATIONAL TRICITY FINANCE LIMITED**
Reference 62623456   On 09/07/99

Useful Addresses

The following addresses are provided should you wish to contact lenders in respect of any Credit Account information or County Courts in respect of any judgment information recorded on your file.

SOUTHPORT COUNTY COURT: DUKES HOUSE, 34, HOGHTON STREET, SOUTHPORT, MERSEYSIDE, PR9 0PU

FIRST NATIONAL TRICITY FINANCE: MRS PAM LONGCROFT, CUSTOMER SERVICES (DATA PROTECTION), TRICITY HOUSE, 284, SOUTHBURY ROAD, ENFIELD, MIDDLESEX, EN1 1HF

CAPITAL BANK: MR A MCELHINNEY, COLLECTION & LITIGATION DEPT, CAPITAL BANK, CAPITAL HOUSE, CITY ROAD, CHESTER, CH99 3AN

Notice of Correction

5007080/SMITH
Mr Edwin Smith wishes it to be made clear to any potential lender that the information in the name Mr Simon R Castle relates to a former business associate with whom he shares a joint account. Mr Smith advises that, while Mr Castle did lodge at his previous address, the joint bank account is the only financial connection they share and any further information in Mr Castle's name has no connection with Mr Smith. Mr Smith stresses that he holds no responsibility for the defaulted account in Mr Castle's name and requests that anyone searching his file takes this into consideration should he make an application for finance. Added 23/05/01 HRL

Remember, neither Equifax nor Experian can 'fix' your credit rating or approve your application for credit. The most they can do is make certain that their reports reflect your past credit history accurately. Anything more that's needed to make you an attractive credit risk is your responsibility.

What a 'good credit rating' means— and how to get one

Being a 'good credit risk' means that you're considered responsible and likely to repay any debt you incur. (Remember what *credit* means: it's the banker's 'I believe in you.') That's a good thing— but it's not without dangers.

For example, what does it mean if you get a lot of credit solicitations in the mail? It's both good and bad. On the good side, it means that the credit card companies know that you pay your bills on time. However, it may also mean that you make the minimum payment each month! That means you pay a lot of interest, and the credit card companies enjoy a lot of profits off you. To be blunt about it, they see SUCKER written on your forehead. No wonder they seem to gather round you like sharks round a wounded dolphin . . .

NO CREDIT HISTORY?

On the other hand, if you've always paid all your bills in cash, you may get turned down when you apply for a loan or a credit card. The reason is simple: never having used credit before, you have no credit history and therefore no credit rating. This may seem unfair: 'Why should I be penalised for managing my money so efficiently that I never have to borrow?' Nonetheless, in the eyes of lenders, paying in cash doesn't make you a good credit risk—it puts you in the same category as drug money launderers!

The same problem sometimes afflicts people who've only recently stepped out on their own financially: recent college graduates, for example, or newly divorced women.

Fortunately, there's a simple solution. Get a credit card, use it a few times a month, and pay your bills promptly and in full. After six months or so, you'll have established a credit history which should help you in borrowing. So if you know, for example, that you're interested in buying a home and therefore will need a mortgage in the next year or two, take steps if necessary to create a good credit history for yourself.

TOO MANY SELF-INFLICTED BLACK MARKS?

On the other hand, if you've got a bad credit record that you fully deserve, the solution is more difficult. Cleaning up a poor credit rating may take some time and patience. If past late payments are a problem, then three to six months of consistently on-time payments should improve your credit rating. However, if your credit history is blotted by a county court judgement (CCJ) against you or a legal bankruptcy, expect to wait six years to be able to borrow again.

Obviously the moral here is: if you've never been in credit trouble, vow to keep it that way. It's much easier to maintain a clean record than to clean one you've previously smudged.

3

THE JOY OF SAVING

It's easier than you think

'I just can't save'

Most of the people I meet and advise on my television programmes seem to believe that they can't save. Some even appear to take a perverse pleasure in it. They boast, 'Oh, I'm terrible at saving! Money just slips through my fingers, and half the time I have no idea where it's gone!' This includes some people you'd never expect to hear talk this way, such as successful business managers. Sometimes they explain, 'After working on budgets and financial plans at work all day, I can't bear to think about money when I get home. No wonder I let my personal finances go to pot!' I suppose it's the old story: the house the builder lives in is never finished.

Oddly enough, the people who boast about their financial ineptitude rarely seem to be apprehensive about their futures. They seem to assume that somehow, someone will save them from their own wasteful ways.

I'm not sure how they expect this to happen. Perhaps they are hoping to inherit money. But depending on the sudden death of people you love isn't the happiest route to financial success—even if it were reliable. You never know whether one of the *other* cousins will turn out to have been Aunt

Mildred's *real* favourite. And getting on *Who Wants To Be a Millionaire?* offers no guarantees either. Haven't you noticed how tricky those last few questions tend to be?

Happily, it's not necessary to rely on a stroke of good fortune for your future financial well-being. In reality, saving is one of the easiest things to do, as we'll shortly demonstrate.

WHY SAVE?

Learning to save is the first essential step towards guaranteeing a better future life for yourself and your family. Unless you are capable of saving, you'll have little chance of ever enjoying real prosperity, let alone wealth. And unless you have a cushion of savings behind you at *all* times, you run the risk of becoming truly destitute at a moment's notice—shocking as that idea may be.

I'm writing this chapter less than two months after the horrific attack by terrorists on New York's World Trade Center. Thankfully, I wasn't downtown on the morning of 11 September 2001. But my livelihood was significantly affected. Many of the financial firms I consult and teach with were located in or around the World Trade Center buildings. In the wake of the tragedy, they cut way back on employee training and other functions that once provided a major source of my income. So even as I grieve, along with millions of others, over the terrible loss of lives, I am also scrambling to deal with the personal impact of a huge loss of income.

Luckily, I took my own advice about saving. Because I'm self-employed, I've always been very conscious of the need to maintain an emergency fund. That fund is keeping me solvent today.

IT CAN HAPPEN TO YOU

You may be thinking, 'But I'm no freelancer. Why do I need an emergency fund?' The truth is that *everyone* is subject to financial emergencies. In fact, statistics show that most people will suffer a significant loss of income at some point in their lives, a loss that can plunge them into poverty if there's no financial cushion to fall back on.

The emergency you face could take many forms, including:

● An injury that prevents you from working.

● A plant closing or business slowdown that eliminates your job.

● A devastating illness.

● An accident that destroys your car.

● A mental, emotional, or social problem that afflicts a family member.

● A fire that destroys your home and property.

● An unexpected legal calamity, such as an arrest or a lawsuit.

On my television programme we profiled a woman who could be the poster girl for savings. A year before I met her, she and her partner had joint earnings of £60,000. They enjoyed that income to the fullest, taking lavish holidays and buying presents for their small child. They even spent £13,000 on a cruise to Jamaica in order to fulfil their dream of being married by a ship's captain.

Within a few months, everything changed. First, her husband's business went bad and the debts began to mount. Then he left her. Weeks later, she was made redundant from her job. Because she had no savings, her parents ended up paying her mortgage. Now, as an unemployed single mum, she's dependent on state benefits to get through each month.

Please don't say, 'It could never happen to me.' Deep inside, you know it could. You owe it to yourself and your family to be prepared for such emergencies.

The goal of saving three months' income strikes some people as very ambitious. It's certainly more than most people have on hand. But I'm convinced it represents a realistic emergency fund, one that will probably allow you to find ways to navigate safely through many of the financial storms you're likely to encounter. Anything less is all too likely to be quickly depleted in the face of a true emergency.

Accumulating three months' income won't happen overnight. For most people who embark on a serious saving programme, it will take four to five years to reach this target. That's all right. Many of life's worthwhile achievements take that much time: graduating from college or university, getting a career off the ground, raising a child to school age. The key is to set your sights on reaching the goal and be persistent in pursuing it. Once you've built up the three-month fund, it can remain in

Begin saving now with the goal of having *three months' after-tax income* in a liquid savings account. *Liquid* means readily accessible at full value. Money invested in property is not liquid, since it may be difficult to sell at a moment's notice, and if you *must* sell it quickly, you may not be able to get full value. Your emergency savings should also be in a safe account—one with virtually no risk of loss. Shares and bonds carry significant risk, and therefore don't qualify on this score. I recommend using a bank or building society account for your three months' savings, since such an account is both liquid (you can withdraw it at any time) and very safe (the value of your funds is insured).

savings untouched, ready to spring into action when an emergency arises.

If you are self-employed

Self-employed people should be diligent in setting aside money for taxes. This will help them avoid the common, self-inflicted horror of having to scramble to come up with the full amount of the tax bill all at one time. Follow these steps:

1. Work out your own potential tax liability—the Inland Revenue sometimes makes mistakes.

2. Deduct the correct percentage from each cheque you receive and deposit that amount into a separate saving account dedicated to taxes.

3. Recalculate your income and tax liability periodically (at least once per quarter) to make sure the money you are saving will be sufficient to cover the amount you will owe the Inland Revenue.

Above all, don't put your head in the sand about your potential tax liability. Inevitably, the Inland Revenue will bite the parts left sticking out.

Put saving first

The problem most people have with saving is that it is the last thing they think of doing with their money. Most spend their income mentally before they get it. You need to reverse that 'spend first, save last' impulse. Here's how.

Begin by deciding how much you want to save. A good target is 10 percent of your take-home pay. (Ten percent will allow you to build your three-month fund in less than five years.) But if that amount seems like a daunting goal, don't make that into an excuse to do nothing. Many people can't start at the 10 percent level. If necessary, start by saving whatever you can afford, even if it's no more than £10 or £20 or £50 a month, and gradually increase the amount when you're able.

Whatever amount you decide to target, take this money out of your pay cheque *up front*, before you spend a penny on anything else. Better still, arrange for automatic withdrawals from your current account into a savings account. Most banks will be happy to set up such a plan for you.

Deposit this 'top 10 percent' into a *limited access* bank account. This is a special account from which only five withdrawals a year are permitted. Ask your banker about such an account; he or she will gladly help you set one up. Then pretend that this account doesn't exist. Don't get a cash card for this account. If the bank sends you one anyway, cut it up. And when making your spending plans, don't factor this money into your income. You know the old saying, 'Out of sight, out of mind.' Keep your savings account out of sight, and soon it will slip out of your mind . . . except when you look up your balance, to congratulate yourself on how nicely it's growing.

SAVING SECRETS

Here are some other tricks that can help make saving easy—or at least easier:

- Maintain your savings account in a different bank from your current account, preferably one that's a few minutes' walk out of your way rather than just a step or two from your office door or your home. This helps to create a psychological barrier that discourages you from withdrawing and spending. Incidentally, searching out a new bank will give you a chance to investigate opportunities for earning a better interest rate on your money—a second benefit that's not to be overlooked.

- After launching your savings programme, look for openings to increase the amount you set aside each week or month. For example, earmark your next salary rise entirely for savings. This is surprisingly easy to do; after all, you've been living on the lower amount all along. Just pretend you never got a rise, and enjoy watching how the rate at which your savings grow suddenly increases. Do the same with end-of-year bonuses, cash gifts or inheritances from relatives, and other windfalls.

- Finally, change your debt habit into a savings habit. Here's what I mean: suppose you've been setting aside an amount each month to pay off your credit cards—£200, let's say. Once you get all your debt paid off, start banking the same £200. You won't miss the money, since you haven't been spending it anyway. Use the same technique when you've finished paying off a car loan or your mortgage.

MATCHING SAVING WITH FUN

Does all this sound rather self-denying and harsh? Perhaps you want to protest, the way small children do, 'I never get to have any fun!' If so, consider building some fun into your savings programme by tying it to giving yourself something you want. Decide in advance what categories of spending are most gratifying and enjoyable for you—the desserts of your daily diet. Then link that kind of spending to saving.

For example, if clothes are your weakness, then every time you spend money on a piece of clothing, deposit the exact same amount into your savings account. Do this with whatever is your weakness—buying books, going to the movies, splurging on fancy tools or cosmetics, whatever. Thus, the pleasure of treating yourself will be associated with (and increased by) the happiness of building up your cash reserve.

The magical payoff: compound interest

Once you begin your savings programme, a magical reward will start to appear automatically. This reward is *compound interest*. Not only do you earn interest on the money you save, but through compounding you earn interest on the interest. The result is that your money grows much faster than you might anticipate. See the tables on page 98 for a simple example of how this works, based on the assumption that you save £100 per month.

As you see, the benefits of compound interest can be truly startling. If you want to get *really* excited, project how much money you can accumulate if you set aside more than £100 per month. It's a simple matter of multiplying the figures in the chart to reflect the amount you are saving. For example, suppose you save £300 per month, a figure that's within easy reach for many people. Multiply the figures in the chart by three. If you earn an average annual rate of 6 percent interest on your money over 30 years, you'll have over £300,000 when you retire. Not a bad nest egg.

THE BRILLIANCE OF COMPOUNDING

Suppose you saved £100 per month for a period of thirty years—say from age thirty-five to sixty-five. How much money would you accumulate *without* earning interest? How much would you accumulate if compound interest *were* paid? The charts below show the answers.

I. WITHOUT INTEREST

Time elapsed	0% interest (£)
1 year	1,200
5 years	6,000
10 years	12,000
15 years	18,000
20 years	24,000
25 years	30,000
30 years	36,000
INTEREST EARNED	**0**

II. WITH INTEREST (COMPOUNDED MONTHLY)

Time elapsed	4% interest (£)	6% interest (£)	8% interest (£)	10% interest (£)
1 year	1,222	1,234	1,245	1,256
5 years	6,623	6,977	7,355	7,736
10 years	14,694	16,388	18,335	20,438
15 years	24,529	29,082	34,727	41,295

20 years	36,513	46,204	59,196	75,544
25 years	51,117	69,299	95,723	131,783
30 years	68,912	100,452	150,252	224,129
INTEREST EARNED	**32,912**	**64,453**	**114,252**	**188,129**

Saving tax-free

With most ordinary savings accounts, you'll have to pay tax on your profits: income tax on the interest you earn, and, in some cases, capital gains tax on the growth in value of the underlying investment. These taxes slow down your accumulation of money. However, you can help your money grow faster by taking advantage of various schemes for accumulating savings tax-free, including ISAs and National Savings and Investments plans.

HOW ISAs WORK

An Individual Savings Account, or ISA, is a special kind of account designed to let you save without paying tax on the growth of your savings. It's not in itself a savings vehicle but rather a 'wrapper' that can hold cash savings or various kinds of investment products, from shares to life insurance. The income and growth of an ISA are free of income tax and capital gains tax, and you don't have to declare an ISA on your tax return.

Each tax year you can put a total of £7,000 into ISAs. (A tax year runs from 6 April of one year through 5 April of the next.) You can have either one 'maxi ISA' or up to three 'mini ISAs' (with different kinds of investments) each tax year. There are limits to the amounts you can pay into each of these accounts, as the table on page 101 shows.

RULES ABOUT ISAs

MINI ISAs

In any given year, you can invest in three mini ISAs. Each must contain a different kind of investment.

There are three basic kinds of investments that can go into a mini ISA. For each one there is an annual payment limit.

CASH ISA. A cash mini ISA may include:

- ISA bank and building society accounts

- Authorised unit trust cash funds

- National Savings and Investments products designed for ISAs

Maximum contribution in any given tax year: £3,000

STOCKS AND SHARES ISA. A stocks and shares mini ISA may include:

- Shares in companies

- Corporate bonds

- Government bonds (gilts)

- Unit trusts

- Investment trusts

- Investment funds

Maximum contribution in any given tax year: £3,000

LIFE INSURANCE ISA. A life insurance mini ISA includes insurance policies designed for ISAs. Maximum contribution in any given tax year: £1,000

MAXI ISAs

If you open one maxi ISA you can contribute up to £7,000 total. This money must be invested in stocks and shares.

Maximum contribution in any given tax year: £7,000

If you exceed any of the annual limits specified above, you will lose the tax benefits on any savings above the limit.

OPENING AN ISA

You can open an ISA with an ISA manager, which is an organisation approved by the Inland Revenue and authorised by the Financial Services Authority (FSA). ISA managers include banks, building societies, investment firms, stockbrokers, insurance firms, solicitors and financial advisers. Not all ISA managers offer all kinds of ISAs. So if you want to invest your ISA money into various kinds of savings and investment plans, you may want to use more than one ISA manager. There's no problem with this at all.

What type of ISA is best for you? It depends on many factors. In later chapters, I'll explain how to think about different kinds of investments and how to decide what forms of investments make sense for you, based on your age, your financial goals, your personal risk tolerance and other considerations. For now, I'll offer the following rules of thumb:

- When building up your three month cash reserve fund, put your money into a virtually risk-free savings vehicle. For this purpose, a cash ISA is best. As explained earlier, a bank or building society account works well for this purpose.

- Once you've accumulated your three month fund, consider investing additional savings in a stocks and shares ISA, especially if you are saving for long-term goals, such as retirement. This kind of investment vehicle carries greater risk than a cash ISA (since stocks and shares go up and down in value), but it usually offers a higher rate of growth over a long time period.

- Invest in a life insurance ISA only to the extent that you need insurance coverage. In a later chapter, I'll discuss life insurance and offer some simple rules for determining how much coverage you need.

ADVANTAGES OF AN ISA

You pay no income tax on any interest you get from your ISA. In addition, your ISA is free from capital gains tax. This is tax that is normally payable on any increase in value in a share or unit trust investment. Finally, you don't have to list your ISAs on your UK tax form.

By the way, ISAs replace the older savings schemes, called TESSAs and PEPs, that have been discontinued since 1999. Although you can't put any new money into a TESSA or PEP, if you already have one of these accounts you can continue to hold it and withdraw funds from it as needed.

NATIONAL SAVINGS AND INVESTMENTS

If you've reached your annual limit on ISA payments, consider using one of the National Savings and Investments plans as an additional source of tax-free money growth. These are tax-free forms of saving that include Savings Certificates, Premium Bonds and Children's Bonus Bonds. They don't need to be listed on your tax return. You can invest in these tax-free on top of any amounts you put away in an ISA, even if you've reached the limit of your allowable ISA payment for the year.

Setting and pursuing your personal saving goals

Once you have your three month cash reserve fund, you're ready to begin saving for other goals. Use these goals to determine the amount of money you want to save by a certain date. These will usually include both short-term and long-term goals.

Short-term goals are those that can be reached through six to sixty months of saving. Typical short-term goals include buying a car, refurbishing your home, taking a special holiday, or buying new appliances.

Long-term goals are those that you will need to save towards for five years or longer. Typical long-term goals include buying a home, starting or buying a business, and funding your retirement. Nowadays many parents also need to save to pay for college education for their children. This is increasingly important now that the British government has become less generous with educational support. Just as Americans have done for decades, people in the UK need to begin building college costs for the kids into their long-term financial goals.

A PLAN FOR BEGINNING SAVERS

If you're new to the saving game, here's my recommended plan:

- Set at least one long-term and one short-term goal, but no more than three of each.

- Put a price on each—a pound value you want to accumulate.

- Decide how long it will take to accumulate this amount and develop a monthly savings plan to reach that goal.

Use the form on page 108 to develop your savings plan. There's a filled-in sample on the following page to show you how it's done. For simplicity's sake, I suggest you ignore the (positive) impact of interest and other income on your savings. Just calculate the amount you need to save each month by dividing the total you want to save by the number of months between today and your target date. The interest you earn on your savings will actually shorten the process, which means you will be able to buy the new car or take that special holiday a few months earlier than you now hope. Or, if you keep saving for the full allotted time, you'll have a little extra money to spend (which always seems to find a purpose).

You'll notice that the sample plan does *not* include retirement as one of the long-term goals listed. There's a special reason for this. Nearly everyone would list retirement as a long-term goal, and it's one of the most important reasons to save.

But retirement planning is a rather complex process. Deciding how much money you'll need to live on after you stop working (considering such factors as price inflation over the coming years) and then figuring out how much you need to save to make that possible (while considering such additional helps as government assistance and company pensions) takes several steps and some detailed mathematics. I'll walk you through the entire process in a later chapter, and after working through that chapter you'll have a complete retirement savings plan.

So for now, omit retirement from your savings plan. We'll deal with that important goal later.

YOUR SAVINGS PLAN

Date

Short term goals

Goal	Cost (£)	Time frame	Per month
1.			
2.			
3.			

Long term goals

Goal	Cost (£)	Time frame	Per month
1.			
2.			
3.			

MONTHLY SAVINGS TOTAL

YOUR SAVINGS PLAN

Date 5 January 2002

Short term goals

Goal	Cost (£)	Time frame	Per month
1. New cooker and fridge	800	10 months	80
2. Special holiday— Greek cruise	3,500	18 months	194
3.			

Long term goals

Goal	Cost (£)	Time frame	Per month
1. vacation home	30,000	10 years	250
2. university for baby Anne	25,000	17 years	123
3.			

MONTHLY SAVINGS TOTAL £647

First steps towards building your personal wealth

If you follow the steps I've outlined so far in this book, your personal financial status will steadily improve. First, you'll reduce, then eliminate your outstanding credit card and other consumer debts. Then you'll begin to save some of your monthly income. In time, you'll build up a three-month cash reserve as protection against emergencies. And once that fund has been accumulated, you'll begin to focus on and save for other personal goals.

These stages will take time. For almost everyone, they will require some months of effort and self-discipline; for some (especially those who have fallen into serious debt), they will require a few years. But as you go through these stages, many good things will begin to happen to you.

Some of these improvements will be intangible. Your stress level will go down. You'll probably have fewer rows with your partner, you'll sleep better at night, and when you do indulge yourself, you'll find that you can enjoy spending money with less guilt and greater pleasure. As anxieties about money recede and your ability to concentrate on the things you care most about grows, you may find yourself experiencing greater success and satisfaction in your career, your schooling and your family life.

There will also be some very tangible results. One of the most important will be the growth of your personal wealth. The best way to measure and track this improvement is by creating a Personal Balance Sheet.

Your Personal Balance Sheet is a tool for measuring your wealth. It's called a balance sheet because it involves listing all your assets (that is, everything of value that you own) and balancing them against your liabilities (that is, money you owe to others).

The balance sheet is a basic tool of business. Every public company must make its balance sheet available to investors, and a company with a strong balance sheet (that is, a good accumulation of wealth on hand) has much better future prospects than a company whose balance sheet is awash in debt.

The same is true for individuals. Drawing up your Personal Balance Sheet today will give you an idea of where you stand in your progress towards accumulating wealth. And it will help you gauge how far you need to go in order to have a level of wealth that will make you feel truly secure for the future.

Use the form on pages 112–114 to develop your Personal Balance Sheet. As usual, we've provided a filled-in sample on the following pages which you may find helpful. It may take you an hour or two to complete this exercise. Most of that time will be spent tracking down figures, such as your current bank balances and the amount due on your home mortgage. As you'll see, the maths required is simple: addition, subtraction and one division (when we show you how to figure your current asset ratio). Use a calculator, and you'll whiz through this exercise easily.

YOUR PERSONAL BALANCE SHEET

Date

Assets

I. Liquid assets (i.e., cash and assets whose full value can be easily accessed).

Cash to hand	£
Current account balance	
Savings account balance	
Shares (current value at which they can be sold)	
Bonds (current value at which they can be sold)	
ISA (PEP, TESSA) balance	
Unit trusts (current value at which they can be sold)	
Other liquid assets	
LIQUID ASSETS TOTAL:	£

II. Illiquid assets (i.e., assets that may be harder to sell for their full cash value). For each item, list the *liquidation value*—the amount you could realistically get if you had to sell it quickly.

House	£
Other property	
Cars	
Jewellery	
Household goods	

Art, antiques, collectibles	
Other illiquid assets	
ILLIQUID ASSETS TOTAL:	£
TOTAL ASSETS (LIQUID + ILLIQUID)	£

Liabilities

III. Short-term liabilities (i.e., debts to be repaid within five years or less).

Bills you currently owe	£
Credit card balances	
Store card balances	
Car loan balances	
Current bank overdrafts	
Revolving credit line balances	
Money owed to friends or relatives	
Other short-term debts	
SHORT-TERM LIABILITIES TOTAL:	£

IV. Long-term liabilities (i.e., debts to be repaid in longer than five years).

Home mortgage balance	£
Second mortgage balance	
Other long-term debts	

**LONG-TERM LIABILITIES
TOTAL:** £

**TOTAL LIABILITIES
(SHORT- + LONG-TERM)** £

ANALYSING YOUR BALANCE SHEET

A. How healthy is your financial status today? One key measure is your *current asset ratio*, calculated by dividing your total liquid assets by your total short-term liabilities:

$$\frac{\text{Total Liquid Assets}}{\text{Total Short-Term Liabilities}} = \underline{\hspace{2cm}} = \underline{\hspace{2cm}}$$

Your current asset ratio should be positive (i.e., it should have a value greater than 1.0). The higher the ratio, the better. A good target is 4.0.

B. How bright is your long-term financial picture? One key measure is your *net worth*, calculated by subtracting your total liabilities from your total assets:

Total Assets–Total Liabilities = _____

Your net worth should be positive (i.e., your total assets should be greater than your total liabilities), and it should be steadily increasing over time.

YOUR PERSONAL BALANCE SHEET

Date: *20 January 2002*

Assets

I. Liquid assets (i.e., cash and assets that can be easily sold for their full cash value).

Cash to hand	£268
Current account balance	1,150
Savings account balance	3,570
Shares (current market value)	0
Bonds (current market value)	0
ISA (PEP, TESSA) balance	9,590
Unit trusts (current market value)	5,200
Other liquid assets	0
LIQUID ASSETS TOTAL:	**£19,778**

II. Illiquid assets (i.e., assets that may be harder to sell for their full cash value). For each item, list the *liquidation value*—the amount you could realistically get if you had to sell it quickly.

House	£70,000
Other property	0
Cars	3,000
Jewellery	600
Household goods	1,000
Art, antiques, collectibles	0
Other fixed assets	0

ILLIQUID ASSETS TOTAL: £74,600

TOTAL ASSETS (LIQUID + FIXED) £94,378

Liabilities

III. Short-term liabilities (i.e., debts to be repaid within five years or less).

Bills you currently owe	£670
Credit card balances	2,359
Store card balances	0
Car loan balances	2,210
Current bank overdrafts	200
Revolving credit line balances	0
Money owed to friends or relatives	100
Other short-term debts	0

SHORT-TERM LIABILITIES TOTAL:
£5,539

IV. Long-term liabilities (i.e., debts to be repaid in longer than five years).

Home mortgage balance	£42,380
Second mortgage balance	0
Other long-term debts	0

LONG-TERM LIABILITIES TOTAL: £42,380

TOTAL LIABILITIES
(SHORT- + LONG-TERM)   £47,919

ANALYSING YOUR BALANCE SHEET

A. How healthy is your financial status today? One key measure is your *current asset ratio*, calculated by dividing your total liquid assets by your total short-term liabilities :

$$\frac{\text{Total Liquid Assets}}{\text{Total Short-Term Liabilities}} = \frac{19,778}{5,539} = 3.6$$

Your current asset ratio should be positive (i.e., it should have a value greater than 1.0). The higher the ratio, the better. A good target is 4.0.

B. How bright is your long-term financial picture? One key measure is your *net worth*, calculated by subtracting your total liabilities from your total assets:

Total Assets–Total Liabilities =

£94,378–47,919 = £46,459

Your net worth should be positive (i.e., your total assets should be greater than your total liabilities), and it should be steadily increasing over time.

Net worth: your financial marker

We've been using the term *wealth* to refer to the level of financial security you have. Maybe the word makes you a little uncomfortable: 'Wealthy? Me? Never!' But don't associate *wealth* only with country estates, flights on Concorde, and annual holidays in the Canary Islands. Any positive sum at the bottom of your balance sheet constitutes wealth—your wealth—which is worth nurturing and building. You may start small, but there's no reason why you can't finish (relatively) big; not necessarily in the league of Madonna, Richard Branson, or J.K. Rowling, but big enough to make a wonderful difference in your life and the lives of those you love.

The key financial marker for tracking the growth of your wealth is your net worth. As the balance sheet exercise shows, your net worth is the difference between your total assets and your total liabilities. Obviously it's important for that to be a positive number, to begin with. And once you've attained that your objective should be to have your net worth grow steadily, month by month and year by year. It is the growth in your net worth that will eventually make possible all your short-term and long-term goals, from a new car or a remodelled kitchen to a retirement home in Spain.

FOUR KEYS TO BUILDING NET WORTH

There are many ways to make your net worth grow. Every item shown on your balance sheet has an impact. But for the vast majority of people, there are four keys to the growth of net worth:

- Keeping short-term liabilities under control.

- Sticking to a regular programme of saving.

- Owning property that gradually increases in value.

- Owning shares or other investments that gradually increase in value.

So far in this book, we've considered the first two items on this list. In the chapters to come, we'll delve into the latter two.

4

PROPERTY CHOICES

The money impact of buying or renting your home

Climbing the property ladder

The biggest purchase most people ever make—by far—is the home they live in. For most people, their home (whether house or flat) is the biggest item on the asset side of their personal balance sheet. And many people consider their home to be their single biggest investment. (This is *not* the best way to think about it, as I'll explain shortly.) For all these reasons, your decisions about property ownership are among the most important financial decisions you'll ever make. That's why I'm devoting an entire chapter to them.

The most fundamental decision concerning property is whether to buy or to rent your home. If you're like most people in the UK, your strong bias is towards buying. Nearly everyone I speak to either owns a home (or two), is planning to buy a home, or is desperately yearning for the chance to do so. (And half the people I meet in the UK seem to feel driven to urge *me* to buy property there.) It is a kind of national obsession.

This bias towards buying isn't wrong. There are distinct benefits to owning a home as opposed to renting. The greatest benefit is the growth of your home's value, or *equity*, which can be very financially beneficial, especially over the long term.

Here's how it works. Most people borrow part of the purchase price of their home. (A long-term loan used for buying property is called a *mortgage*.) Because the mortgage is secured by the value of the home, the bank or building society has a claim on a portion of the home's value.

As the homeowners pay off the mortgage over a period of years, the percentage of the home's equity that the bank has a right to shrinks, and the percentage owned by the homeowners increases. Eventually, when the mortgage is completely paid off, the entire value of the home belongs to the homeowners. The house is theirs, free and clear, representing a big amount on the asset side of their personal balance sheet.

The good news doesn't stop there. In most places, at most times, houses and flats have tended to increase in value. This means that when you're ready someday to sell the home you own, the chances are good that you'll profit from the sale, perhaps handsomely. You may want to use this profit to buy a larger, nicer home, perhaps to accommodate a growing family, or simply to provide a more enjoyable lifestyle. Some people repeat this process several times, until they're ready to scale back to a more modest home—after the kids have grown up, for example. And the profits realised from the sale of their grandest home help swell their retirement nest egg (or their kids' inheritance).

Many have benefited from climbing the property ladder in this fashion. It's a financial strategy that works well when used with care. So *most* people should plan on owning the home in which they live—eventually.

But this doesn't mean that everything—including financial safety—should be sacrificed in the interest of buying a home *now*. I've found that many young people in the UK are too eager to hop aboard the property ladder. Under pressure from peers or parents, or led astray by misleading advice in the media, they borrow heavily to buy a house they can't really afford. Unable to keep up the payments, they fall behind in all their obligations, running the risk of ruining their credit rating for several years and perhaps having to sell the property under duress.

So rent a home until you can really afford to buy. Money you spend on renting is *not* 'thrown away', 'tossed into a black hole', or simply 'put into someone else's pocket', as some people like to claim. Instead, think of it as a necessary living expense during the years when you are saving to be able to buy a home.

NO DEPOSIT? NO WAY

I strongly urge you not to hop aboard the property ladder until you've saved enough to put down a significant deposit on your home. You can then take out a mortgage to pay the remainder.

As you may have heard, it's possible to borrow the entire purchase price for a home. Some lenders will even let you borrow *more* than the property's purchase price. Neither action is wise. There are two big disadvantages to a mortgage of 100 percent (or more):

● When you borrow the entire purchase price of

your home, you'll be charged a higher interest rate on the mortgage loan. This will increase the lifetime cost of your home, often by many thousands of pounds.

- What's worse, if you happen to live through a period when property values fall, and you need to sell your home at that time, the home may be worth *less* than the amount you owe on your mortgage. This is known as *negative equity*. As a result, you may find yourself so deep in debt that you can't get out of it. Bankruptcy may result.

In effect, when you borrow *all* the money to buy your home, you are betting that property values will rise quickly in the future. In most years, property values do rise, but not in all.

Take a look at the table on page 124. It shows how the average UK house price has varied from year to year since 1969. Obviously, the overall trend is up. In most years, the average house price has increased from the year before. In some years, the increase has been huge; for example, the 1979 average price of £20,000 represents a 29 percent increase over the 1978 average.

But look at the period from 1989 through 1996. House prices were *lower* at the end of this seven-year period than they were at the beginning. Factoring in the inflation of other prices during the same period, the decline in house prices was actually greater than the raw pound figures would indicate. And in specific districts, house values shrank faster than the national average. In the south-east, for instance, the average house price fell from £98,200 in 1989 to a low of £75,900 in 1993, a decline of almost 23 percent.

If you'd bought a house at the top of the market and then sold it at the bottom, you'd have suffered a big loss. And it's very possible that the amount you'd still owe on your mortgage loan after selling the house would be *greater* than the amount you'd realise from the sale. You'd have to make up the difference from your own pocket.

So, contrary to general belief, house prices do carry some risk of decline. That's why paying up front for a significant percentage of your home's equity is far safer than borrowing without a deposit.

Average UK house price, 1969–2000
(Source: Council of Mortgage Lenders)

Year	(£)	Year	(£)
1969	4,600	1985	34,900
1970	4,900	1986	39,800
1971	5,500	1987	46,400
1972	7,300	1988	58,200
1973	9,900	1989	70,400
1974	10,800	1990	69,500
1975	11,400	1991	68,600
1976	12,400	1992	66,000
1977	13,400	1993	64,300
1978	15,500	1994	66,200
1979	20,000	1995	66,600
1980	24,300	1996	69,000
1981	25,600	1997	75,500
1982	26,200	1998	83,700
1983	29,400	1999	93,300
1984	32,000	2000	106,700

How much mortgage? How much home?

All right, I've convinced you that borrowing up to the full value of your home is foolhardy. But what amount *should* you borrow? How much mortgage debt is a reasonable amount? There are some rules of thumb that are commonly applied to mortgage debt. Some of these reflect the common practice of mortgage lenders (primarily banks and building societies):

- If you're single, you can usually get a mortgage equal to three or 3.5 times your annual salary. Thus, if you have an annual salary of £35,000, you can probably qualify for a mortgage loan of up to £105,000 (since 35,000 × 3 = 105,000).

- If you're part of a couple that is buying a home, you can usually get a mortgage equal to 2.5 times your total salaries. Thus, if you have an annual salary of £35,000 and your partner has an annual salary of £25,000, you can probably qualify for a mortgage loan equal to £150,000 (since 35,000 + 25,000 = 60,000, and 60,000 × 2.5 = 150,000).

- Your monthly mortgage payments should equal no more than 30 to 40 percent of your take-home pay. Thus, if you have a monthly take-home salary of £3,000, your monthly mortgage payment should be no greater than £900 to £1,200.

These rules of thumb are all right. But I recommend that you be a bit more conservative, especially if you're a first-time homebuyer with no experience of owning property *or* if there's any doubt in your mind about your employment prospects. (And very few people today can honestly say that there's *no* chance they'll be laid off from their jobs some time in the future.)

Following the 80 percent rule will reduce the cost of your mortgage. (Remember, lenders do charge extra interest when there's little or no homeowner's deposit, because the risk of default on the loan is greater.) It will also help ensure that you won't be biting off more than you can chew. You should certainly steer away from following the prevailing wisdom, which is to mortgage yourself to the max. That can be a prescription for disaster, especially if there's a downturn in the economy.

Don't forget that there are many other costs involved in buying a home. These can add up quickly, draining your bank account. You also need to limit what you spend on home-related items. For example, after buying your home, don't rush out to remodel, add a room, redecorate, or buy a houseful of furniture. If you borrow or use your credit cards for these purchases, you'll be carrying even more debt.

Maybe you'll feel a little disappointed after doing these calculations. Maybe you were expecting to spend a lot more on a house, despite the possible risk. Time for an attitude adjustment. Remember the concept of the property ladder: most people trade up from one property to another, living in two, three, four or more homes over the course of a lifetime. It's silly to assume that your first or even your second home will represent your dream house. Instead, be patient. Buy the home you can really afford, and let the usual growth in property values, like a rising tide, gradually lift you to the next level.

Believe me, you'll get much more pleasure out of living happily in a modest house than you'd get out of living in a palace burdened with excessive debt and constant anxiety.

Plumbing the mortgage mystery

There are many different kinds of mortgages, the varieties limited only by the ingenuity of banks and building societies. Eager to find new lending 'products' they can push, these financial firms are forever devising new variations on the old mortgage theme. Many prospective homebuyers find the proliferation of mortgage types (and the terminology that goes with them) confusing. In this section, I'll try to bring some order to the cacophony of words you'll be hearing.

Most fundamentally, you need to know the difference between two kinds of mortgage: the *repayment mortgage* and the *interest-only mortgage*. The most common form of the latter is the *endowment mortgage*. Here's how they work.

- With a repayment mortgage, you make a single monthly payment which includes both interest on the loan and a portion of the principal (that is, the amount you originally borrowed). The loan will be entirely repaid at the end of the *mortgage term*, a pre-set length of time which commonly ranges between ten and thirty years.

- With an interest-only (endowment) mortgage, you give the bank two payments every month. One pays for interest on your mortgage loan only. The other provides money which goes into a unit trust or other investment vehicle that invests in the stock market. The hope is that the total value of the invested funds (the 'endowment') should grow to equal the principal you owe by end of your mortgage term.

There's more to the endowment mortgage than this; for example, the mortgage also includes life insurance coverage which will pay off the debt if you die during the term of the loan. But here's the key thing to understand: the endowment mortgage concept relies on the stock market investment growing in line with projections made at the time you take out the loan. Since the performance of stock investments varies, three possible situations may result:

128

- If the investment grows as predicted, your endowment will cover the principal you owe, and at the end of your mortgage term you and the bank will be all square.

- If the endowment does *better* than anticipated—if the stock market enjoys a period of significant growth, for example—then your endowment will have earned extra money, and at the end of your mortgage term you'll receive a cheque for the difference.

- But if the endowment does *worse* than anticipated, then you'll end up with insufficient funds to pay off the mortgage. Therefore, you still owe money. When that happens, many people remortgage their homes; that is, they take out a fresh loan to cover what they owe, and they start the repayment process all over.

PLAYING ENDOWMENT ROULETTE

When weighing mortgage options, many people feel attracted to the endowment mortgage because the monthly payments are less than with a repayment mortgage. And during the 1990s, when the stock market rose rather steadily, few people with endowment mortgages experienced shortfalls when the loan came due. But more recently the stock market has provided a bumpy ride, with more downs than ups. As a result, many endowment borrowers have been (or soon will be) left without enough money from the endowment to pay off the remaining mortgage—a painful dilemma to face.

Of course, the stock market's current doldrums will eventually pass. Similar stock downturns in the past have always given way to renewed growth. But exactly when will this happen? No one can say. If your mortgage comes due during the bear market, you will be in an unfortunate situation.

STAYING ON TRACK

If you do take out an endowment mortgage, the company that handles the investment part of the scheme (usually referred to as the *endowment company*) should keep you informed as to how your investment is growing. Approximately once every two years you should receive a *re-projection letter*. This letter will tell you whether your endowment policy is on track to pay off your mortgage loan or whether there is a risk that the policy will not pay off the whole loan.

If there is such a risk, take action! There are three options to consider:

- One option is to begin putting extra money into savings every month so that you'll be able to pay off the loan at the end of the term.

- A second option is to convert all or part of your interest-only mortgage into a repayment mortgage. Your lender should be able to arrange this conversion. But before you pick this option, ask about fees—they can be significant.

- A third option is to extend the term of your loan. This gives you additional time in which to pay off the amount you borrowed. Again, your lender can explain how this works.

If at all possible, avoid the third option. You'll be much better off getting out from under your debt sooner rather than later. In general, the longer you take to pay off your loan, the more it will cost you.

Other mortgage choices you must make

Once you've decided between a repayment mortgage and an interest-only mortgage, your choices aren't finished. You'll need to make decisions concerning the interest rate you'll pay on your loan, the term of the loan, and other special mortgage features.

131

INTEREST RATE OPTIONS

How mortgage interest rates are determined varies from one type of mortgage to another. Here are brief descriptions of the most common types of mortgage interest rates, with an explanation of how each one works:

- *Variable rate*. This is the most typical mortgage type. The interest rate varies from time to time, usually tracking a benchmark rate (such as the base rate set by the Bank of England). Thus, if interest rates rise, your monthly payment will increase; if they fall, your payment will decrease.

- *Fixed rate*. Here, you pay an interest rate that is guaranteed not to change for a set period of time, typically from one to five years. During that time, you can be certain that your monthly payments won't change. After that time, however, the rate becomes variable, moving up and down in accordance with a specified benchmark rate.

- *Capped rate*. In this hybrid mortgage type, the interest rate varies, but it cannot increase above a specified level (although it may fall if other interest rates decline). Because you enjoy a degree of protection against the risk of higher rates, the capped-rate deal will probably be set at a slightly higher interest rate than with a fixed-rate mortgage.

- *Discount rate*. You receive a discount on the

132

standard variable rate for a set period. The discounted rate often increases in stages over a year or more until it reaches the standard variable-rate level. (Not all lenders offer a discount-rate loan. Ask about it when talking to prospective lenders.)

Which of these mortgage types is best for you? There's no one-size-fits-all answer. It depends on a number of specific variables, including current interest rates and the likelihood that those rates will rise or fall in the coming months and years; the length of time you expect to own your home; and your degree of risk tolerance (that is, your psychological and emotional willingness to place a financial wager on the economic future).

The graph on page 136 shows how consumer interest rates in the UK have varied over the past two decades. As you can see, the swings have been substantial. If you want a forecast for the future, you can probably get one from a financial adviser, your bank manager, or the financial media. Unfortunately, these forecasts are about as accurate as forecasts of the weather in the UK— not very. As the American baseball player Yogi Berra, famous for his fractured words of wisdom, once said, 'It's very hard to make predictions, especially about the future.'

My best advice on the subject: if you feel interest rates are likely to go up, look for a fixed-rate mortgage. If you feel they are likely to go down, choose a variable-rate mortgage. If you want above all to protect yourself against a major upward swing, consider a capped-rate mortgage. And in any case, ask whether a discount rate is available.

MORTGAGE TERM OPTIONS

As I've mentioned, the term of your mortgage loan is the length of time you'll take to repay it. Naturally, the longer the term, the smaller your monthly payments. However, since you will be making many *more* payments with a longer term, you'll end up paying a lot more in total.

You can save enormously by borrowing for the shortest length possible. You will have to pay more each month, but it will save you tens of thousands of pounds over time. Furthermore, you'll be thrilled when you finish paying off the loan at age forty-five rather than age sixty, and you'll enjoy many more years of financial freedom as a result. So a twenty-year mortgage is a much better choice than a thirty-year mortgage. And a fifteen-year mortgage is better still.

See the chart on page 135 for a vivid illustration of how great the difference can be. By paying an extra £100 a month—not very much more, really—you can save more than £36,000 over the lifetime of the loan. Can't you think of any better uses for that money than handing it over to the building society?

Opting for the shortest possible mortgage term will mean that your mortgage payments may be a bit steeper than you'd like, especially at first. But if you're like most young people, you can expect (or at least hope) that your income will gradually increase over the years to come. The monthly payment of £450 that's quite painful today (when your annual income is, say, £15,000) will feel much

How you can save with a shorter mortgage term

Suppose you are borrowing £80,000 at an interest rate of 6.25 percent. The following chart compares the monthly and lifetime cost for a repayment mortgage at various term lengths.

Term (years)	Monthly payment	Lifetime cost	Amount saved
	(£)	(£)	(£)
30	497.35	179,046	0
25	533.96	160,188	18,858
20	593.08	142,339	36,707
15	697.67	125,581	53,465
10	916.54	109,985	69,061

more bearable when your income has increased to £30,000. And when, thanks to your hard work and diligence, your income has grown to £60,000, you'll wonder how £450 ever felt like a burden.

OTHER MORTGAGE VARIATIONS

As if these choices weren't complex enough, here are three other mortgage options you may want to consider:

● *Cash-back mortgage.* You get a cash payment at the time the loan is made, generally a percentage of the loan amount. In effect, you are simply borrowing extra money beyond what's needed to make the home purchase.

Graph showing the trend of the UK base interest rate since 1985. This rate, currently set by the Bank of England, is the basic interest rate that strongly influences the rates paid and charged by banks, mortgage lenders, and other financial institutions.

Some people choose the cash-back option in order to have extra funds for renovating or decorating their new home, but you know my feeling about debt. I suggest you avoid extra borrowing. Instead, save your pounds until you can afford to decorate out of cash you have in the bank.

● *Flexible mortgage.* This is a repayment option

which allows you to vary your repayment schedule. For example, you can pay back your mortgage earlier with no penalty (known as *prepayment*), or take a 'payment holiday' when unexpected financial difficulties arise for a given month. The flexible mortgage option is a good one, since the prepayment penalties imposed by many lenders are quite onerous. Getting out from under these is a good thing.

- *Flexible consolidated mortgage with equity line of credit.* Here your savings, mortgage and current account are consolidated into a single account. You're given an equity line of credit against the value of your property. Your savings are used to reduce the amount of your mortgage. (In some accounts, the savings amount is nonetheless posted separately from the mortgage.) Your total pay cheque, when it enters the current account, is also automatically applied against the mortgage. Both of these features reduce the mortgage balance on which you pay interest. Then, when you start paying your monthly bills, you tap first into the equity amount released by your pay cheque. This is not a bad system, especially for artists and other self-employed people, who may need access to the equity line to help them live through the ups and downs of their income. But it requires real self-discipline. If you overspend you are dipping into your home equity and your savings (if any), and the account makes this mistake easy by showing a large available balance, posing an enormous temptation. In a worst-case scenario, you could fritter away the equity in your home without

137

even realising it.

For easy reference purposes, key items to consider when applying for a mortgage are summarised in Your Mortgage Checklist on page 139.

YOUR MORTGAGE CHECKLIST

When applying for a home mortgage be sure to consider each of the following items. Taken together, they can make an enormous difference in the lifetime cost of your home.

☐ Be clear what you need and want from your mortgage. Do you want to repay the loan as quickly as possible, or do you need to keep your monthly payments as low as possible? You can't do both.

☐ Shop around for the best deal. Packages from different lenders vary widely. On a £100,000 mortgage, saving a single point on your interest rate could save you £18,000 over a twenty-five-year term.

☐ Let lenders know that you are comparison-shopping. Some may sweeten the deal— for example, by refunding your legal fees or survey costs—to get your business.

☐ Also shop around for other home-buying services. For example, before choosing a solicitor, ask about fees. You may be able to save if your mortgage lender agrees to use the same solicitor as you. Ask about policies and restrictions your lender may impose.

☐ Understand how the interest rate on your loan will be determined, and how it may change when benchmark rates change.

☐ Make sure that every fee and charge associated with your mortgage is clearly explained and reflected in the paperwork.

☐ Ask whether you *must* purchase home insurance through your mortgage lender. If so, you may lose most or all of what you save on your lower mortgage interest in the form of higher insurance premiums.

☐ Some lenders will automatically tack on a life insurance policy to your mortgage loan. Ask whether this is required. If not, you may be able to save money by omitting the policy.

☐ If you are considering working with a mortgage broker, ask whether they comply with the Mortgage Code. If the answer is no, don't use them.

☐ Ask about schedules and dates. Make sure your timetable for closing the deal and moving into your home matches the capabilities of your lender.

☐ Don't sign any mortgage document until you understand what you're signing and approve of the terms. Ask for an explanation of any clause you don't follow, and insist that everything you're told orally be reflected in writing.

☐ For further information, consult the Council of Mortgage Lenders. They offer a range of useful publications on home buying. Their website can be found at www.cml.org.uk.

ASK THE TOUGH QUESTIONS, AND INSIST ON GETTING ANSWERS

In any case, when you're mortgage-shopping, be certain you fully understand your options. Both the charges you are accepting and the commitments you are undertaking should be crystal-clear before you put your initials on any document.

Bankers may be wonderful people, but they are sometimes *not* great communicators. (If they were, they'd be teachers, politicians, or hosts of financial advice programmes!) Your banker may fail to explain the penalties, such as the prepayment penalties, with sufficient clarity. Sometimes this is because he doesn't fully understand the rules himself. In other cases, he understands the mortgage contract but has forgotten how to explain it in terms ordinary humans can follow. Don't be shy about asking for an explanation, and asking again until you *really* understand the answer.

Prepaying and refinancing

PREPAYING YOUR MORTGAGE

I've mentioned that some people like to have the option of prepaying their mortgage—that is, making more than the minimum payment each month, as often as they can afford to do so. The advantage of prepaying is that you save enormously on interest over time, even when your prepayments are relatively small. Eventually, you can pay off your mortgage some months or years ahead of schedule and begin living a mortgage-free life earlier than you expected.

There is, however, a subtle disadvantage to consider. When you make extra mortgage payments, you are placing your cash into an investment vehicle (your home) that is considered *illiquid*—that is, sometimes difficult to sell. In a worse-case scenario, you might need access to the cash that is locked up in the value of your property during a time when house prices are falling. Under these circumstances, it may be better to have the cash sitting safe and sound in a building society account.

REFINANCING YOUR MORTGAGE

The issue of prepayment penalties is relevant to another mortgage strategy question—namely, when to consider *refinancing*.

First, a bit of background. As I've mentioned, like other interest rates, mortgage interest rates charged by banks vary from time to time. In times of inflation, the rates tend to rise; in times of price stability, they tend to fall. When mortgage rates fall, people who've taken out loans at relatively high rates of interest sometimes become interested in the possibility of refinancing; that is, replacing their higher-interest loan with a new loan at a lower rate. This means, in effect, paying off the old loan using money borrowed at the new, lower rate. The idea is to save money by reducing the monthly interest charges you pay.

Is refinancing to save on mortgage interest a good idea? It can be. You will definitely save on interest payments when interest rates go down significantly. But there is a downside: many UK lenders impose penalties for prepayment of your original loan. These penalties can be quite steep. For example, if you refinance during the first five years of the mortgage term, you may have to pay a full year's interest as a penalty. It's important to know what penalties your bank imposes and to take them into account in deciding whether or not it pays to refinance.

You also need to consider the costs involved in taking out the new mortgage. The application fee, valuation fee and solicitors' fees may amount to £700–800 or even more. However, some of the usual mortgage charges may *not* apply if you refinance with the same lender that gave you your original loan. And if you switch lenders, the new firm may willingly waive or pick up some of these charges as a reward for bringing them your business.

So take nothing for granted: ask about the deals you can get. And, as always, don't rely purely on oral responses. Get the answers in writing so you know you can depend on them.

The gold-plated castle

You know the old saying, 'My home is my castle.' It captures a very common attitude. If it means simply that your home is a cherished refuge from the troubles and worries of the outside world, that's wonderful. But if it means that you feel entitled to decorate it in a style befitting a Renaissance warrior prince, think again. Your home may be your castle—but does it have a moat wide enough and deep enough to keep creditors from knocking on the door?

This isn't an idle question. Decorating is enormously popular in the UK, and many of the families I've advised have run themselves into terrible debt problems by succumbing too deeply and too often to the lure of new furniture, drapes, rugs, appliances and a new conservatory. I recommend that you treat decorating as a step-by-step process. Don't give in to the temptation to use your credit cards to do the whole house at once. The pressure of carrying the debt incurred in spending money on fix-ups is likely to negate the pleasure you'd otherwise derive from living in the house.

The home-as-castle attitude leads to over-spending and over-borrowing. It also helps produce renovations whose value is unlikely to be gained back when it comes time to sell. Thoughtfully planned DIY projects can enhance your home's value. But many people fix up their homes in ways that are so—well, unique (a polite way of saying 'odd')—that whoever buys the house from them will probably want to rip out the insides and start all over again. Those who make this mistake will almost never get back the money they've spent on renovations.

Property as an investment

Is property a shrewd investment? It depends on how you define the word *investment* and what you hope to gain from the money you spend on a home.

Unlike most of the things you buy for your own use and enjoyment—cars, clothing, furniture, appliances—property does tend to increase in value over time, provided it's well maintained and located in an area where other people want to live. There are exceptions, however. As I've explained, the property market, like any other market, is subject to downturns. If you need to sell your home during a slump, you may actually lose money on the deal.

However, most people find that they can sell their homes for more than they paid for them. By that definition, then, a home can be a good investment. And in certain places at certain times, the growth in the value of houses has been so rapid that some lucky people have found themselves enjoying enormous windfalls. Maybe you've heard stories about people who bought houses for £30,000 or £40,000 during the 1960s and were able to sell them for many times that amount in the late 1990s. For these people, a home turned into a fabulous investment that may have helped to secure a comfortable retirement.

CAN YOU 'RETIRE ON THE HOUSE'?

Despite the stories you may have heard, it's a bad idea to try to build a personal investment programme totally around your home. This is true for several reasons:

- The super-fast growth of home values during the 1960s and 1970s and during the late 1990s was an aberration, not the norm. You can't expect the same kind of growth in the future.

- Unlike other investments, the home you live in doesn't produce income. When you own shares, you usually receive dividends; when you own bonds, you receive interest payments. But a house or flat doesn't send you any cheques (unless of course you rent out a room). In fact, you have to spend money to heat, light, maintain, refurbish and repair it.

- As your home's value increases, so do the values of other properties. So when the time comes to sell your home, you'll probably find that buying the *new* home into which you'll move eats up most of the profits from selling the old home.

For all these reasons, don't expect to 'retire on your house'. Life just doesn't usually work that way. Instead, buy a home you can enjoy living in and take care of it in a way that enhances your comfort and pleasure. If you profit handsomely when you sell it, fine. (Later in this book I'll outline the kind of investment portfolio you *should* be developing to fund your retirement and other long-term goals.)

BUYING TO LET

What about investing in properties other than your own home? Here the picture is a little different.

Buying property to rent out is very popular, especially among older people. My friend Sheila, a manager of public relations for theatre companies and other arts organisations, is saving her pounds in hopes of buying a place to rent out as an ongoing source of income. She is pursuing this dream even though she herself lives in a rental property! For Sheila, buying property isn't a matter of owning her own castle; rather, it's a business venture, like buying a stationer's or a tobacconist's shop.

If you dream of becoming a property mogul, approach it in the same business-like spirit. Do a lot of homework before you buy. Make certain that you're buying a property that is likely to command a worthwhile rent: one in a location and with an architectural style and amenities that will be popular among the mass of renters.

If you plan to handle the property directly rather than using the services of a property manager, be prepared for the complications of being a landlord. You'll be responsible for all the various nuisances involved: the paperwork related to leases and taxes; collecting rent regularly (and when necessary pursuing negligent renters for the money); keeping the property in repair; working with contractors and utility companies, and so on. When the heating breaks down or the roof springs a leak, *you* will be the person who gets the irate phone call—and you can count on it happening most often after midnight on Saturday!

When considering the profit potential in managing property, weigh all the costs involved. They will probably be greater than you expect. Wear and tear on an apartment can be high and the expense of repainting, refinishing floors, and fixing wiring and plumbing between tenants can be shocking. And you should assume that the property will be vacant for an average of two months a year. If you can't carry the expenses without income for that long, you could be in trouble.

Having offered all these warnings, let's end on a more positive note. For those who are prepared to do all the necessary homework and to spend the time required to maintain the property and deal with tenants, investing in property can be a fine source of income and growing wealth. If you buy a well-chosen flat or house, mortgage it conservatively, and collect a rent that's large enough to cover the mortgage cost and all other expenses as well as providing a significant profit, you can do well. You may be able to buy a second property with the profits thrown off by the first, and then eventually a third property and a fourth. Some people end up building modest property empires that they devote full-time to managing.

If this idea appeals to you, go for it! But expect it to be just as much work as any other full-time job.

BUYING WITH A PARTNER

One final point about buying property. If you're part of an unmarried couple that plan on buying a home together, you should really have a partnership agreement that includes a clause about how the property will be handled if the relationship breaks up. More once-loving people end up fighting over property than any other subject (save children).

In the next chapter, I'll offer more advice about how to manage the volatile combination of love and money.

5

FINANCIAL PARTNERSHIP

*Love, marriage, family, and the
money choices they bring*

The talking cure

I'm no expert on love and romance. Like most
people, I've had my share of heartthrobs and
heartbreaks, but I'd suggest you turn to an agony
aunt if your hormones are your chief problem.

One thing I *do* know about, however, is the
effect of money on a love relationship. At its worst,
I can tell you, it's far from pretty.

Experts say that other problems—spats over the
children and the in-laws, arguments about careers,
even sexual differences—can be overcome with a
little goodwill and accommodation. But conflicts in
regard to money are different. For most couples,
these are harder to resolve. One reason is that
attitudes towards money are deep-seated, largely
unconscious, and often virtually non-negotiable. So
disagreements about how money should be earned,
managed, spent, saved, invested, and passed on can
be almost impossible to reconcile.

Therefore it's important to talk about your
differing attitudes in regard to money *before*
making a serious life commitment to one another,
whether through marriage, living together, or
through some other drastic step, such as buying a
home, having a child, or chucking it all to move to

Tahiti. This is not to say that talking about money *afterwards* isn't important and valuable, too—of course it is. And if you find that you've got involved in a serious relationship with someone without having talked through your financial attitudes, don't despair; you can deal with those issues now. My point simply is that sooner is better, before assumptions harden into positions that must be defended at all costs.

One couple on my TV programme *Your Money or Your Life* discovered that they had radically different points of view about money which they'd never discussed in five years of living together. Just a week after we filmed the programme, she left him, convinced that their differences about money could never be overcome and that her personal financial well-being was in danger from her partner's seeming indifference. An extreme case? Yes, but don't think it could never happen to you.

Your Money Partnership Quiz

On pages 153–156, you'll find Your Money Partnership Quiz. Make two copies: one for yourself, one for your partner. Answer the questions separately (no peeking at your partner's responses). Then set aside an hour or two to go through the questions together and *seriously* discuss the areas of agreement and disagreement that you uncover. You'll learn a lot about the values you and your partner hold in regard to money, the (often unspoken) assumptions you each make, and the dreams, fears, and desires you each have concerning money.

You'll also learn a bit about how to listen to one

151

another and talk to one another in a mutually respectful, sympathetic way. These skills can go a long way towards helping you keep your relationship strong and healthy even when serious arguments about money arise.

YOUR MONEY PARTNERSHIP QUIZ

Each partner should answer the following questions individually. Then review and discuss your answers together. There are no right or wrong answers. Instead, the quiz is designed to launch a conversation between the two of you about your attitudes towards money and your financial goals, dreams and desires. The objective is to learn about yourself and your partner, and to lay the foundation for developing a money plan for life that you can *both* be happy with.

YOUR CURRENT MONEY SITUATION

☐ **How satisfied am I with my current income?**

☐ **How satisfied am I with my current degree of wealth?**

☐ **How much debt do I currently have? Is my current debt load comfortable or is it too great?**

☐ **How satisfied am I with my career and income prospects for the near future (one to three years)? How about for the longer term (three to twenty years)?**

☐ **Are there things I would like to do to improve my career and income prospects? If so, what are they? Am I taking steps to pursue those goals?**

☐ **How satisfied am I with my current spending patterns? Why?**

- [ ] What would I like to spend *less* money on?
- [ ] What would I like to spend *more* money on?
- [ ] What do I wish I could buy that I can't currently afford?
- [ ] How satisfied am I with my current saving patterns?
- [ ] How much money do I have set aside for an emergency? Is it enough?
- [ ] How much money do I have invested in shares, unit trusts, bonds, or other financial investments?
- [ ] How satisfied am I with the current results of my investments? Why?

HOW YOU MANAGE YOUR MONEY

- [ ] Do I enjoy managing money? Specifically, how do I feel about paying bills? About saving? About investing?
- [ ] Would I like to turn over the management of my money to another person if I could?
- [ ] Where do I turn for advice and information about money?
- [ ] Do I have a professional money adviser? If so, am I satisfied with the help he or she gives me? Why or why not?

YOUR FUTURE FINANCIAL PLANS

- [ ] What plans do I have for a family? Do I plan to have children? If so, how many?

When?

- [ ] If I plan to have children, do I expect to have enough income to raise them in a style I consider appropriate?

- [ ] What 'special things' (beyond basic food and shelter) would I want to provide for my children? Which are most important? Do I expect to be able to afford them?

- [ ] What level of income do I hope to enjoy ten years from now? Twenty years? Thirty years?

- [ ] What lifestyle would I like to enjoy ten years from now? Twenty years? Thirty years?

- [ ] How long do I intend to keep working?

- [ ] What is my idea of a rewarding retirement?

- [ ] Where do I hope to live in retirement?

- [ ] What activities do I hope to pursue in retirement?

- [ ] How much income will I need to enjoy my desired retirement lifestyle?

- [ ] How much savings will I need to make my desired retirement lifestyle possible?

MONEY AND YOUR PARTNERSHIP

- [ ] To what extent do my partner and I share income and expenses?

- [ ] Am I satisfied with the current sharing of money rights and responsibilities between me and my partner? Why or why not?

☐ What money matters, if any, would I prefer *not* to share with my partner? Why?

☐ Do I have any other emotional or psychological concerns related to money that this quiz has *not* uncovered? If so, what are they?

Your family money history

Another valuable exercise is shown on pages 158–160. This involves creating Your Family Money History. It's a process you can work through together with your partner. It includes creating a simple 'genogram', or family tree, for you and your partner. This is a starting point for an in-depth discussion of the role money played in both your families and how this influences your present attitudes towards money.

A couple of points regarding the creation of your genogram:

- In a traditional family tree, squares are used to symbolise males, circles to symbolise females. If you or your family are part of a non-traditional partnership (two males, for example), simply ignore the shapes of the symbols.

- If births, remarriages, adoptions, or other events added additional members to any generation of your family, just add squares or circles as needed to include all the relevant family members.

As you'll see, the purpose of the genogram is simply to provide an easy way to talk with your partner about the ways in which money was handled in your family and the meanings money took on over time.

YOUR FAMILY MONEY HISTORY

Create a simple 'genogram' for yourself and your partner. Fill in the names of the family members as shown in the sample genogram (family tree) on page 159. The two large boxes at the bottom of the diagram represent you and your partner. Prior generations appear above. Draw horizontal lines to represent marriages or other committed partnerships. Draw vertical lines to represent parent-child relationships. Add brothers, sisters, aunts, uncles and other relatives to the genogram as appropriate, depending on which family members were significant in your upbringing and family history.

Your Money Genogram

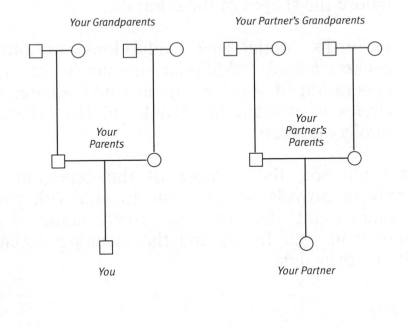

Your Money Genogram

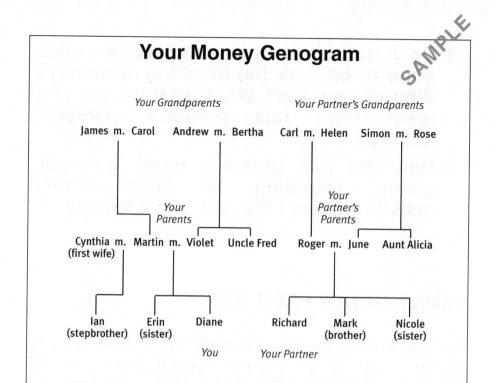

Next, for *each* person named on your genogram, answer the following questions as fully and accurately as you can:

1. **What work did s/he do?**
2. **How did s/he use or invest money? Was s/he a 'saver', a 'spender', or a bit of both?**
3. **What kind of wealth or property did this person accumulate?**
4. **What stories regarding money and this person were told in your family?**
5. **Is there any money connection between this person and you (for example, by way of gift, loan, or inheritance)?**

6. **Do you consider this person a role model, good or bad, for the handling of money? Why or why not? What lessons can you learn from this person's personal history?**

7. **How did this person's work, property, giving, spending, or other money activities impact the rest of the family?**

FAMILY MONEY PATTERNS

As you work your way through the Family Money History with your partner, you'll find yourself discussing how money was earned, accumulated, invested, enjoyed, used, and lost in your family. You may remember events, family stories, and sayings that you haven't thought about for years, and you'll undoubtedly discover things about your partner that you never knew. Among the themes you may want to explore as you carry out this exercise are:

- How was money viewed in the families you and your partner grew up in? Was it a source of worry, tension, and discord? Was it a source of happiness and pride? Was it viewed as something to hoard against disaster, or something to spend freely, even carelessly?

- Was money discussed around the family dinner table? Or was it regarded as a 'secret' to be talked about only behind closed doors?

160

- What were the preferred 'truths' about money that you inherited from your family? Were there certain sayings or lessons concerning money that were passed on from generation to generation? (For example, sayings like, 'A penny saved is a penny earned,' or 'The rich get richer, the poor get children,' convey specific money attitudes that often influence how people feel and behave, perhaps unconsciously.)

- What rights and responsibilities regarding money did children have? Were they expected to earn money? To save money? Did they receive pocket money or allowances? Was money given as a 'treat', a reward for good behaviour, or a 'bribe' to win affection?

- What assumptions were made about the differing roles of men and women in regard to money? Was one sex expected to assume the responsibility of earning money? Did one sex manage the family finances? Did one sex handle most of the shopping and spending? Did one sex handle the investing? Did family stories, jokes, and remarks convey any stereotyped assumptions about money and men, or about money and women?

- How did money figure in the family history? Was there a 'family fortune', either in the past or present? If so, how was it amassed? Who controlled it? What disputes about money occurred in the family? How were they resolved? Were there certain family members with notable attitudes towards money or relationships towards money? Was there a family member generally regarded as a 'miser', a 'spendthrift', a 'Rock of Gibraltar', a 'worrywart', a 'financial genius', a 'money magnet', a 'squirrel', a 'generous giver', and so on?

● How did money figure in the important family events? How was money used or regarded in connection with significant holidays (Christmas, for example) or family milestones (weddings, anniversaries, births, deaths)? What messages about the importance or meaning of money were conveyed by these activities?

As you talk with your partner about these questions, you may find patterns emerging. Money habits (like other ways of behaving) tend to run in families. If your father was a feckless dreamer, forever throwing money away on get-rich-quick schemes that 'can't fail'—but always did—look back a generation or two. It's likely you'll discover that *his* father, or perhaps an uncle or a grandfather, exhibited much the same behaviour. Uncovering patterns like these can serve as an early warning device about your own tendencies. Chances are good that the idiosyncrasies of your family members will reappear in your own life at some point.

When I was around ten years old, my mother inherited a small sum from her uncle. About six months later, I heard my grandmother ask what had become of the money. Mother admitted that it was all gone. I still remember the tone of disappointment and frustration in my grandmother's voice as she asked, 'Didn't you save *any* of it?'

I mention this episode because I can see in all my mother's children—including me—the same tendency to spend quickly any money that comes into our hands. For all of us, saving is a constant struggle. Recognising this as an inherited trait makes it a little easier to deal with and keep in check.

TALKING ABOUT MONEY

The Money Partnership Quiz and the Family Money History are designed to provoke an in-depth conversation about money with your partner. For many people, it will be the first such conversation ever. And you may find that it raises some uncomfortable issues. You'll probably uncover differences in your attitudes towards money, your desires and fears, and your experiences in handling money. That's all right!

163

Differences can be the spice in a relationship, provided you approach them in a spirit of mutual acceptance, honesty and respect.

Try hard to avoid blaming, criticism and attack. There is no one right way to manage money, and virtually everyone is gifted with *some* valuable talent or attitude in regard to money. Yes, everyone has something beneficial to contribute to the money dialogue. Even in the classic case where a frugal, highly responsible, conservative person is partnered with someone who cannot keep track of money for more than five minutes and is much better at spending money (usually on needless things) than at earning or saving it—even in a case like this, *both* partners should realise that they can learn useful lessons from one another. Frugal Fred can teach Spendthrift Susan the pleasures of accumulating wealth and gaining control over her impulses; but Susan can also teach Fred about the fun of (occasionally) tossing self-control to the wind and using money simply for the joy it can bring to oneself and others.

Don't use the facts and stories that emerge from your Family Money History dialogue as tools of argument. Believe me, you'll be tempted to do so! The next time your partner does something that annoys you, you'll want to blurt out, 'You *would* squander half your bonus on a night out with the boys—it's just what your granddad used to do!' or 'No wonder you can't stop buying shoes—you're just picking up where your mum left off!' When this urge surfaces, bite your tongue. When family secrets are turned into weapons, it only fosters mistrust. Deal forthrightly with your current disagreements, and don't drag the past into the conversation—relevant as it may seem.

Above all, don't allow money differences to turn into a battle for control of the relationship. The goals and dreams that each of you harbours are important and worth while, and the best shared money plan is one that gives you *both* a chance to make those dreams come true.

Sharing the responsibilities

The overall responsibility for your shared financial future must be 'owned' by both partners. It's foolish and unrealistic for anyone to say (or feel), 'Oh, I never have to think about money—Jane [or Harold] handles everything.' This doesn't mean, however, that both partners must participate equally in every money activity. One outcome of your shared money conversation should be an honest appreciation for the unique skills and interests that each of you have. Try to talk through what you both enjoy doing with money, and use the insights you develop to decide who should do what in your partnership. Of course, issues such as the amount of time you each have available should also be taken into account. You need to determine which partner is best equipped to:

- Pay the routine bills (mortgage or rent, heating, telephone, credit cards).

- Shop for food and other routine items.

- Monitor and reconcile your bank account(s).

- Handle spending money (possibly including

165

giving an 'allowance' to the other partner).

- Shop for special purchases (major gifts, furniture, appliances).

- Save for short-term goals (holidays, for example) and long-term goals (a home deposit).

- Make investment decisions.

- Monitor investment accounts.

- Deal with banks, brokers, insurance companies, and financial advisers.

In most relationships, these chores will be divvied up between the partners. And in some cases, a chore will become a shared responsibility, perhaps with one partner taking the lead. For example, consider the important issue of making investment decisions. You might agree that Sharon will research investment ideas and make *tentative* plans, but that she must run her decisions by John before actually writing a cheque to the broker; with the understanding that John will not second-guess Sharon unless he has some special knowledge or insight to offer.

Exactly how you divide up the money chores is completely up to you, of course. And you may want to change the division of labour from time to time, as your interests, abilities, needs, and time availability change. There are just two important rules to remember:

- Be certain there's a clear understanding between the two of you as to who is responsible for a particular task, and what approval (if any) is needed from the other partner. This is the only way to avoid needless misunderstandings and rows: 'But I thought *you* were handling the insurance bills!' 'Wasn't it clear that I expect to be consulted any time you want to spend more than £100?'

- Don't allow yourself the luxury of total, blissful ignorance concerning any money activity. The fact that your partner handles the monthly bills (for example) is no excuse for you to be unaware of how much they amount to and how they impact your budget. Remember that death, disability, divorce, and separation are unfortunate, unpredictable facts of life. If you suddenly find yourself having to handle *all* the financial chores, you want to be at least generally familiar with what's required. So make it your business to share the basic information about every money activity with your partner at least twice a year.

In many couples on my TV show, one partner decides that handling money is the *other* partner's responsibility. Sometimes they make this decision and cling to it even when they know that their partner is undisciplined, disorganised, bad with numbers, or otherwise unfit to manage their joint finances. Most often it's the female member of a male-female partnership who takes this position, psychologically trapped by the tradition that money management is a man's responsibility. 'But it's *his job!*' she insists, even as she watches the bank balances vanish and the debts mount.

Putting it in writing

Once you've gone through the exercises described in the earlier parts of this chapter, you're just a short step away from creating a full-blown partnership agreement, setting out the financial rights and responsibilities that you and your partner will take on.

I can hear your objections already: 'A *contract* defining our love? How cold! How unromantic!' And you may want to add, 'We don't need some kind of financial agreement, anyway. We're not royalty, film stars, or tycoons! We have so little it wouldn't even be *worth* fighting over.'

I understand your feelings. I've been young and in love, and I know that young partners are rarely preoccupied with legal and financial matters. And the news media do encourage us to think of 'cohabitation agreements' and 'pre-nuptial contracts' as the special prerogative of the rich and famous. Recently the gossip pages were abuzz with the rumour that Michael Douglas had agreed to pay his new bride Catherine Zeta-Jones $10 million for every year of their marriage in the event of a divorce. You probably don't have assets like that to worry about.

Nonetheless, a partnership agreement is important for both unmarried and married couples, especially if:

● One or both partners have significant net worth

(£100,000 or more) or significant annual income (£70,000 or more).

- Either has children from a previous partnership.

- Either has inherited assets (cash, shares, property).

- Either owns a business.

The partnership agreement is simply a way of setting down on paper the plans and understanding you've reached together through the open discussions we've described in this chapter. Creating it will have several powerful benefits:

- Putting your agreement in writing forces you both to think clearly about how you want to handle your money matters and to express your understandings with no ambiguity or confusion.

- It also forces you both to think through *all* your financial rights and responsibilities without ignoring or forgetting any of them.

- Having a written document to refer to prevents future rows due to honest forgetfulness about what you've agreed.

- In the event of a break-up, the agreement provides a basis for splitting your assets and liabilities fairly, preventing needless (and expensive) wrangling.

- It will also help to protect children and others who may have a legitimate claim on part of your resources.

Frankly, creating a partnership agreement is also an important stepping-stone in the development of a lasting relationship. The process calls for honesty, trust, respect and generosity from both partners. If you can work through the process together and emerge with an agreement you are both happy with, your love will be greatly strengthened. And if you discover that the process is impossible because you have disagreements that are simply too deep-seated to resolve—well, maybe you need to question whether it makes sense to plan a lifetime connection with a partner whose basic values you can't share.

You may think that the amount of money or other assets you have doesn't justify the bother of producing a written agreement. Maybe so. But many couples are a little startled to discover how *much* they've accumulated when they take the time to produce a written list.

Furthermore, there are almost certainly assets of emotional and psychological significance that ought to be handled appropriately, even if their monetary value isn't enormous. (Think about that painting you bought together the last time you were on holiday; or your pet budgie, for that matter. Is it really clear who ought to have it if you two break up?)

Finally, having an agreement as a basis for your financial future is important even if you feel fairly poor today. Perhaps the little business you launch tomorrow may grow into a tidy, profitable operation over the next five years. If that happens, your agreement will spell out who owns what portion of that business in the event that it becomes an issue. And it'll be relatively easy to revise the agreement as needed should your circumstances change dramatically; far easier than starting from scratch.

For all these reasons, it's worth while to create a partnership agreement even if the two of you have only modest financial means.

PARTNERSHIPS AND THE LAW

What I've been referring to as a partnership agreement actually includes several components. They're listed in the checklist on page 172. Taken together, the various documents that go into the partnership agreement serve to spell out how the financial rights and responsibilities of the two partners will be shared and how assets and liabilities should be handled in the event of a break-up or the death of a partner.

You'll need the help of a lawyer in putting your wishes into legal written form. But you can save time and money by thinking and talking through the details with your partner before visiting a lawyer, who can then use legal knowledge to create documents with the proper form and wording.

YOUR PARTNERSHIP AGREEMENT CHECKLIST

Most committed couples should put in writing the following kinds of financial partnership documents. The advice of a lawyer is strongly recommended, and all relevant documents should be considered together, so that the provisions of one document do not clash with those of another.

☐ *Cohabitation agreement (if unmarried) or pre-nuptial agreement (if married).* This document spells out who will pay for which living expenses, who controls which assets (such as individual or joint bank accounts), who is responsible for debts incurred by each partner, what should happen if one partner is disabled or otherwise unable to contribute financially, and how assets will be divided in the event of a break-up.

☐ *Agreement concerning titles and deeds to any properties.* This document spells out whose name (or names) will appear on the titles and deeds for any land, houses, flats, or other properties you own.

☐ *Wills for each party.* These documents spell out what should happen to your assets upon your death. With the help of a lawyer, committed partners should make wills that are designed to work together, so that children or other dependants will be properly taken care of no matter whether Partner A dies first, Partner B dies first, or both partners die at the same time (as in a car crash, for example). More on wills in chapter ten.

☐ *Parental responsibility agreement.* This document spells out how children of either or both partners should be cared for in the event of a break-up or the death of either or both partners.

Cohabitation agreements (between unmarried couples, including same-sex couples) and pre-nuptial agreements (between married couples) have somewhat different legal statuses in the UK today. Cohabitation agreements are generally considered legally enforceable, on the ground that two unrelated persons who enter into a contract together deserve to have their wishes recognised and enforced.

By contrast, pre-nuptial agreements may or may not be upheld by a court. The reason for this is that, over the centuries, an extensive body of law has grown up which spells out how courts are supposed to divide property and income, and to provide for the maintenance of children in the event of a divorce. Courts are supposed to consider the assets and the requirements of both parties, the needs of children, the standard of living to which all parties are accustomed, the length of the marriage, and other factors in determining a fair divorce settlement. The terms of a pre-nuptial agreement will probably influence the settlement, but they may not control it.

However, courts have been showing an increasing readiness to give weight to pre-nuptial agreements when making divorce settlements. If you and your spouse do agree on fair divorce terms as embodied in a pre-nup, the chances are good that the acrimony and cost of your break-up can be greatly reduced.

PLAYING FAIR

I've been touting all the good things a partnership agreement can do for your relationship. But these benefits will be negated if you don't handle the process in a way that is fair to both of you. Here are some tips to follow to make sure that your agreement is truly mutual:

- Be sure your legal advice is even-handed. Choose your lawyer together. He or she should be equally sympathetic and attentive to the interests of both partners. If you have any concerns about the fairness of the agreement, or if you have large or complicated interests that it's important to protect, consider having a lawyer for *each* partner—at least to review and bless the finished document.

- Work to equalise the balance of power in your relationship. Neither partner should accept any agreement under duress. If there is any provision you feel uncomfortable with or don't understand, don't go along for the sake of harmony. Insist on having your questions answered (by a professional if necessary) and make certain that the final agreement respects your legitimate concerns.

- Be prepared to compromise as needed. In the best agreement, neither partner gets everything he or she wants. Instead, both partners should expect to give up some things in return for getting others.

When baby makes three (or more)

When I meet couples with a new-born baby or with one on the way, I'm often amazed at how ill-prepared they are to deal with the financial realities of parenthood. Maybe the denial they experience is a hormonal thing. Whatever the cause, many young parents seem to assume they can go on living with a child just like single people, making no changes in their spending or saving patterns, as if the baby were some sort of a decorative accessory for their home rather than a living, breathing human being with steadily increasing needs and wants.

The fact is that having a baby—or two, or three—is very expensive. Periodically, surveys are published that purport to show the amount you can expect to spend on raising a child. One recent story, alarmingly headlined 'The £296,000 baby', presented this breakdown:

	(£)
● Pregnancy and birth	6,000
● Day care	30,000
● Extra costs for food and clothes	43,000
● Holidays, leisure activities and birthdays	21,000
● Private education (ages 2 to 18)	171,000
● University	25,000

Add these up, and you get the total of £296,000. Feeling frightened yet?

The responsibilities of parenthood are very

serious, and a baby is something that must be planned and saved for. However, I would take figures like those shown above with a grain of salt. For one thing, remember that the total cost of child rearing (whether it amounts to £296,000 or some other total) isn't demanded in a lump sum in the delivery room but rather is paid out in dribs and drabs over eighteen years. These expenses tend to increase gradually over time. During the first year of life, the cost of nappies, juice and cereal, and a few items of equipment can usually be kept within affordable limits; by contrast, the clothes, shoes, toys and activities of a twelve-year-old can be quite expensive. Hopefully your career, and the income it generates, will grow as your baby does.

Also notice that the largest single expense in the table above is private schooling at the primary and secondary level. Strictly speaking, this is not a necessity but rather a luxury, since state schools are available free of charge to all. Does the quality of a private education justify the financial burden it imposes? Only you can answer that question. Investigate the schools in your area, gather the opinions of other parents (and their children), and weigh the trade-offs you'll have to make to invest several thousand pounds a year in tuition. In the end, the choice you'll make will be a personal one.

For what it's worth, I'm convinced that the most important factor in a child's success is not the kind of school he or she attends but the attitudes instilled by the parents. If you raise your youngster to love reading, to be curious about many subjects, and to aspire to an interesting career, the chances are good that he or she will get a lot out of school no matter what kind of school it is.

The cost of a university education, however, is an obligation I'd take very seriously. In the twenty-first century, most of the lucrative careers will require a university degree, and tuition costs (as well as living expenses during three or four years of college) continue to rise steadily. If you're a parent (or a prospective parent), university expenses ought to find a place in your list of long-term savings goals.

Fortunately, you'll have eighteen years in which to amass the amount needed. And there are tax-free plans available that make saving for a child's education easier. These include ISAs, National Savings Children's Bonus Bonds (which accumulate interest tax-free until your child is twenty-one years old), and various tax-free savings plans offered by friendly societies (that is, mutually owned assurance companies). Investigate these and begin saving sooner rather than later. The more time you allow for the brilliance of compounding to work on your money, the easier it'll be to amass the sum needed to pay for the years of schooling.

Affluenza: the spreading blight

Paradoxically, one of the biggest financial problems that I encounter on my television programmes grows out of the increasing *prosperity* of many British families. I call it *affluenza*: the sense of entitlement that infects the money attitudes of many well-off families. It's paradoxical, because most parents are of two minds. They want their children to benefit from the greater incomes they've achieved and the relative wealth they've accumulated, yet they don't want their children to

178

be spoiled, unwilling to work hard, unable to cope with adversity, and unrealistic in their expectations. For these families, achieving the right balance is an ongoing challenge.

One family on my TV programme had received a large payoff from selling a successful window-glazing business. I interviewed the three grown-up sons, all of whom were either non-working or working at undemanding jobs. Curious, I asked them point-blank, 'Do you think that your family's financial good fortune has taken away your own sense of ambition?' Without hesitation, they all answered, simply, 'Yes.'

One symptom of affluenza is the drop-off in employment by teenage youngsters. Fewer and fewer kids today work at part-time jobs as a way of earning pocket money or saving for tuition. Instead, most just look to their parents for the money. Things have changed a lot from my own boyhood in the 1960s and 1970s, when lots of kids worked at fast-food shops, groceries, car washes, and other local places. Nowadays, many teenagers, especially those with well-off parents, actually look down on such work as beneath them.

Don't misunderstand me, I don't advocate paid employment for every teenager. Part-time work can cause problems, especially if it interferes with school work or with worthwhile activities such as sports and clubs. But it can have many good effects as well. Looking back, I can see that part-time jobs helped my friends and me to learn such lessons as the importance of hard work, the discipline of budgeting and saving, and the pride of achieving a goal through our personal efforts. Along with classroom schooling, this was a good training

179

ground for adult life.

So when your children reach their teenage years, don't dismiss the notion of part-time work, or encourage them to regard the idea with scorn. In moderation, it can be a wonderful school for money lessons they'll benefit from for a lifetime.

EARLY LESSONS IN MONEY MANAGEMENT

In any case, I *do* advocate having children help around the home from an early age—not for pay, but simply as a way of shouldering part of the responsibility for keeping the family going. The smallest youngsters can help to set the dinner table, take out the trash, and make their beds. Older kids can be assigned such chores as caring for the family pet, washing the car, doing the laundry, and helping with the grocery shopping. Is this financial advice? Strictly speaking, no. But when kids learn from an early age that life involves responsibilities as well as fun, they develop attitudes that will make them smarter handlers of money.

It's also beneficial to give kids a regular allowance and to require that they manage some of their own recurring expenses through that allowance. For example, they might be expected to use their allowance to pay for bus fare, cinema tickets, CDs, or school supplies. The lessons this teaches are many: how to create and stick to a simple budget; how to save money towards a goal; how to choose among competing priorities; how to shop and spend wisely.

Almost every youngster will make a financial blunder or two. Ten-year-old Matt may sign up to join a CD club and order more music than he can really afford to pay for; fifteen-year-old Nancy may blow her allowance on a concert ticket and wind up with no money to pay for next week's lunches. When this happens, bail them out—one time. Take the opportunity to teach a lesson (firmly but not heavy-handedly). Then, if the problem recurs, make the child fix it. Perhaps Matt can earn a little money by walking the neighbours' dogs for a week; Nancy can do some baby-sitting. If he or she has no choice but to borrow money from Mum or Dad, handle it as a business transaction: write up the debt and the repayment schedule and make your youngster stick to it.

If instead you simply provide your child the money he or she needs to undo the mistake, or make a loan and 'forget' to insist on repayment, you will be teaching exactly the *wrong* lessons. You'll convince your child—unconsciously, but powerfully—that no matter how irresponsibly he or she behaves, there will always be someone around to pick up the pieces.

I've met many thirty- and forty-year-olds who are still trying to unlearn this faulty childhood lesson; for example, the adult going through a divorce whose first instinct is to move back in with his or her parents or to borrow money from them so as to avoid having to scale back a comfortable lifestyle.

SET THE RIGHT EXAMPLE

Most important, parents should teach their kids how to handle money responsibly through the power of personal example. This means getting your own act together: identifying and exorcising

181

your own financial demons, getting debt under control, launching and maintaining a savings programme, and all the other steps I've discussed (and will discuss) in this book. Children are amazingly observant. If they see you thinking before you spend and making careful, deliberate plans for saving money and building the family wealth, they will learn to behave in the same ways without a lot of scolding. If they see you doing the opposite, they'll do so too.

One way in which too many parents send the *wrong* message to their children centres around gift-giving. I interviewed one mother who admitted—proudly!—that she'd bought a gift for each of her three children every single week of their lives, a six-year-old habit by the time I met her. 'I love to see the look in their eyes when I hand them a present,' she declared. Meanwhile, the family had not a penny in savings.

Gift-giving has a way of getting out of hand especially on birthdays and at holiday time. We all love giving (and receiving) gifts. A thoughtful, appropriate present is a lasting source of happiness that deepens the bond between people. But the orgy of buying we see at Christmas time is another thing altogether. When a child (or an adult, for that matter) is swamped with ten or fifteen expensive toys, games, and other presents, the real meaning of the holiday and the true joy of exchanging gifts are both lost. Each individual gift is diminished in value. Often, a week after Christmas, the child is hard pressed to remember more than one or two presents, and he or she may not even know who gave what. Overwhelmed with competing demands on his or her attention, the child responds by becoming bored. Half the toys end up broken; the other half wind up under the bed or in the back of the closet. What a waste of energy and resources!

I'm sure that most parents are at least dimly aware of this pattern. Why do they continue to give in to the holiday madness? I put part of the blame on advertising and our consumerist media. But only a small part. The real responsibility lies with parents. In too many cases, they equate gifts with love—at least unconsciously—and lavish their children with presents as a way of proving their devotion. And perhaps they hope to buy an equal amount of love from their children in return.

Once again, I'm wading into deep psychological waters. Hopefully the exercises you've done to examine your own money attitudes and the role of money in your family upbringing have given you some awareness of the existence of emotional patterns like these. If you've fallen victim to this syndrome, make a vow to change your behaviour, beginning with this holiday season. Buy a few meaningful gifts, and then spend time with your family rather than spending more money on them. The result may be a Christmas that goes down in family lore as the best ever.

The costs of divorce

I can't conclude a chapter on financial partnerships without a word on the costs of divorce.

You've probably heard some of the statistics. They're fairly staggering. Over 40 percent of all UK marriages can now be expected to end in divorce. As a result, the number of families headed by just one parent is steadily increasing. There are now 1.6 million such families with children under sixteen in the UK. Over 90 percent of these are headed by mothers, and the number of single-mum families is increasing by an average of 7 percent every year. Consequently, the percentage of children in fatherless families in the UK is now 20.7 percent, nearly as high as the figure in the US (22 percent).

The rising rates of divorce entail serious social costs, though these are hard to quantify. In the US, where the problem has been studied in depth, statistics show that fatherless children are five times more likely to commit suicide, nine times more likely to drop out of school, ten times more likely to abuse drugs, and twenty times more likely to end up in prison. Anecdotal evidence suggests that the impact of divorce is similar in the UK.

Aside from this, however, there's no doubt that divorce involves heavy costs on the individual level. To begin with, the process of divorce is a burdensome one: the average legal fees incurred by a father undergoing a divorce are over £29,000. And over the long term, every member of a broken family is apt to suffer financially. It's obviously far harder to maintain two households than one on the same income, and many divorcing mothers (who generally obtain custody of young children) are forced to return to the workforce sooner than they expected, or, if they've been working all along, to get second jobs to make ends meet.

Some groups, including those with fundamentalist Christian views, use these facts to support their contention that divorce should be made far more difficult to obtain. I don't agree. For some people, divorce is the only way out of an impossible situation. For some women in particular, it may save them from serious physical or mental abuse. Forcing people to stay in bitter, destructive marriages is no answer to the problems of divorce.

Instead, my advice for minimising the destructive effects of divorce on your life is of a piece with my general suggestions for managing your financial partnership:

- Look before you leap. Make choices about marriage with your eyes wide open. In particular, be certain that you and your partner have compatible attitudes towards money before you tie the knot. That way, you can at least minimise the chances that financial troubles will lead to a break-up.

- Use a thoughtful and fair pre-nuptial agreement to guard the well-being of both partners and of any children in the event a divorce becomes inevitable.

- While you're married, stay informed about your family finances, keep debt under control, and maintain a healthy savings plan. This will help reduce your chance of becoming so dependent on your spouse (or anyone else) financially that you have no choice but to remain trapped in a destructive relationship. It will also enable you to stay on track financially if a break-up does happen.

- Make divorce a last resort. Be willing to try counselling or psychotherapy as long as there is hope of saving your marriage. And have the maturity to balance your personal quest for self-fulfilment with the inevitability of compromise and sharing that marriage entails.

Love is wonderful. But it's no excuse for behaving in ways that are unrealistic, immature, or self-destructive. Thinking hard about the financial impact of your life decisions will help prevent money matters from becoming the cause of a marital breakup—and give your love for one another a far better chance to thrive.

6

INVESTMENT BASICS

First steps in building your personal wealth

Saving, investing and speculating

Many people think of *saving*, *investing*, and *speculating* as being the same thing. In fact, they're quite different:

- *Saving* is putting money into a virtually risk-free financial vehicle, where it can grow slowly and safely over time.

- *Investing* is putting money into financial vehicles with some degree of risk in the hope of seeing the money grow significantly over time.

- *Speculating* is putting money into financial vehicles with a high degree of risk in the hope of enjoying rapid growth.

Both saving and investing should have a place in your personal money plan, and speculating *may* have a place (though a limited one). But you need to be conscious of the purpose and potential of each of these activities. The failure to draw these distinctions clearly leads to serious investment mistakes. In particular, it leads people to take greater than necessary risks with investment vehicles they assume are safe—especially the stock market.

Savings come first

As we've already suggested, your *first* financial goal should be to build up savings to protect yourself in case of an emergency. In chapter three, we urged you to set a goal of accumulating the equivalent of three to six months' salary. This money should be put into an interest-bearing account with little or no risk, such as a high-interest savings account at a building society or an ISA invested in a unit trust cash fund.

Don't plan to invest (and certainly not to speculate) until after you have accumulated your emergency fund, and the money you use for investing should be separate from it.

Basic investment vehicles

Once you've accumulated your emergency cash fund and are ready to consider investing, you'll find that there are many choices of investment vehicles—that is, types of investments (also called *securities*). Those suitable to most people are:

● *Shares*. A share is a certificate representing part-ownership in a company. When you buy a share, you are buying a small part of the company and are entitled to a portion of its profits. These profits are generally paid to the shareholders annually in the form of dividends. In addition, if the revenues and profits of the

188

company increase over time, the value of the company generally increases, and with it the value of the shares, which can then be sold at a profit.

- *Bonds.* A bond is basically an IOU. When you buy a bond, you are lending money to a company, a government agency, or another institution. The institution that issues the bond promises to pay you a fixed amount of interest at regular intervals over a set period of time (the *term*). It also promises to repay the amount borrowed (the *principal*) on a fixed date, which is known as the *maturity date* of the bond.

- *Unit trusts.* A unit trust is a portfolio of securities (usually shares or bonds) managed by a professional. Each unit trust has a stated investment objective (such as income or capital growth) which the manager must adhere to when selecting securities for the portfolio. When you invest in a unit trust you are buying a portion of that portfolio, and you will share in the dividends or interest, as well as the increase (or decrease) in value of the portfolio. There are other kinds of pooled investments similar to unit trusts, called *open-ended investment companies (OEICs)*, which operate according to slightly different rules. For simplicity, we'll refer to all pooled investments as unit trusts.

Within these categories, there are many variations: numerous kinds of shares, bonds and unit trusts, each designed to cater to a particular type of investor or investment objective. As you'll see, they

189

range widely in their suitability for the average investor. So don't assume that all investments in a single category are similar. The obvious rule is: know what you are buying.

There are also many other kinds of investments you'll see touted. Some are *derivative instruments* of various kinds, such as options, futures, real estate investment trusts (REITs), and so on. These are complex, generally speculative (that is, high-risk), and *not* suitable for the beginning investor.

Some people consider such things as antiques, fine art, precious metals, rare books, and postage stamps as investments. These, too, should *not* be chosen as investment vehicles by the average person. Most of those who sink their money into such collectible items lose more than they gain; the only ones who profit (beside the dealers) are a few collectors with deep knowledge of the field, inside connections, and good luck. Of course, if you love pictures or pottery or Persian rugs, by all means buy some and enjoy them. If they grow in value, wonderful! But don't bet your home or your retirement on them.

In this book, we'll focus our attention on shares, bonds, and unit trusts, which are the investment vehicles of choice for the overwhelming majority of people.

Realities of risk

When the time comes to consider investing, many people completely ignore the risk factor. Even worse, they ignore their own emotional reactions to risk. To see what I mean, try the following simple test.

Imagine I gave you £1,000 in cash as a gift, free and clear. You are on your way to your favourite store to spend this windfall on whatever your heart desires. Now imagine that, when you arrive at the store, you discover that you somehow lost £200 on the way. (Maybe it slipped out of your purse or wallet.) How badly would that loss bother you?

If your answer is, 'Not very much—after all, I still have £800,' then imagine the amount you lost was £300. How do you feel about *that*? What about £400? What about £600? At some point, you'll find that your sense of anxiety and dismay (even in thinking about this imaginary situation) kicks in. The higher the figure, the greater your emotional risk tolerance.

When I use this test with ordinary investors, it becomes clear that most people are not nearly as risk tolerant as they believe. (If you want further help in determining your own attitude towards risk, try one of the self-quizzes available on many financial websites. You can find a good one at the website associated with my television programme found at www.bbc.co.uk/yourmoney.) So step one in considering your personal investment strategy is to ask yourself, 'How much risk am I willing to accept?'

What is risk? Many definitions have been suggested, but I prefer a simple one: *risk is the possibility of financial loss*. If I had a pound for every time somebody asked me for a totally risk-free security, I'd be richer than David Beckham. In truth, *no* investment is completely free of risk. No matter what investment vehicle you put your money into, there is always at least a small chance that you may lose some or all of your money. But the degree of risk varies greatly from one type of investment to the next. For example, if you invest in the shares of a small, relatively unknown new company, the possibility that the company will go bankrupt and that you will lose your entire investment is quite significant. By contrast, if you invest in gilts—that is, bonds issued by the British government—the possibility of loss is very, very slight. It would probably take some kind of worldwide financial disaster to cause Her Majesty's government to refuse to pay off its debts, in which case collecting the interest on your bonds would probably not be your only worry!

The risk involved in investing, therefore, runs on a spectrum from very high to very low, depending largely on the kind of investment vehicles you choose. The figure below offers one possible presentation of the risk spectrum, from a building society savings account to so-called derivative instruments such as financial futures. (Don't worry if some of the terms on this chart are unfamiliar to you now. I'll explain them later.) Depending on your personal risk tolerance, you may choose to spend most of your time at the bottom of the pyramid (in the low-risk arena) or venture more boldly towards the middle and top of the pyramid with at least a portion of your money.

There *is* a rationale for accepting somewhat

greater risk: namely, the potential for greater gain. But for now I want to stay focused on the downside of risk, since I believe so many investors, especially novices, underestimate this.

THE RISK PYRAMID

RISKIEST

Derivatives (futures, options, etc)

Small-cap shares

Mid-cap shares

Blue-chip shares (also known as large-cap shares)

Unit trusts (invested in shares)

Corporate bonds

Unit trusts (invested in bonds)

Gilts (UK government bonds)

Building society savings account

SAFEST

KINDS OF RISK

In fact, the concept of risk is a little more complicated than the risk spectrum might suggest. There are actually several distinct kinds of risk, each of which can affect the value of your investments in different ways. It's important to know a little about these different kinds of risk so that you can make intelligent decisions not only about *how much* risk you can accept but also about *which* kinds of risk you're willing to take on.

The kinds of risk include:

- *Market risk.* Also called systematic risk, this is the possibility that an entire investment marketplace—the stock market, for example—will suffer a decline, causing you to lose all or part of your investment in that market. In fact, such declines do happen. They're often referred to as *bear markets,* and they occasion much wailing and gnashing of teeth among investors. Bear markets pass in time, giving way to renewed price increases. But if you need to cash in your investment in the meantime, you may suffer a real and unavoidable loss.

- *Sector risk.* This is the possibility that shares in a particular *sector* or industry will decline due to factors specific to that industry. For example, when fears of terrorism caused many people to cancel travel plans in late 2001, shares of airlines and other travel-related companies suffered a sector decline. Again, most sectors rebound eventually. But if you invest heavily in one or two sectors, you may lose a lot of money if they take a tumble.

- *Company-specific risk.* This is the possibility that shares or bonds issued by a particular company will decline. It may happen for any of a variety of reasons: bad management, increased business competition, an ill-advised company expansion, excessive debt and so on.

If you've invested substantially in the shares or bonds of a specific company whose value falls, you may lose all or part of your money. (Early in 2001, my broker strongly urged me to invest in a highly touted American company called Enron, which was then trading at $49 a share. I did. By now, you've probably heard the story of Enron's collapse—as of this writing, each share is worth 42 cents. When the firm's bankruptcy becomes final, I plan on using the share certificates to wallpaper my guest bathroom, which is about the only use to which they can be put.)

- *Inflation risk.* This is the possibility that your investment money will lose part of its value due to price inflation (that is, the increase in the price of goods and services we use every day). During a high-inflation period (such as the 1970s), otherwise sound investments may grow more slowly than the inflation rate. As a result, the purchasing power of your money actually shrinks. It's impossible to forecast future inflation rates precisely, but the possibility of inflation needs to be considered when measuring the potential future value of any investment.

- *Currency risk.* This risk primarily affects investments in foreign companies, although it can also affect investments in UK companies with large overseas operations. Currency risk is the possibility that the value of your investment will decline due to changes in the relative value of a foreign currency against the pound. For example, suppose you buy shares in a Japanese

195

company. If the value of the yen suddenly collapses, you may find that the value of your shares declines dramatically, even though the Japanese firm may be as well run and solvent as ever.

- *Political risk.* This is another risk related to overseas investments. It is the possibility of losing part of your investment due to governmental instability. When you invest in countries that are politically secure, with strong legal systems and free-market traditions (such as the United States, for example), political risk is minimal. But when you invest in countries that are struggling to establish secure, law-based, free-market systems (such as the countries of the former Soviet empire, for example), political risk may be a significant factor.

Most people are more risk-averse than they realise. The current bear market in stocks (I am writing in late 2001) offers a vivid illustration of my point. Many of my friends who invested in unit trusts for their kids' college expenses are now bitter because those funds have dropped more than 60 percent in the last couple of years.

On the surface, this is an illogical and foolish reaction. After all, at the time they invested their money, my friends were well aware that the stock market may go down as well as up. During the 1990s they enjoyed many years of spectacular growth. And their kids, by and large, aren't yet ready for college, so there's still a good chance that their parents' portfolios will rebound in time.

Nonetheless, my friends are very upset over the decline their shares have suffered. What does it prove? That in reality my friends were far less risk tolerant than they thought.

So it's important to have a realistic sense of what it will feel like to lose real money before you invest. If you're nervous about it, think twice about investing in shares or any other vehicle that carries significant risk. (In chapter seven, we'll show you a risk-free way to try your hand at share investing, which will permit you to experience the highs and lows of the market and see first-hand how you react.)

The paradox of risk

Since risk is the possibility of loss, most investors are eager to reduce their risk exposure. And there are various ways of minimising your exposure to each kind of risk. For example, it's possible to reduce your market risk by spreading your investment money among two or more different kinds of markets, including markets that often move in different directions (rather than in tandem). Since stock markets and bond markets often move in opposite directions, you can reduce your market risk by investing part of your money in shares, part in bonds.

Similarly, it's possible to reduce both sector risk and stock-specific risk through the strategy of *diversification*. This means investing in shares or bonds issued by companies from several different sectors, including sectors that tend to move in opposite directions. For example, if some of your money is invested in shares of consumer products companies (such as retailers and food suppliers), you may want to invest a separate sum in shares of industrial companies (such as aerospace manufacturers and information technology firms). The chances are good that, when one sector is down, the other will be up, minimising your chance of suffering a catastrophic loss.

But here is the paradox of risk: *in general, the greater the risk you are willing to undertake, the greater the potential gains you may enjoy.* In other words, for most investments, the size of the potential upside is closely related to the size of the potential downside.

The paradox of risk means that a very conservative strategy, designed to virtually eliminate risk, is likely to yield steady but very modest gains. By contrast, a very risky strategy— one that accepts high risk in hopes of a big payoff—could produce results ranging from spectacularly good to horrendously bad, depending on your timing, your cleverness and your luck.

Adjusting your risk to your time frame

Of course, this is still only the start of the risk

conversation. It leaves open the question: exactly *where* on the risk spectrum should I fall? As we've seen, the answer to this question depends in part on your psychology. Any investment mix that would make it hard for you to sleep at night is wrong for you. But the answer should also depend in part on your age and your financial objectives. Here's why.

Ideally, you should adjust your risk tolerance depending on the time frame of your main investment goals. Suppose you are investing mainly for a short-term goal: a new car, say, or a once-in-a-lifetime vacation to Hawaii planned for next year. In that case, it makes sense to avoid high-risk vehicles, because if you suffer a loss you'll have little time in which to make it back.

By contrast, suppose you are investing mainly for a long-term goal: your retirement in thirty years, for example. In that case, you can afford to incur somewhat greater risk. Why? Because most investment vehicles will increase in value, given enough time. For example, if you invest in shares, even if the stock market goes through a down period, the chances are good that the market will bounce back and rise again before your retirement

199

rolls around.

For the same reason, many investors like to shift their investment strategy over time, as dictated by the changing time frame of their personal financial goals.

Doing your homework

Another issue that every would-be investor must consider is this: how much homework are you willing to do before you invest?

Smart investing isn't easy. Everyone wants to meet a financial magician, an adviser who can show you how to triple your money, risk-free, overnight. But there is no one who can honestly make such a promise. People in search of this kind of certainty go badly wrong, mistakenly relying on 'hot ideas' published in papers, newsletters and tip sheets or on rumours about 'sure bets' they hear from friends.

It *is* possible to improve your investment choices, but not by discovering a magic formula. The truth is more mundane. If you're willing to learn the basic principles of investing, to work on developing a personalised strategy that makes sense for you, to read the reports compiled by investment analysts, and to follow company news and share prices in the financial press, then you're ready to invest. Remember, investing will never be both easy *and* profitable—one or the other, yes, but not both.

READY TO INVEST?

Let's say you're financially ready to invest; that is, you've squirrelled away your three to six months' fund in a safe and secure place and have accumulated an additional sum for investment purposes. And let's say further that you're ready to do your homework about the basics of investing and work on developing an investment strategy that makes sense for you and for your personal risk tolerance.

If both are true, then you're ready to think seriously about investing. In the pages that follow, I'll lay out some of the facts you need to know to create your own investment strategy. I'll start with shares, partly because they are such an important investment vehicle, partly because understanding shares will make it easier to understand both bonds and unit trusts.

Basic facts about shares

As I've explained, shares represent partial ownership of a company. They are issued by companies as a way of raising money, and they are subsequently traded among investors on stock exchanges, which are marketplaces established for the purpose. Share prices rise and fall along with the company's prospects, and a large part of the art of share investing lies in learning how to spot companies that are ready to expand and become more profitable. The shares of such companies will usually respond by rising in value, to the benefit of the investors who own them.

When you own shares in a company, you are

entitled to some of the company's profits, which are paid out in the form of dividends. Some companies pay out most of their profits to the investors, which means that dividend payments are high. Others invest most of their profits in future growth, by buying new equipment or expanding into new marketplaces, for example. These companies pay smaller dividends or none at all; investors hang on to their shares in hopes that the share price will increase as the company grows. Depending on your investment goals, you may prefer to invest in high-dividend shares (often called *income* or *high-yielding* shares) or in *capital growth* shares.

If you want to buy shares, you'll need the help of a *stockbroker* (also simply called a *broker*). This is an individual or company authorised to trade shares on the exchange. The broker is paid a fee, called a *commission*, for this service. Some brokers do nothing more than carry out customers' orders to buy or sell shares; these are called *execution-only* brokers. Others also provide investment ideas and financial guidance; these are called *advisory* brokers. Advisory brokers generally charge higher fees than execution-only brokers. (More on the types of brokers and the services they offer in chapter eleven.)

Many people, especially in the UK, still assume that the stock market is not for them. They think the stock market is only for insiders and 'old money' types. (In this respect, the British are some two decades behind Americans, who have become quite savvy about the stock market in recent years.)

Nonetheless, British stock markets have been made much more accessible to individuals in recent years. In the 1987 financial deregulation act known as the Big Bang commissions were deregulated. This introduced price competition to the formerly stodgy financial field. Since then, the inroads of so-called discount brokerage firms such as Schwab, T D Waterhouse, and Self Trade, which cater to the average investor and specialise in customer-friendly service, have helped force more competitiveness and openness.

Opening a brokerage account is now a fairly simple and easy process. You'll have to fill out a form requesting information like that shown on page 204. Note that it includes basic questions about your financial status and the level of investment risk you're prepared to assume. This information will help the broker recommend investments that are suitable for you. But remember! The main responsibility for picking investments you can live with is yours and yours alone.

OPENING A BROKERAGE ACCOUNT

This checklist shows the kind of information typically requested when opening a brokerage account. (Adapted from the account opening form used by Killik & Co.)

PERSONAL DETAILS

- [ ] Name, address, phone, fax, and email address
- [ ] Date of birth
- [ ] National Insurance number
- [ ] Pension number
- [ ] Tax ID number
- [ ] Marital Status

BANK ACCOUNT DETAILS

- [ ] Bank
- [ ] Account title
- [ ] Branch
- [ ] Account Number

FINANCIAL CIRCUMSTANCES

- [ ] Occupation
- [ ] Annual Income (Gross)
- [ ] Rate of Tax (Basic or Higher)
- [ ] Value of Investments
- [ ] Value of Property
- [ ] Outstanding mortgage

- ☐ Details of any liabilities (e.g. school fees, etc.)
- ☐ Number and ages of children/dependants

MANAGEMENT OF ACCOUNT

Who will manage your portfolio? Your options:

- ☐ You are the investment manager of the portfolio
- ☐ Your broker is the investment manager of the portfolio

What level of risk are you prepared to accept on individual stocks to meet your overall objectives taking your portfolio as a whole? Your options:

- ☐ Low Risk only
- ☐ Low and Medium Risk only
- ☐ Low, Medium and High Risk

ACCOUNT INFORMATION

Dividends and interest accruing on securities or cash can be:

- ☐ Retained
- ☐ Paid into your bank account
- ☐ Paid into your brokerage account.

For online access to investment information and/or dealing, you will need a password. You can request a password for:

- ☐ Portfolio Valuation only
- ☐ Portfolio Valuation and Online Dealing
- ☐ Research Centre Online

LEGAL REQUIREMENTS

The Money Laundering Regulations require all financial institutions to verify the identity of their clients. Accordingly, your broker will require two of the following items—one item from each list. Photocopies are not acceptable unless certified by a lawyer, banker, or a regulated professional person.

Personal Identification—one of the following:

☐ Your current signed passport

☐ A current photo-card driving licence or current full UK driving licence [provisional licence will not be accepted]

☐ An Inland Revenue Tax Notification [valid for the current year]

☐ A bank or building society statement or passbook issued in the last 3 months

Address Verification—one of the following:

☐ A recent utility bill

☐ A bank or building society statement or passbook issued in the last 3 months

☐ Record of home visit within last 3 months from an employee of the brokerage firm which confirms that address

☐ An Inland Revenue Income Tax bill or coding notice issued within the last year [if not already used to verify name]

☐ A local authority tax bill [valid for the

current year]

- [ ] A current UK photo-card driving licence [if not used for evidence of name]
- [ ] Your most recent original mortgage statement from a recognised lender

AUTHORITY TO DEAL

In addition to receiving instructions from you, you can also authorise your spouse, agent or other person to provide investment instructions on your behalf. If you wish to do so, provide that person's name and sign the authorisation statement.

SIGNATURE

In signing the new account form, you declare that:

- [ ] This application form has been completed to the best of my knowledge and that the information provided is accurate.
- [ ] I/we acknowledge receipt of the brokerage firm Terms & Conditions and Rate Card and have read and agreed to the terms.
- [ ] I/we understand the applicable risk ratings and will notify my broker in writing of any change.
- [ ] I/we authorise the broker to provide safe custody of investments and/or cash under the terms and conditions provided.
- [ ] Unless indicated otherwise, I/we expressly

invite unsolicited communications (i.e. telephone calls). Personal visits will not be made without prior approval.

Your signature indicates your acceptance of these terms.

TYPES OF SHARES

There are almost as many kinds of shares as there are companies. One of the basic breakdowns to be aware of is based on company size or *capitalisation*. Capitalisation is calculated by multiplying the price of a company's ordinary shares by the number of shares outstanding in the market. The result is the total market value of all the outstanding shares. The three broad categories of companies based on size are:

- *Large caps* or *blue chips*. These are shares in large, well-established companies in major industry sectors that generally have a track record of increasing revenues and profits. (They're often called blue chips because these are the highest-value chips used in gambling casinos.) Blue-chip stocks make relatively safe investments that are unlikely either to rise or to fall precipitously. But when major changes sweep the economy, even blue-chip companies may collapse, so don't assume that blue-chip stocks are risk-free.

- *Mid caps*. These are shares in medium-sized companies, so called because their *market capitalisation*—that is, the total value of all the shares on the market—is in the middle range. Mid-cap stocks tend to be somewhat more risky than blue chips; share prices are likely to rise and fall more quickly and unpredictably. However, at any given time, much of the nation's (and the world's) economic growth is concentrated in strong mid-cap companies.

- *Small caps*. These are shares in small companies. They tend to be relatively risky investments, since small companies are often newer, sometimes based on unknown or experimental products, technologies, or markets, and subject to rapid swings in value, both up and down. Some of the great investment success stories involve small caps that grow to become great companies. But more people who invest in small caps lose than gain.

As you can see, the spectrum of stock-issuing companies from large to small generally corresponds to the degree of risk (and the growth potential) offered. We haven't even mentioned the riskiest category of stocks: the very small, so-called *microcaps*. (This category overlaps with another category, so-called *penny stocks*, which get their name from the fact that their per-share price is very low, often under £1.)

A CHEAP SHARE IS NOT NECESSARILY A BARGAIN

Too often people want to invest in something cheap, assuming it's good value. This leads them to invest in a company that is small and often new. But low price isn't the key: quality is. Most inexpensive shares (like most small, new companies) are quite speculative. A few of the companies that issue such shares will become very profitable and successful, but most will not. Thus, buying cheap stocks is a little like buying lottery tickets: there's the chance of a great payoff, but most people will lose their money and have nothing at all to show for it. As tempting as those low prices may seem, I urge you to steer clear of microcaps and penny stocks, especially as a beginning investor.

GOING WITH THE BIG NAMES

Many new investors feel most comfortable starting off with blue-chip shares. The leading UK blue chips belong to the FTSE 100 (pronounced 'footsie'). This is a collection of one hundred companies representing Britain's major industries. Their share prices, combined according to a complex formula, go to make up the FTSE 100 Index, which is reported on the news and in the financial pages as a convenient way of measuring the progress of big business in the UK. Some of the familiar company names included in the FTSE 100 are British Telecom, Vodafone, British Petroleum, Glaxo Smithkline, Unilever, Tesco, Sainsbury's, Associated British Food, Scottish & Newcastle, and ICI.

MARKET SECTORS

People also break down the stock market in terms of sectors—that is, industries. There are various sector breakdowns. To give you a feeling for how companies can be grouped in sectors, here's a random sampling of the sectors into which the FTSE companies are divided:

- Electronic and electrical equipment

- Steel and other metals
- Information technology hardware
- Mining
- Oil and gas
- Personal care and household products
- Life assurance
- Aerospace and defence
- Food and drug retailers

As you can imagine, different sectors tend to react differently to different economic conditions. In the boom days of the Internet, information technology shares were on the rise. When devastating hurricanes or earthquakes strike, property insurance firms suffer. In times of military crisis, the defence sector benefits.

When considering a share purchase, it makes sense to evaluate both the industry sector and the individual company. First, consider the overall strength of the sector and the likelihood that it will grow in sales and profits in the coming years. Then consider the individual company. How does it compare to other companies in the sector? Is it one of the best managed, most profitable, and fastest growing companies in the sector? If so, it stands a good chance of outperforming the rest of the sector. (I'll provide many more tips about choosing individual shares in chapter seven.)

INVESTING OVERSEAS

Investing in foreign shares is increasingly important

in today's globalised economy. But most British people invest almost exclusively in British companies. Perhaps they're discouraged by the higher costs that are usually involved in foreign share purchases. Perhaps they simply feel uncertain about how to evaluate foreign companies. Whatever the reason, I'd urge you to consider investing some portion of your money in foreign shares, including those of companies in my own native land, America.

A recent Company REFS page for Unilever. The graph at upper left over the page shows recent movements in the company's share price. The rest of the page shows basic information about the firm, including a wealth of historical financial data and (at bottom left) recent ratings and forecasts from brokerage firm analysts. The Company REFS website provides detailed explanations of the unique symbols and abbreviations used.

Reproduced by permission of HS Financial Publishing Ltd.

UNILEVER

PRICE (p)   1.4p Ords vs FTSE All-Share vs norm eps

	98	99	00	01	02	03	04
HIGH	707	695	584	610	577		
LOW	460	401	335	478	545		
AVE PER	22.7x	22.6x	15.5x	16.9x	17.7x		

RELATIVE	%
1M	+6.8
3M	+10.4
6M	+4.1
1Y	+33.9
Beta rel	0.59

SEDOL: 574873
EPIC: ULVR   **BLMBG:** ULVR

PRICE (NMS 200)   4-FEB-02   **577p**

ACTIVITIES ANALYSIS (00AR)			
		T/O	Pr
Food products	%	50	48
Home & personal care	%	48	52
Other operations	%	2	1
Europe	%	42	43
North America	%	24	26
Africa & Middle East	%	5	5
Asia & Pacific	%	17	16
Latin America	%	12	11

			m	s
market cap		£39,665m		
position		9th		
index		FTSE 100		
norm eps (pr)		35.8p		
turnover (00AR)		£29,691m		
pretax (00AR)		£1,699m		
DY (pr)	%	2.68	◖	◖
PER (pr)	x	16.1	◖	◖
PEG	f	na	⊕	⊕
GR (pr)	%	12.0	◖	◖
ROCE	%	33.4	●	●
MARGIN	%	12.0	◖	●
GEAR	%	332	◻	◻
PBV	x	4.13	◖	◻
PTBV	x	–1.36		
PCF	x	14.4	◖	◖
PSR	x	1.28	◖	●
PRR	x	51.3	◖	●
nav ps (00AR)			140p	
net cash ps (00AR)			na	

SECTOR: Food producers & processors. **ACTIVITIES:** Foods, home and personal care products.

DIRS: N W A FitzGerald (ch), A Burgmans (vch), R H P Markham (fd), A C Butler, P J Cescau, K B Dadiseth, A R van Heemstra, C B Strauss, Dr H O Ruding*, B Collomb*, O Fanjul*, Baroness Lynda Chalker of Wallasey*, H Kopper*, C R Shoemate*. **HEAD OFF:** Unilever House, PO Box 68, Blackfriars, London, EC4P 4BQ. Tel: (020) 7822 5252. Tlx: 28395. Fax: (020) 7822 5951. **REG OFF:** Port Sunlight, Wirral, Merseyside, CH62 4UJ. Tel: (0151) 644 8211. **REGISTRAR:** Lloyds TSB Registrars, Birmingham. Tel: (0870) 600 0158

BROKERS: UBS Warburg Ltd. **FINANCIAL ADVISERS:** UBS Warburg Ltd. **AUDITORS:** PricewaterhouseCoopers.

3RD QTR: (2-Nov-01) 9 mths to 29 Sep 01. T/O £24,030m (£20,856m). Pre tax profit £1,921m (£2,122m). EPS 14.5p (18.6p). 3rd qtr div 4.65p making 4.65p (4.40p). **OUTLOOK:** (24-Sep-01) Ann: "...we continue to plan for low double digit earnings per share growth in 2001. Our business depends on people's continuing need to eat, clean and groom themselves, however, at this stage no one can predict the full consequences of the terrible events of 11th September with certainty". (2-Nov-01) 3rd Qtr: ch - "In general, conditions have become more challenging but our business is naturally resilient and has been further strengthened by the path to growth programme which focuses our resources...We remain confident of achieving our targets". (19-Dec-01) Ann: "...business conditions in the second half have been more challenging...we remain confident of delivering our low double digit earnings per share growth target in 2001".

NEWSFLOW: (19-Jun-01) Ann: The company intends to seek buyers for its womens's health diagnostics subsidiary, Unipath Ltd, as part of its Path to Growth strategy. (20-Nov-01) Ann: Unilever announces a definitive agreement to sell to Johnson Wax Professional its DiverseyLever institutional and industrial cleaning business. Unilever will receive US$1,000m in cash and a loan note of US$279m. (20-Dec-01) Ann: The company has sold Unipath Ltd to Inverness Innovations Inc for £103m in cash. (9-Jan-02) Ann: AOL Time Warner and Unilever PLC announce a multi-million dollar enhanced cross-platform advertising and marketing partnership under which AOL Time Warner will bring Unilever's product brands to consumers through AOL Time Warner's broad range of online, on-air and print media.

SHARE CAPITAL, HOLDINGS, DEALINGS		
(1) 2911m 1.4p Ords (Maj 16.5%, Dirs 0.01% [d]); (2) 572m NLG1.12 Ord.		
Brandes Investment Partners	%	6.11
Leverhulme Trust	%	5.39
The Capital Group Companies	%	5.00
N W A FitzGerald (ch)	k	73.2
R H P Markham (fd)	k	58.1
A Burgmans (vch)	k	38.7
A C Butler	k	42.1
P J Cescau	k	14.3
K B Dadiseth	k	8.53 3+

year ended 31 Dec		1996	1997	1998	1999	2000	2001E	2002E
turnover	£m	33522	29766	27094	26994	29691		
depreciation	£m	849	736	624	741	948		
int paid (net)	£m	251	73.0	–105	9.00	395		
FRS3 pretax	£m	2657	4719	3085	2860	1699		
norm pretax	£m	2884	2900	3007	3049	3217	3457	3867
turnover ps	£	4.45	4.00	3.64	3.87	4.50		
op margin	%	9.28	9.90	10.6	11.2	12.0		
ROCE	%	27.4	23.7	33.5	31.5	33.4		
ROE	%	22.5	18.9	30.0	29.7	26.7		
FRS3 eps	p	21.5	43.7	25.8	25.4	9.55		
norm eps	p	24.5	26.3	24.8	28.0	32.0	32.0	35.8
norm eps growth	%	+8.60	+7.39	–5.78	+13.0	+14.2	–0.10	+12.0
tax rate	%	36	27	33	32	32	34	33
norm per	x					18.0	18.0	16.1
provisional peg	f							
cash flow ps	p	37.7	31.1	30.1	42.1	40.1		
capex ps	p	11.6	11.6	9.74	10.1	8.42		
dividend ps	p	8.01	8.42	10.7	12.5	13.1	14.2	15.5
dps growth	%	+8.98	+5.12	+27.1	+16.8	+4.56	+8.53	+8.99
dividend yield	%						2.27	2.46
dividend cover	x	3.06	3.12	2.32	2.24	2.45	2.25	2.32
shrholders funds	£m	5181	7416	3352	4825	5097		
net borrowings	£m	2068	–672	–597	493	16927		
net curr assets	£m	3058	7071	2747	3821	–5108		
ntav ps	p	67.6	98.7	40.9	49.6	–424		

	2001 ESTIMATES				2002 ESTIMATES			
Broker	Date	Rec	Pretax £m	Eps p	Dps p	Pretax £m	Eps p	Dps p
Tilney I/M	30-Mar-01	MPER	3380	31.3	14.0	3750	33.6	15.0
Gilbert Eliott	26-Apr-01	BUY +	3500	34.0	14.3	4000	38.0	15.4
Williams de Broe	17-Oct-01	BUY	3485 –	32.5 –	14.3	3900 –	36.5 –	15.8
Lloyds TSB Private Banking	12-Nov-01	HOLD	3430 +	33.0 +	14.0	3650 +	35.0 +	15.2 +
Prudential-Bache Ltd	15-Nov-01		2605	24.0 +	14.0			
Pereire Tod Ltd	26-Nov-01	ADD		32.4 +	14.0 +		36.5	15.1
DrKW	20-Dec-01	BUY	3854 –	32.1 +		4549 –	39.6 +	
Schroder Salomon SB	20-Dec-01	3M		20.1 +	14.2		27.8 +	15.2
ING Barings Charterhouse	4-Jan-02	HOLD	3548 +	32.6 +	13.9	3880 –	35.9 –	14.8
ABN AMRO	14-Jan-02	HOLD –	2509 –	31.4 –	14.2	2882 –	35.0 –	15.5
BNP Paribas	18-Jan-02	NEUT	3486 +	32.4 +	14.4	4009	36.3 –	15.8
Numis Securities Ltd	21-Jan-02	BUY +	3198	29.9	14.9	3550	33.3	17.2
UBS Warburg	22-Jan-02	BUY	3556 –	32.2 –	14.9 –	4108 –	37.8 –	16.5 –
Investec Hend Crosthwaite	1-Feb-02	Embargoed						
Consensus			**3457**	**32.0**	**14.2**	**3867**	**35.8**	**15.5**
1M change			–16.2	+0.48	+0.01	–29.9	+0.23	+0.04
3M change			+13.3	+0.17	+0.02	–24.9	–0.34	+0.08

GEARING, COVER (00AR)			
intangibles		Incl	Excl
net gearing	%	332	neg
cash	%	32.0	neg
gross gearing	%	364	neg
under 5 yrs	%	324	neg
under 1 yr	%	204	neg
quick ratio	r		0.52
current ratio	r		0.71
interest cover	x		6.11

KEY DATES	
next AR year end	31-Dec-01
year end	31-Dec-00
prelim results	8-Feb-01
annual report	5-Mar-01
fin xd (8.67p)	25-Apr-01
1st qtr results	27-Apr-01
agm	9-May-01
int results	3-Aug-01
3rd qtr results	2-Nov-01
3qtr xd (4.65p)	14-Nov-01

LEARNING MORE ABOUT SHARES

There are several excellent sources of information on shares. One is *Company REFS*, a monthly book with a page of detailed data on each company covered (now available on CD as well, and also online from www.companyrefs.com). Or you can call your broker and ask him or her to send you the latest analyst's report on a company you're interested in.

The bond alternative

As I've explained, a bond is an IOU. When you buy a bond you are lending money to a company or a government agency, which promises to repay the loan, with interest, over a specific period of time, known as the term.

As an investment, bonds are generally considered lower risk than shares. There are several reasons for this. For one thing, the amount of income you'll enjoy from your bond is spelled out in advance, in the form of the fixed rate of interest promised by the bond issuer. (This rate is referred to as the *coupon*.) Bond issuers are obligated to make these payments when they are due; if they miss a payment, they are said to be in default.

Another reason bonds are considered relatively low-risk is that when a company goes bankrupt and its assets are sold off, the law generally stipulates that the claims of bondholders take precedence over those of shareholders. Hopefully bankruptcy will never strike any company you invest in, but if it does you will be better off as a bondholder, since

A recent brokerage firm report on Unilever.
Compare the information provided here with the data offered on the Company REFS page. In this presentation, the emphasis is on the analysis and forecast developed by the share analysts at the brokerage firm (Killik & Co.). No analyst is always correct, but expert opinions like the ones presented here can be very helpful to you in making your own decisions about how to invest. Reproduced by permission of Killik & Co

---

UNILEVER

21st December 2001

Accumulate

Showing resilience in the downturn

FUNDAMENTALS

Price	556p
Sector	Food producers & processors
Risk rating	3 (1 is low, 9 is high)
EPIC	ULVR
52 week range	478p – 610p
Market capitalisation	£38.5bn
Position in All-Share	9th
Net debt	£16.7bn (At half-year 2001)
Beta	0.63 (5 year, rel. FTSE All-Share)
Q4 Results	14th February 2002

PERFORMANCE

Unilever, p

Unilever
(relative FTSE All Share Food Prod & Proc. Index)

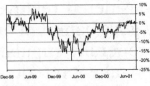

Sources: Bloomberg, Company Refs, Company information

PROFILE

Unilever is one of the world's largest consumer goods groups, selling its home, personal care and food products in around 150 countries. Unilever's portfolio of brands includes well-known names such as Dove soap, Lipton tea, Magnum ice cream and Hellmann's mayonnaise.

KILLIK VIEW

➢ Unilever is actively managing its brand portfolio, focusing on growing its leading brands and disposing of non-core and under-performing businesses. In 1999, Unilever's top 400 brands accounted for about 75% of the group's sales. It estimates that by 2004, around 380 top brands will contribute over 90% of group sales. The group expects leading brands to grow by 5% in the year to end-December, 2001.

➢ Unilever has targeted low double-digit growth in underlying earnings per share for the full year. It recently confirmed that it is on track to achieve this target. It has seen strong growth in the first two months of the fourth quarter, and expects fourth quarter earnings per share growth, before exceptionals and amortisation, to be about 35% higher than last year.

➢ Unilever should continue to derive cost savings from its restructuring programme, and benefit from global purchasing and synergies from the Bestfoods integration. Additionally, the group is benefiting from lower media rates, which have helped reduce the cost of its advertising and promotion activities. This is helping to improve margins in the short term.

➢ Capitalised at £38.5bn, Unilever trades on a 2002 P/E of 15.5. The group has a clear focus, has programmes in place to drive cost savings, and is proving resilient in a tough environment.

FINANCIALS

Year end 31st Dec	1998A	1999A	2000A	2001E	2002E
Pretax profit (normalised) £m	3007	3049	3217	3490	3872
Earnings per share (norm), p	24.8	28.0	32.0	31.4	35.8
Price earnings ratio	-	-	17.4	17.7	15.5
Dividend / share, net, p	10.7	12.5	13.1	14.1	15.4
Yield, gross, %	-	-	2.6	2.8	3.1

ordinary shareholders come last in line among those to be paid off and typically get nothing.

Of course, bonds are not completely risk-free—no investment is. As I've mentioned, companies do go bankrupt, and sometimes the bondholders are left high and dry, or paid off just a fraction of their investment money. Even governments occasionally default on their debts, as Russia did in 1998, and as Argentina did in 2002, for example. But most nations will do everything possible to avoid default, since it makes it nearly impossible for them to borrow additional money for years to come. Obviously the British government is one of the most stable and secure in the world, and the risk of default on UK-issued bonds is very, very small.

Bonds also carry other, more subtle forms of risk. After they've been issued, bonds can be bought and sold in the open marketplace (generally through a broker or dealer, like shares). The price of a bond on this *aftermarket* will vary from time to time, based mainly on changes in interest rates. Here's how this works. Suppose you buy a bond that is paying interest at an annual rate of 5.5 percent. If interest rates rise, so that comparable bonds are paying (say) 6.5 percent, your coupon will become less desirable to other investors. As a result, the selling price of your bond will fall. On the other hand, if interest rates fall to (say) 4.5 percent, your 5.5 percent coupon will look very attractive, and the price of your bond will rise. Thus, the market value of your bond is subject to interest rate risk.

Similarly, bonds are subject to inflation risk. When inflation accelerates, the value of a rate of interest that seemed fair at the time a bond was

217

issued will be eroded as the buying power of the pound shrinks. If you hold a bond with a 4 percent coupon, and inflation rises to 6 percent annually, your investment will actually be *losing* value every year, despite the interest payments you are receiving. When the bond principal is repaid, you'll be able to buy fewer groceries and haircuts than you would have been able to when you initially invested the money.

Of course, all risks work both ways; whenever you take on the possibility of losing money, you also take on the possibility of profit. This applies to bonds, as my co-author Karl discovered. He bought long-term US Treasury bonds (the American equivalent of gilts) back in the 1970s as investments for his children's university education. At the time, inflation was rampant and interest rates were very high. Accordingly, Karl's bonds carried a coupon of over 13 percent. These bonds were still paying the same high rate of interest in the late 1980s, when other interest rates had fallen into single digits. In this case, market risk worked in Karl's favour, and his investment suddenly looked brilliant.

TYPES OF BONDS

Just as there are many kinds of shares with differing degrees of risk (and potential reward), there are various kinds of bonds. Although as a generalisation it's correct to say that bonds carry lower risk than shares, there are exceptions at both ends of the spectrum. Some of the most important types of bonds are:

• *Gilts* or *government bonds*. These are bonds

issued by the British government, considered extremely safe as investments. Every gilt has a so-called *par value* of £100. This is the amount you'll receive as a repayment if you hold the bond to maturity (that is, throughout its term). In addition, of course, you'll receive regular interest payments as long as you hold the bond. Most gilts have terms of five, ten, or fifteen years, and they can be purchased through a stockbroker, a bank, or direct from the government at any Post Office.

- *Corporate bonds.* These are issued by companies as a way of raising funds. The risk you assume when you buy a corporate bond depends on the financial strength of the company that issued it. Bonds issued by large, profitable, long-established businesses in stable industries are almost as safe as government bonds, while bonds issued by small, new firms may be quite risky. The most risky corporate bonds are sometimes called *junk bonds* or *high-yield bonds*. (For obvious reasons, the bond salespeople prefer the latter term!)

The interest rates paid by bonds will usually vary directly with the degree of risk entailed. Bonds issued by blue-chip firms pay relatively low interest rates; risky junk bonds promise high interest payments—but of course there's the chance the company may go belly-up, and you may receive nothing at all.

WHY OWN BONDS?

There are several good reasons why an investor might want to own bonds. The most important are:

- *To generate low-risk income.* An investor who is mainly interested in producing a reliable, steady stream of current income (rather than in building a nest egg for the future through growth) will probably want to put a significant part of his or her portfolio into bonds. Many retirees use government bonds or low-risk corporate bonds for this purpose.

- *To balance the risk involved in owning shares.* Generally speaking, shares grow in value along with the companies they represent. Therefore, during hard times, when the national or world economy (or large sectors of the economy) fail to grow, shares are apt to stagnate or fall in value. By contrast, bond values often increase at such times. Therefore, you may want to put some of your investment money into bonds to balance, or *hedge*, the risk in your shares portfolio.

One easy way of getting started in bond investing is by buying shares in a unit trust whose portfolio is made up of bonds. I'll explain how this works in the next section.

Your best first choice: unit trusts

As I explained earlier, a unit trust is a pooled investment: a portfolio of shares, bonds, or both selected and managed by a professional investor using money pooled from thousands of individual investors. When you invest in a unit trust, you buy a *unit* of the fund. As the value of all the shares in the trust portfolio rises (or falls), so does the value of each unit you own. As an investor in the unit trust, you can elect to have dividends earned by the shares in the portfolio either paid out to you or reinvested in the fund. If you choose the latter, the total value of the portfolio increases, as does as the number of units you own.

For most people, a unit trust is an excellent first investment choice. A unit trust is easy to buy directly from the company that manages it, and you can start investing for a modest sum. You can even sign up for a savings scheme by which £20 or £50 per month is automatically invested in the unit trust of your choice. Best of all, a unit trust offers the average investor a quick and easy way of achieving diversification—that is, of investing in shares in a wide range of different companies. This reduces the degree of stock-specific risk you are exposed to. When a particular company suffers a downturn, chances are good that other stocks owned by your unit trust will be moving up, thus making up for some of the decline. (Of course, when the entire stock market is in the tank, many unit trusts will go downhill as well.)

A unit trust also has the advantage of professional management. The investment managers who buy and sell shares or bonds on behalf of unit trusts spend all their time evaluating specific companies and their management, studying the economic environment, and developing strategies they hope will produce profits for their investors. Although like anyone else they are fallible, they are probably better informed than the average amateur investor.

Naturally, the managers of the unit trust expect to be compensated for their work on your behalf. They are paid in two basic ways. The first is through an initial charge when you buy into the unit trust, which averages 5 percent of the amount you invest. The second is through an on-going annual charge, which is deducted from the overall value of your holdings. The annual charge averages between 1 and 1 ½ percent of the fund's value. It's worth considering these charges when deciding on a unit trust investment. All things being equal, a unit trust that charges lower fees may be a more profitable long-term investment.

TYPES OF UNIT TRUSTS

There are almost 1,800 different unit trusts to choose from in the UK. Each is managed by a different individual or team, and each operates according to a slightly different investment philosophy. However, the many types of trusts tend to fall into several general categories. What follows is a list of the most popular types of trusts, with some indication of the kind of investor who ought to consider each.

● *Index-tracker funds* are designed to follow the performance of a popular stock-market index, such as the FTSE 100. The managers of a tracker fund either buy shares in all the companies that make up the index or buy shares in a representative sampling of those companies. For various reasons, tracker funds have generally outperformed most other unit trusts, and because they usually have relatively low charges they are an attractive option for most investors.

- *Equity income funds* focus on companies that pay high dividends. These trusts are a good choice for investors who seek a low-risk investment that offers relatively high current income (though with limited long-term growth prospects). Thus, retirees often favour equity income funds in their investment portfolios.

- *Capital growth funds* invest in companies whose share prices are expected to increase substantially. Young investors with long time horizons who are able to tolerate the ups and downs of the market should consider investing in capital growth funds.

- *Small-cap funds* invest in smaller companies that are considered to have strong growth prospects. Since the long-term performance of companies in this category is very hard to predict, these trusts are relatively risky. In a bad year you could lose 20, 30, or even 50 percent of your total investment in a small-cap fund. But in a good year you could double your money. You may want to invest a portion of your long-term money in a small-cap fund, but if you do be prepared for a rocky ride.

- *Global funds* (also known as *world funds*) invest in foreign shares and shares of UK companies that do significant business overseas. Depending on the mix of countries, regions, and industries that are selected by the trust manager, global funds can be rather risky. During the Asian financial crisis of the mid-1990s, for example, many global funds suffered badly. But because the economies of the emerging world (Latin America, Asia, and the former Iron Curtain countries) are growing faster than those of Europe and North America, well-managed global funds have relatively strong long-term growth prospects.

- *International funds* invest solely outside the UK. They have many of the same characteristics as global funds but are generally even more risky.

- *Regional funds* invest in shares of companies from a particular region of the world: Asia, the former Soviet bloc, or Latin America, for example.

- *Sector funds* invest in specific industries. These funds perform as well or as poorly as the industries they focus on. During the high-tech boom of the late 1990s, technology funds performed spectacularly. Since the bust of 2000, most of those gains have evaporated. Don't invest money that you can't afford to lose in a sector fund. But if you feel strongly that a particular industry (whether it's pharmaceuticals, entertainment, health care, or consumer goods) is due for a period of rapid growth, consider buying shares in an appropriate sector fund.

- *Bond funds* invest in bonds rather than shares. Some concentrate on government bonds (gilts), others on corporate bonds. Buying bond funds can be a convenient, low-risk way of including some bonds in your investment portfolio. Since bonds and shares generally move in opposite directions, this can help to balance some of the risk involved in owning shares.

- *Ethical funds* invest in shares of companies that meet specified moral criteria. For example, some ethical funds avoid companies that make military equipment, tobacco products, or alcoholic beverages. Others choose companies with stellar environmental records or a strong track record of hiring and promoting women and minority group members. Many ethical funds have performed well over time, so consider investing in such a fund if you have strong moral principles you'd like to back up with your pocketbook.

This is just a sampling of the kinds of trusts currently available. New trust types are emerging all the time, limited only by the ingenuity of fund managers (and of the marketing arms of the financial firms). Take some time to read about the various fund types and try to compare your investment interests and objectives with those of the funds you're considering. When you find a good match, you may want to make a purchase.

EVALUATING PERFORMANCE

Many investors try to select a unit trust on the basis of past performance. That is, they look at the growth of the value of the trust over the past one, three, or five years and use this to extrapolate future performance. The assumption is that the fund that has earned the greatest profits for investors in the recent past is likely to do the same in the future.

It's certainly worthwhile to consider past performance when evaluating a unit trust. (And managers whose funds have performed well will certainly encourage you to do so!) History shows that past performance is no guarantee of future returns. Only a few investment managers have been able to earn significantly better returns for their clients when compared to the overall stock market or their competitors over time.

However, it's easy to give past performance more weight than it deserves. This is true for several reasons:

- Short-term performance is partly a matter of luck, good or bad. Quite often the fund at the top of its category in a given year does no better than middling or even below average in the following year, while last year's low-rated fund rises to the top of the heap.

- Fund managers switch jobs from time to time. The fund that earned huge profits last year may be headed by an entirely different team this year, making past performance that much harder to replicate.

● Funds often rise or fall based on unpredictable or cyclic economic factors. Money managers who looked like geniuses when the dot.com shares were booming suddenly looked like imbeciles when the bottom fell out of that marketplace. In truth, they were neither geniuses nor imbeciles; they just happened to be in the right place one year and in the wrong place the next.

Does this mean that the performance of unit trusts is purely a matter of dumb luck? Should you pick a trust simply by tossing a dart at the listings in the *Financial Times*? Not quite.

A good source of information on unit trusts is Micropol. co.uk, which is owned by the large American financial information firm Standard & Poors. Micropol rates unit trusts by risk and tracks their long-term results. It's an excellent source of basic data that can be very helpful in selecting one or two trusts to get started with.

From unit trusts to shares

As we've discussed, investing in unit trusts is a good starting point for most investors. However, at some point in your financial life, especially if you begin to accumulate a significant amount of investment money, you'll probably want to consider direct investment in shares. I'll turn to that topic in the next chapter.

7

INVESTING FOR LIFE

Developing a personal strategy to make your money grow

Getting started in share investing

I've suggested that the best place for most people to start investing is with a unit trust. After a while, however, you may want to 'graduate' to investing directly in shares.

Most investors agree that *smart* share investing is the best way to amass really significant wealth. For one thing, the direct stock investor doesn't have to pay the management fees and other on-going charges that investors in unit trusts must bear.

Furthermore, the individual investor has a potentially significant advantage over the professional money manager. A professional fund manager is under constant pressure to invest, since more money keeps flowing into the fund from investors, particularly if the fund is successful. This pressure makes it hard for a fund manager to maintain a consistently successful track record over time. By contrast, the individual investor can simply refrain from buying shares until a really good opportunity appears.

So when you're ready, investing to create your own share portfolio can present some exciting opportunities. But how to begin?

There's one piece of advice offered by all the

great share investors, from Warren Buffett (director of the ultra-successful holding company Berkshire Hathaway) to Peter Lynch (the legendary former investment manager of the Magellan Fund): *invest in what you know*.

'How can I follow that advice?' you may wonder. 'I'm no financial expert. And when it comes to shares, I'm a novice. How can I invest in what I know?'

The answer is that you probably know more than you realise. Based on your career, your personal interests, your family background, and what you observe in your community, you in fact know quite a bit about the world of business. For example, you know:

- Which new products you, your family, and your friends love to use—and which ones you hate.

- Which shops in your neighbourhood are always crowded—and which ones are usually devoid of customers.

- Which toys, games, movies, theme parks, music, and clothing styles your kids and their friends consider cool—and which ones they shun.

- Which companies in the industry you work in are well managed—and which ones are run by incompetents.

- Which local businesses are hiring workers and expanding—and which ones are contracting or shutting down.

Each of these facts represents a possible clue as to which companies are likely to enjoy growing sales in the future and which ones are apt to decline. As you'll discover, everything you know about the world of business can be applied to finding worthwhile companies to invest in.

Of course, before buying shares, you'll also want to add to your stock of specific knowledge about the companies you are considering investing in. This is the process rather grandly known as *fundamental analysis*. Although this is a serious discipline to which some experts devote a lifetime, it's not hard to learn and begin practising the basics. As you'll see, analysing and choosing shares isn't necessarily much more complicated than examining the pros and cons of a dozen different resorts and then choosing the place you'll visit on your next holiday.

If you are intrigued by the brief presentation in this chapter, there are many books (including my own *Winning with Shares*) that you can study for a more in-depth introduction to share investing strategy.

The least you should know about stock analysis

There are many approaches to stock analysis. Every stock-picking expert—and many of those who'd like to consider themselves experts—have their own favoured methods. In this section, I'll suggest a few items I consider basic to any analysis of the fundamentals of a company and its shares. You can locate this information about a particular company in several ways. Sources such as *Company*

231

Refs (mentioned in the last chapter) present all this information and much more besides. A lot of the data can be found in the share listings and the columns about investing in your daily newspaper. And your stockbroker can probably provide you with analysts' reports on any company you are considering as an investment.

The key items I like to examine concerning any company include:

- *The story of the company.* This refers to the basic history of the company: the products or services it sells, the markets it serves, how it is organised, how creatively and progressively it is managed, and what strategies it is pursuing to grow in the future. A convincing, positive story that makes sense in the light of everything you know about business is not enough in itself to make a company's shares worth buying, but it's not a bad starting point.

- *The company's turnover and profit history.* Turnover (also known as revenue) refers to the company's total sales of products and services. Profit, on the other hand, is the portion of revenues remaining after operating expenses, interests and taxes have been deducted. Generally speaking, a company with a history of strong and steady growth in turnover over the past several years is a better investment prospect than one whose sales are flat or declining. It is also important to look at the *sources* of the increased turnover. If they come mainly from acquisitions of competing companies, there's a chance that the growth may soon falter because of the many unknowns associated with acquiring and integrating a new company. Similarly, the more consistent the company's profits, the better. And a pattern of steadily increasing profits over time is better still.

- *The company's earnings per share (EPS) and earnings growth.* Earnings are the amount of a company's profit that it has available to distribute to ordinary shareholders. Earnings per share (EPS) is this amount divided by the number of ordinary shares outstanding. This is 'the bottom line' for investors. Consistent annual growth in EPS over a period of five years or more is a sign of a strong company, especially if that growth comes from increased turnover or from improved company productivity and efficiency. Conversely, a decline in EPS may indicate problems within the company or reflect a slowdown in the overall economy.

- *Recent movements in the company's share price.* These will indicate how investors have reacted to recent developments in the company's business as well as to news about the current and future expectations of its sector and of the overall economy. All share prices have their ups and downs, but a generally upward trend is a sign that the marketplace has confidence in the company's management and its strategy, while a declining stock price suggests that many investors have doubts about the company's future. Of course, it's dangerous to assume that the share price trend of the past year will continue. When a basically sound company has a lagging share price, it may mean there is a bargain to be had, while a high share price may be too high, suggesting that the company may be heading for a sharp pull back. So look at past share price movements, but analyse their meaning sceptically. Use this information to get a better understanding of how news affects the company's shares.

- *Share price volatility.* When examining recent share price movements, also consider the size of the up-and-down price swings exhibited by the shares over the past year. If you are uncomfortable with a high degree of risk, you may want to avoid shares that have a pattern of very large price gyrations (often referred to as high volatility). Instead, look for less volatile shares—that is, those with generally smaller price movements.

- *The stock's P/E ratio.* This refers to the ratio of the ordinary share's current market price to the company's annual earnings per share—hence, price/earnings ratio, or P/E. For example, if a company's shares are currently selling at a price of £24, and the company had earnings of £2 per share during the past twelve months, the P/E ratio is 12 [24 ÷ 2]. One way to understand this is to think of that twelve as representing the number of years it would take for you to recoup the cost of the shares from company's earnings. The higher the P/E ratio, the more positive—some would say exuberant—are the

234

expectations of most investors and analysts concerning the company's future prospects, particularly the growth of its earnings. They're hoping that earnings will grow at a rate that will enable them to earn back the cost of the initial investment more quickly. However a high P/E ratio generally means that the share price will be more volatile. Any disappointing news about the company's earning growth will cause investors to sell in droves, driving the price of the stock down sharply. And positive news will prompt a wave of buying that can drive the price of the stock up quickly. Other investors like to buy shares whose P/E ratio is low compared to other companies in the same business sector. They feel that this indicates that the shares are a relative bargain. However, a low P/E ratio can also indicate that a company is heading for trouble. Investors may have sold off their shares, driving the price down, in anticipation of bad news about the company's earnings. A company's P/E ratio must therefore be analysed in the light of other news about the company's future financial prospects and relative to other companies in the same sector.

- *The company's dividend history.* Remember that dividends represent the portion of a company's earnings that the Board of Directors decides to pay out to investors. Examining the consistency and size of the dividend payout over the past several years can offer a partial indication of the financial health of the company. After all, only a company that is consistently profitable can afford to pay and periodically increase the dividends year after year. This is an especially important indicator if you are seeking shares primarily for current income.

- *The company's gearing (or leverage).* This refers to the amount of debt owed by the company. Owing some money isn't necessarily a bad thing; an expanding business often must borrow to finance the construction of new factories or stores, for example. But excessive debt is a red flag. Servicing the debt (industry jargon for paying interest on the money borrowed) can be a huge drain on a company's financial resources. This situation gets worse if turnover or revenues slow down for any reason. Since average gearing ratios vary greatly from industry to industry, the best way to evaluate a company's indebtedness is by comparing it with others in the same sector. Other things being equal, a company with less gearing (and therefore a stronger corporate balance sheet) is likely to be a better investment.

- *How share analysts view the company.* Finally, consider the opinions of the experts who track shares and issue reports about them for brokerage houses and other financial firms. These are often cited in the financial press and on television, as well as in reports published by the financial firms themselves. Like anyone else, the analysts working in the City are human and fallible. They've been known to overrate a company because of a convincing presentation by a charismatic chief executive. And sometimes the analysts fall prey to fads, crazes, and manias (which occur in finance just as in other human activities). Nonetheless, you may find it informative and educational to read what the professional analysts have to say, especially *after* you've studied a company and drawn your own conclusions.

Does this list of indicators add up to a perfect formula for profitable share investing? Unfortunately, no. The factors that determine the ultimate success of a company (and therefore the value of its shares) are too complex and unpredictable to be easily reduced to a formula. Even the best investors (including Buffett and Lynch) have picked their share of losers. If you want to invest in shares, you'll need to study, experiment, and learn from your successes and failures.

Think of it as being a bit like taking up golf or any other challenging sport. No one shoots a hole in one every time out. But those who take the game seriously and put in the necessary practice can expect to improve their performance steadily.

A risk-free way to try your hand at share investing

If you're intrigued by the possibilities of share investing but uncertain whether you're ready to risk real money in the markets, I have an ideal method to suggest that can bridge the gap. On pages 239–244, I present a risk-free plan for testing your aptitude for share investing. I call it the Portfolio Game.

THE PORTFOLIO GAME: A BEGINNER'S PATH INTO SHARE INVESTING

1. PICK THREE SECTORS. Select three business sectors you are interested in considering for an investment. They may include the sector you work in, the sector someone close to you works in, a sector you are interested in, a sector you happen to be knowledgeable about, a sector you have heard is 'hot', or just a sector you'd like to learn more about. You can use the *Financial Times* to identify the names of various sectors. List your three sector choices below:

SECTOR A:

_____

SECTOR B:

_____

SECTOR C:

_____

2. PICK FOUR COMPANIES IN EACH SECTOR. List four companies that are active in each of the sectors you've chosen. You can find these companies in several ways. If you already know a company in the sector, list it. You can also find names in the stock market pages of your daily newspaper, in *Company Refs*, or by consulting a stock broker. Don't worry yet about whether the companies you list are 'good' companies or not. Just choose them at random. List your choices below.

SECTOR A:	SECTOR B:	SECTOR C:
1.	1.	1.
2.	2.	2.
3.	3.	3.
4.	4.	4.

3. RESEARCH ALL TWELVE COMPANIES.
Here's where you will have a bit of homework to do. For each of the twelve companies you listed, get the relevant page from *Company Refs* or hemscott.co.uk. Or use information from a share analyst's report or an information sheet from a broker. For each company, fill out the Share Study Form shown on page 242. (Make as many photocopies as you need.)

4. PICK THREE POTENTIAL WINNERS.
Based on what you've learned about the twelve companies, pick three (one from each sector) that you think have the best chance of increasing in value over the next six months.

5. 'PURCHASE' SHARES OF YOUR THREE POTENTIAL WINNERS. Pretend that you buy shares of each of your three favoured companies. Allocate the same amount of investment money to each. For example, if you want to 'invest' a total of £15,000, you will allocate £5,000 to each share. Then determine the number of shares that you can purchase with that amount of money. Simply divide the amount to be invested by the latest price per share. (If you were really investing, broker commissions would also be charged. For this exercise, ignore such costs.) Round off to the nearest share. For example, if you are investing £5,000 in a company whose most recent share price is £36, you will purchase 139 shares [£5,000 ÷ £36 = about 139].

6. TRACK THE PRICE MOVEMENTS OF YOUR 'PURCHASES' FOR SIX MONTHS. Use the Share Tracking Form on page 243.

THE SHARE STUDY FORM

Complete this form for each share you are considering.

1. Story of the company

2. Turnover and profit history

3. Earnings per share (EPS) history

4. Past price movement

5. P/E ratio. Compare to others in the same sector and to the overall market

6. Dividend history

7. Gearing (leverage). Compares to others in the sector

8. Analysts' assessments

SHARE TRACKING FORM

Name of company

Date purchased

Per-share purchase price

Number of shares purchased

Total invested

Week	Price per-share (£)	Total value (price per-share x number of shares purchased) (£)
1		
2		
3		
4		
5		
6		
7		
8		
9		
10		
11		
12		
13		
14		
15		

16	
17	
18	
19	
20	
21	
22	
23	
24	
25	
26	

Final per-share price

Final value of total investment

Increase or (loss) from initial value

Percentage increase or (loss)

(Mark any loss by enclosing it in parentheses.) Determine the percentage increase or (loss) by dividing the amount of the increase or (loss) by the initial investment value. The result will be a decimal value. Multiply that value by 100 to obtain a percentage. For example, suppose your initial investment of £5,000 grows in value to £5,470. The increase from the initial value is £470 [£5,470–£5,000]. The percentage increase is 9.4 percent, which is calculated as follows: [£470 ÷ £5,000 = 0.094; then 0.094 × 100 = 9.4%].

THE SHARE STUDY FORM

Complete this form for each share you are considering. (For this example I used the information from the research reports from Company Refs and Killik & Co. on pages 214 and 216.)

1. Story of the company: *Unilever is an international company that makes food, home, and personal care products—everything from Dove soap to Lipton tea. Its product base includes products known worldwide that people use every day. How good is the company's management?*

2. Turnover and profit history: *After four years of decline, revenues rose last year from £26.9 billion to £29.7 billion. Profits have been up and down—last year went down from £2.8 billion to £1.7 billion. What caused the decline? Is the company ready to rebound?*

3. Earnings per share (EPS) history: *Shows steady growth, from 24.8 in 1998 to an estimated 35.8 for 2002. How did earning continue to grow when profits were down?*

4. Past price movement: *Over past six months, fluctuated from a low of 478p to a high of 610p. Recently*

closed near its 6-month high and the overall price trend is upward? downward?

5. P/E ratio. Compare to others in the same sector and to the overall market: *currently at 9—pretty low compared to the sector and overall stock market. Does this mean that Unilever is undervalued relative to its competitors? Is it therefore a good time to buy?*

6. Dividend history: *Since 1996 has paid dividends per share of 8.01, 8.42, 10.7, 12.5, and 13.1 annually. Nice upward trend there! But can it continue with the increase given the variability of its turnover and profit? What might cause it to cut its dividend payment?*

7. Gearing (leverage). Compares to others in the sector: *Pretty high: 67.3 percent! A bad sign?*

8. Analysts' assessments: *Consensus—14 percent growth in revenues, 15 percent growth in earnings for next year. Do they see any danger signs in the company's future?*

SHARE TRACKING FORM

Name of company	*unilever*
Date purchased	*1 July 2001*
Per-share purchase price	*£5.40*
Number of shares purchased	*929*
Total invested	*£5,000*

Week	Price per-share (£)	Total value (price per-share x number of shares purchased) (£)
1	5.42	5,040.06
2	5.70	5,300.43
3	5.62	5,226.04
4	5.84	5,430.62
5	5.88	5,467.81
6	6.08	5,653.79
7	5.94	5,523.61
8	6.16	5,728.18
9	6.00	5,579.40
10	5.92	5,505.01
11	5.81	5,402.72
12	5.85	5,439.92
13	6.12	5,690.99
14	5.86	5,449.21
15	5.67	5,272.53
16	5.47	5,086.55

17	5.13	4,770.39
18	4.95	4,603.01
19	5.03	4,677.40
20	5.28	4,909.87
21	4.86	4,519.31
22	5.10	4,742.49
23	5.22	4,854.08
24	5.30	4,928.47
25	5.50	5,114.45
26	5.62	5,226.04

Final per-share price	£5.62
Final value of total investment	£5,226.04
Increase or (loss) from initial value	£226.04
Percentage increase or (loss)	4.5

(Mark any loss by enclosing it in parentheses.) Determine the percentage increase or (loss) by dividing the amount of the increase or (loss) by the initial investment value. The result will be a decimal value. Multiply that value by 100 to obtain a percentage. For example, suppose your initial investment of £5,000 grows in value to £5,470. The increase from the initial value is £470 [£5,470–£5,000]. The percentage increase is 9.4 percent, which is calculated as follows: [£470 ÷ £5,000 = 0.094; then 0.094 × 100 = 9.4%]

PLAYING THE PORTFOLIO GAME

When you play the Portfolio Game, you'll identify and research several companies (using the Share Study form on page 242). You'll select and 'invest' in three companies on paper for six months without actually spending money. Choose an amount you might really invest—an amount it would hurt a bit to lose. Then you'll track the shares using the Share Tracker form (pages 243–244). Look up the prices at least once a week, for example, every Sunday. (I like using Sunday for this purpose, since I'm sometimes moved to prayer by what I find!) On pages 245–248, you'll find filled-in samples to show what the forms might look like.

Many share investors like to create charts (that is, line graphs) that capture the up-and-down price movement of their shares. You can do this as you play the Portfolio Game if you like. There are many computer software packages and online services, including AOL, that can help you do this, but I strongly recommend that first-time investors make charts by hand. You'll get a much better 'feel' for price activity that way. Charts are nice because they're visual, providing a vivid, concrete sense of how prices go up and down.

You may also want to jot down news events that may affect the price of your shares. (You can use the margins of the Share Tracker form for this purpose.) They might include:

● Major pieces of economic news: a change in interest rates, for example, or an important government announcement about unemployment.

249

- Events related to a particular industry you are tracking: for example, a merger between two companies, or an announcement concerning quarterly sales or profit results.

- Major price moves for the stock market as a whole.

Finally, you may want to jot a note about your emotional reactions when these are strong. If shares you 'own' are doing exceptionally well, you may want to record your jubilation on the Share Tracking form ('Up 25 percent in one week—fabulous!'). If they take a tumble, record those feelings as well ('Lost one-fifth of my stake. This makes me very nervous. What will happen next week?'). The entire process of recording prices and making notes about your holdings shouldn't take very long. Expect to spend a total of between thirty minutes and one hour per week.

After six months, look back at your performance. How many winners and losers did you have? How much did your entire portfolio grow? You may discover that you're not really a very good share picker! If so, stick with unit trusts for now. Or you may find that your instincts were excellent. If so, consider taking the plunge carefully with some *real* money.

In any case, playing the Portfolio Game will give you a feeling for how events affect share prices. You'll begin to understand your strengths and weaknesses as an investor, and you'll get a sense for how you react to ups and downs in the market. One of the keys to successful investing is the ability to keep your head and make rational decisions in times of euphoria and gloom. Naturally, your feelings as you play the Portfolio Game won't be as powerful as those you'll experience when the investments are real. But at least they'll give you some inkling of the highs and lows that share investors experience, and a feeling as to whether you have the temperament to stay cool as you ride those waves.

PLAY THE GAME IN REAL TIME

One warning: it's important to play the Portfolio Game in real time—that is, to track the share price movements as they actually occur, week by week. Some clever people think that they can speed up the process of testing their investment ideas by picking shares and then tracking the price movements backward, gathering historical data from the Internet or old newspapers. (This technique even has a name: it's called *back-fitting*.) Resist this temptation. Back-fitting is not the same as really living with the ups and downs of the market. And it's deceptively easy to pick shares that have performed well in recent months (even to do so unconsciously) and then congratulate yourself on your investment wisdom.

Play the game looking forward, not backward. After all, that's what you'll have to do when you put real pounds on the line.

Developing your personal investment strategy

As you've seen, it's important to do your

homework so as to choose investment vehicles wisely. But research is not enough to make a successful investor. It's also necessary to develop an investment strategy—an overall approach that will guide you in managing your money and increase your chances of reaching your financial goals, no matter how the markets behave. In this section, I'll offer some hints about how to develop a strategy that will work for you.

FOCUS

One key is to set some reasonable limits as to how much of the market you will try to master. It's impossible to know everything about the whole stock market. There are just too many widely varying business sectors, interacting in complex ways with one another and with larger economic and social trends, for any one person to comprehend fully. So if you decide to get involved in shares, focus on a limited group of sectors that you understand and that appear promising in today's economy. Look for the best companies within those sectors, ones with strong business and financial fundamentals. Buy shares when their prices appear to be reasonable, and hold them patiently for as long as the business prospects continue to look solid.

Also focus on a limited number of companies. For most people, five or six shares are enough to study at once. I have a friend who invests his money in five stocks at any one time. John generally drops one company each year and replaces it with a different one whose prospects he's impressed with. I don't recommend this unusual plan to everyone, but it has the advantage of being very focused. John keeps close tabs on just five companies at a time, which is a manageable number of firms for him to be truly knowledgeable about.

In most cases, a focused approach will bring success in the long run. In fact (in a simplified form), this is how Warren Buffett made his billions. Of course, this approach is simpler to describe than to carry out. Otherwise, every share investor would be as rich as Buffett. But it does provide a proven framework for the ongoing learning you'll need to carry out if you hope to become a skilled and successful investor.

REMEMBER TO DIVERSIFY

As I explained in chapter six, the share investor needs to guard against two kinds of risk in particular: sector risk and company-specific risk. The former is the possibility of loss due to a collapse of a particular industry; the latter is the possibility of loss due to the failure of a single company.

Both kinds of risk can be reduced through the strategy of diversification. This means making certain that your portfolio includes holdings from more than one company and more than one sector. If you select shares from companies whose business fundamentals are quite different, it's likely that a decline in one company will be offset by an increase in others, reducing the risk of an overall loss to your portfolio.

Therefore, as you buy shares, be aware of the need to diversify. Don't buy exclusively shares of companies in the same industries, or in closely related ones: computer hardware and software, for example, or retailing and fashion. Otherwise, when one falls, your whole share portfolio is apt to collapse along with it.

BUY AND HOLD—BUT FOR HOW LONG?

Yet another strategic issue has to do with the time horizon of your investments—that is, how long you will hold a share after you've bought it. Conventional wisdom used to say, 'Buy a good investment and let it run.' That is, simply hold on to the stock, bond, or unit trust indefinitely or until you need the money, for example, when your child is ready for university or you reach retirement age.

THE DANGERS OF OVER-TRADING

The traditional wisdom wasn't far wrong. Buy and hold is a far better strategy than trade trade trade. The overall trend of the stock market over the long term has always been upward; naturally so, since the national and world economies, in general, continue to grow. Therefore, if you buy shares in a variety of good and solid companies (either directly or through a unit trust) and hold on to them for a period of years, the chances are pretty good that your investment will increase in value—probably faster than inflation.

By contrast, day traders—that is, those who buy and sell investments frequently—tend to hurt themselves. Why is this so? There are several reasons:

- The trader is trying to 'outsmart' the market. That is, he is trying to anticipate price movements in the shares he owns so that he can buy them at or near the lowest possible price and sell them at the highest possible price. But outsmarting the market is a lot tougher than it looks. After all, share prices represent the consensus judgement of thousands of large and small investors concerning the value of a company. It's not so easy to out-think such a large number of investors. No wonder it's hard for any individual, no matter how clever, to remain ahead of the market curve for long.

- The day trader is also apt to make errors in

255

judgement due to emotions. When you watch stock price movements every day (or even, thanks to today's electronic means of communication, every hour or every minute), it's easy to get caught up in the excitement of the market roller-coaster. But emotions aren't a sound guide to actions. Many traders lose money by selling shares when feeling despondent over a downturn, or by buying more when exhilarated by an upswing—moods that may *not* reflect the true long-term value of the shares.

● Every time you buy or sell a share, you incur costs, especially the dealing costs and commission payable to the broker or brokerage firm that handles the transaction. When these costs are factored into the equation, they can seriously erode the profits you make on such short-term investing.

So the old buy-and-hold philosophy of investment is a fundamentally sound one, and far better for most people than active trading.

HAVE AN EXIT STRATEGY

Nonetheless, many of us have slightly shifted our thinking about investments in recent months (I'm writing this at the end of 2001). The current downturn in share prices has made it clear that many investors would have been better off if they'd taken some money off the table—that is, if they'd sold some of their share holdings in the late 1990s. If they'd done so, they'd have turned some of the enormous gains that the market had enjoyed during the decade into cash. Relatively few investors did this. Instead, they held on to stocks, believing—and hoping—that the price rises of the 1990s would continue indefinitely. When the tide turned, they lost a lot of their profits, at least on paper.

It is therefore prudent for you to make a plan for how and when you will consider selling your shares. At the time you buy them, I recommend that you set two parameters:

- How far the investment has to drop before you sell; and

- How far it has to rise before you consider selling.

For example, suppose you buy shares of Company M at a price of £15 per share. Based on your analysis of the firm's fundamentals, you believe that Company M is poised to double its sales and profits over the next three to five years, and you hope that the share price will grow at a similar rate. Of course, there's always a chance that your analysis may prove wrong, that some change in the economy or in Company M's industry may hurt the firm's prospects. So a downturn is possible as well. Under these circumstances, you might decide to:

- Sell your shares of Company M if they drop by 20 percent or more below your purchase price or the share's current market price if they have gone up. Thus, if the price per share falls to £12, you will sell (thereby *cutting your losses*, in investment lingo).

- Sell your shares of Company M if they rise by 100 percent. Thus, if the price per share doubles to £30, you will sell (thereby *taking your profits*).

Is either of these tactics foolproof? No. In the former case, it's possible that Company M might fall 20 percent, then suddenly rebound. If you sell your shares when they are down, you'll be upset over missing the rebound. On the other hand, millions of investors can tell stories about losing wads of money by trying to wait out downturns they hoped were temporary ('It's *sure* to come back, isn't it? Let's hold on just another week or two . . . or a few months . . . maybe next year . . .'). Setting a target price for selling, and sticking to it, will help you avoid that trap.

In the latter case, it's possible that Company M might double in value, then go on rising for months or years longer. If you sell when the shares are only halfway up their climb, you'll feel a bit frustrated over missing some of the upside ('If only I'd held on to those shares!'). But again, you'll avoid another all-too-common trap: the danger of trying to squeeze out the last pound of profit from a success story, only to lose most of your gains when the shares finally stop rising and take a tumble.

Periodic investing

If you've accumulated a sum of money you want to invest (or have received a lump sum from some windfall, such as an inheritance), don't put all your money into the market at once. Instead, 'feather' it in at regular intervals over a period of time. Experience shows that investing gradually can be less risky than taking a single big gamble. This strategy is particularly effective when investing in unit trusts.

When you invest over a period of months, you'll be buying shares at several different price levels, sometimes during periods of euphoria, when prices are riding high, sometimes during periods of gloom, when prices are low. Your overall potential return can be better if you spread out your investing over such a range of price moves.

POUND-COST AVERAGING

The concept of pound-cost averaging illustrates one of the benefits of periodic investing. This investment technique can actually *reduce* the average purchase price of your investments, thereby improving your potential return over time. Here's how it works.

The investor who wants the benefit of pound-cost averaging invests the same amount of money in a unit trust at regular intervals. One easy way of doing this is to arrange for automatic investments in a unit trust of a fixed monthly sum—£100, £200, or whatever amount you feel comfortable with. Since the price of a unit trust fluctuates from time to time, this fixed monthly sum will sometimes buy more units, sometimes fewer.

Now here's the beauty of pound-cost averaging: because you buy more units when the price is lower than when the price is higher, the average amount you spend per unit over the time you're making the investment is actually *less* than the average price of the investment during the same time period. Thus, your overall gains on the investment will be greater as a result.

The chart on page 261 illustrates how pound-cost averaging works. If you find the maths a little tricky, don't worry. The point is that you will benefit from regularly investing the same sum of money. And since this strategy also fits into the good habits of saving and investing that I've stressed throughout this book, the benefits of pound-cost averaging are simply another good reason to do something you ought to do anyway.

HOW POUND-COST AVERAGING WORKS

Suppose you invest the fixed sum of £100 every month in a unit trust. The price of the unit trust will vary from month to month, as shown in the third column below. (In this case, we'll assume that it varies between a low of £8.50 per unit and a high of £14.75 per unit.) Therefore, the number of units you can buy with £100 will vary, as shown in the fourth column.

Month	Sum invested (£)	Price per unit (£)	Units bought
1	100	8.50	11.76
2	100	9.50	10.53
3	100	10.00	10.00
4	100	11.25	8.89
5	100	13.50	7.41
6	100	14.75	6.78
7	100	11.00	9.09
8	100	10.50	9.52
9	100	10.25	9.76
10	100	9.50	10.53
11	100	10.50	9.52
12	100	11.00	9.09
TOTALS	**1,200**		**112.88**

The average **cost** (i.e. price you paid) of the units bought is £10.63 [£1,200 ÷ 112.88 = £10.63].

The average **price** of the units over the twelve-month period was actually £10.85. (This is the sum of all the prices in the third column divided by twelve.) Thus, the amount you *paid* per unit is £0.22 less than the average price over the same period. Your gain on your investment is calculated from the lower amount (£10.63), therefore your return on your investment is higher.

Tending your growing portfolio

As your investment portfolio grows in value (and complexity), you'll need to consider one more level of investment strategy. *Asset allocation* is the art of deciding how to divide your portfolio among various kinds of investment holdings so as to produce a risk-reward scenario that is suitable for you.

First, recall a couple of basic facts about risk:

- Risk and potential reward tend to vary together. The greater the risk you undertake, the greater the potential for profit. The lower the risk, the lower your potential return.

- The amount of risk you should assume depends partly on your own psychology—how comfortable you are with the possibility of loss.

- It should also depend partly on your financial goals and especially on their time horizon. Money for short-term goals should be invested in less risky vehicles; money for long-term goals may be invested in more risky vehicles.

Based on these principles, investment experts have developed a number of models for asset allocation. These models are designed to combine different kinds of investments into a single portfolio that matches a particular investment style and objective to a person's risk tolerance. In general, these formulas involve blends of two or three kinds of holdings, commonly referred to as asset classes.

- Shares, including unit trusts that own shares.

- Bonds, including unit trusts that own bonds.

- Cash, including savings accounts with banks or building societies and cash ISAs.

The charts on pages 265–267 illustrate four classic asset allocation models). Which model is best for you? That depends. Consider a combination of factors that include your personal risk tolerance, your age, how far you are from your main financial goals, and the overall size of your portfolio. Generally speaking, if you are younger, with a longer time horizon to reach your financial goals, or have a relatively large portfolio, you can probably afford to assume greater risk. If you are older, closer to your goals, or have a small portfolio, you will probably want to be more conservative.

Naturally, you may want to develop your own customised asset allocation model which is slightly different from any of the four classics shown in our charts. Asset allocation is *not* a one-size-fits-all exercise.

Furthermore, you may want to change models when economic conditions change. If you sense that the stock market is about to suffer a serious downturn, consider shifting some of your money from shares into bonds or cash. When the market is about to rally, load up on shares. Naturally, no one can hope to time such shifts perfectly, so don't buy and sell constantly in hopes of catching every wave. But you can't afford to ignore the business climate altogether. Over time, you'll develop a style of responding to shifts in the securities markets and the economy that fits your personality and your overall investment philosophy.

ASSET ALLOCATION: FOUR CLASSIC MODELS

MODEL 1: LOW RISK: THE BALANCED MIX

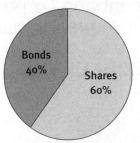

By allocating a full 40 percent to bonds, this model greatly reduces exposure to the risk involved in share investing. Of course, the types of shares held will have a large impact on the overall degree of risk. If only blue chips are included, the overall portfolio will be low risk. If some of the stocks are small caps or foreign stocks, for example, the portfolio will have a greater level of risk.

MODEL 2: MODERATE RISK BUT STILL CONSERVATIVE: THE ROBOT MIX

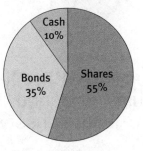

Like the balanced mix, the robot mix includes a

sizeable proportion of bonds. However, the suggested 10 percent allocation to cash is intended to create opportunities to buy shares or bonds when either is attractive. Thus, the actual proportion of shares in this mix may vary between 55 percent and 65 percent, depending on how optimistic you feel about share prices.

MODEL 3: FLEXIBLE: THE AGE-ADJUSTED MIX

At age 30:

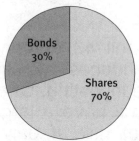

At age 50:

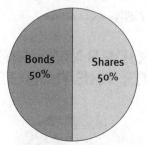

The age-adjusted mix is not a fixed model but rather a formula designed to move from relatively risky to fairly conservative over time. The formula is:

100%—your age = Percentage in stocks

The remainder would be allocated to bonds (or to a combination of bonds and cash). Thus, when you are thirty years old, this model would allocate 70 percent of your portfolio to stocks (30 percent to bonds). When you are fifty, this model would allocate 50 percent of your portfolio to stocks (50 percent to bonds). The first graph above illustrates the proportions for a thirty-year-old investor; the second shows how the proportions would change for a fifty-year-old.

MODEL 4: HIGH RISK: THE SO-CALLED OPTIMUM MIX

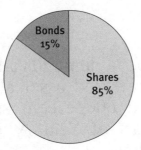

This is an aggressive portfolio model. If you have high psychological risk tolerance and believe strongly in the price potential of shares, consider this mix. However, be careful about the types of shares you choose. If most or all of your share holdings are in risky share types (such as small caps or foreign shares), you will run the risk of severe losses in the event of a market downturn.

REBALANCING YOUR PORTFOLIO

Once a year, reconsider your asset allocation strategy. This is important for three reasons:

- Increases and decreases in the value of the holdings in your portfolio may have changed the allocation percentages from those recommended in the model.

- You may have reached one or more of your financial goals, which makes it useful to reconsider the blend of short-term and long-term money in your portfolio.

- Changes in the economic and business climate may make you want to reconsider your approach.

The first point above demands a bit of explanation. Let's say your preferred asset allocation model is the balanced mix: 60 percent stocks, 40 percent bonds. At the start of Year A, the value of your portfolio is as follows:

Shares and unit trusts owning shares:	£30,000 (60 percent)
Bonds and unit trusts owning bonds:	£20,000 (40 percent)

This means that your portfolio matches the balanced mix formula perfectly. However, suppose that, during Year A, the stock market performs famously. Consequently, the shares you own rise in value by a full £10,000. Meanwhile, your bond holdings remain stagnant and barely change in value. Now your portfolio looks like this:

Shares and unit trusts
owning shares: £40,000 (67 percent)
Bonds and unit trusts
owning bonds: £20,000 (33 percent)

Suddenly your holdings no longer match the model you prefer. The solution lies in *rebalancing your portfolio*. This means buying and selling investments in order to reset the percentages to the desired blend of shares and bonds in the model. In this case, you would sell £4,000 worth of shares and use the proceeds to buy bonds. Your rebalanced portfolio would look like this:

Shares and unit trusts
owning shares: £36,000 (60 percent)
Bonds and unit trusts
owning bonds: £24,000 (40 percent)

One advantage of rebalancing is that it creates an automatic mechanism for taking profits, protecting the overall safety of your portfolio, and benefiting from the usual ups and downs of markets. If share prices have grown significantly, rebalancing forces you to capture some of the gains produced by your big winners and invest the money in bonds. Thus, you'll have taken some of your more risky money and put it into something safer. Conversely, if shares have plummeted, you'll sell some of your bonds and put the money into shares, taking advantage of the relatively bargain prices.

There's no need to obsess about rebalancing. If your portfolio varies from the ideal mix by a few percent, you may decide to leave it alone till next year. (After all, it does cost money to buy or sell an investment.) That's fine. But *do* examine your holdings at least once a year, so you'll recognise when your portfolio has got seriously out of whack.

Investing can be fun

You can probably tell I'm enthusiastic about share investing. Why not? Thanks to the steady growth of the world economy, I've been able to build a nice nest egg through share ownership. So have millions of other people. I hope this chapter has convinced you to consider joining them.

If you are bitten by the investment bug you may find, as I did, that learning about businesses, trying to choose tomorrow's winning companies, and developing an individual portfolio strategy is genuinely interesting and fun—at least as challenging as crossword puzzles or *The Weakest Link*, and far more rewarding! Approach share investing in a spirit of curiosity and adventure, and in time you're likely to find that your personal balance sheet is reflecting a steadily growing share of the national wealth. Doesn't that sound appealing?

8

INSURANCE OPTIONS

*The coverage you need,
the coverage you can skip*

Insurance is *not* fun

I admit it: there's nothing glamorous about insurance. After dazzling audiences in the role of Gordon Gekko, the rapacious investment tycoon in *Wall Street*, Michael Douglas did *not* appear next in a movie about a fabulously successfully life insurance salesman. By comparison to some other money topics, life insurance is drab, humdrum, b-o-r-i-n-g.

What's worse, it deals with topics most of us would rather not think about: illness, accidents, unemployment, death. Especially when we're young, most of us would prefer to pretend we'll never get sick, get hurt, be made redundant, or die. And surely we can think of more enjoyable things to spend money on than insurance premiums.

I understand. So I plan on keeping this chapter short and sweet. I'll tell you only what you absolutely need to know about insurance, and I'll try to quickly zero in on the issues of greatest concern: what kinds of insurance you really ought to have, what kinds you can skip, and how to spend the least possible money on the coverage you absolutely need. I know that the sooner you can get back to planning your next holiday, the happier

271

you'll be.

A price on your head: basics of life insurance

As you probably know, life insurance is a financial product that provides a payment (known as a *benefit*) when you die. The association with death makes many people feel there's something ghoulish about life insurance. 'Let's not discuss insurance. It gives me the creeps to talk about dying,' they say. And some people refuse to buy life insurance because 'I don't want to be worth more dead than alive.'

The truth is, not everyone needs life insurance. The whole point, as with any form of insurance, is *to protect you or those you care about from financial loss*. If there is no one who would be financially harmed by your death, then life insurance is probably unnecessary. Therefore, if you are single and have no children or other dependants, you can skip to the next section.

However, if you are married or in a committed relationship; if you have a child; or if you have a mortgage or other significant obligations, then you probably need life insurance. The questions then become: how much? and what kind?

Let's start with the first question. How much life insurance do you need? Some people—especially insurance salespeople—will suggest one-size-fits-all answers. For example, they offer the rule of thumb that everyone ought to have insurance coverage equal to fifteen times their annual salary. That would amount to a whopping £450,000 if you earn £30,000 per year. But I suggest a slightly more

272

analytical approach.

Here are my guidelines:

- If you are responsible for paying a mortgage, begin by assuming that you need life insurance coverage equal to the outstanding amount of your mortgage debt. This way, if you die, your spouse or loved one will be able to pay off the mortgage in full, despite the fact that you'll no longer be around to contribute to the payments. Without this coverage, it might be impossible for your surviving spouse or partner to make the payments and the home might have to be sold.

- If you have a loved one whose life is intertwined with yours financially, figure out what his or her needs would be in the event of your death. This amount may vary greatly. If you have a partner with a job and a good income, then the needs your life insurance will have to cover might be few. If you have a stay-at-home partner who might need training or retraining before getting into the workforce and becoming self-supporting, then one to four years' income might be needed. And if you have a partner who for some reason is completely unable to be self-supporting, then lifetime maintenance may be appropriate.

- If you have children, consider the financial needs that would arise should you die. Depending on the age of the children and the resources of your spouse or other caregivers, these needs might include daycare, partial support throughout childhood, primary and secondary schooling, and university education.

As you can see, life insurance needs are likely to vary widely from one person to another. Nigel, who is married to a successful solicitor and childless, may want some £65,000 of life insurance coverage—just enough to pay off the mortgage that he and Fiona are carrying. Bryony, with two small children (and no mortgage), may need £150,000 of coverage—one-third to help her spouse pay for daycare while the kids are little, one-third to help with expenses during their school years, and one-third to cover university tuition. And Craig, a prominent physician with a stay-at-home spouse and three teenage kids, may want £500,000 of insurance, so that his wife and children can continue to live the high life—boarding schools, posh holidays, designer clothes—even in his absence.

Naturally, the larger the death benefit you want, the more costly the insurance coverage will be. Life insurance payments, or *premiums*, are based on several factors, including your age, your sex, your occupation, and your health status. The insurers rely on statistical models that help them predict the likelihood that you'll die in a given time frame. Based on these models, they charge premiums that should cover the death benefits they must pay out, the expenses of running the insurance business, and a little left over for profit. So think carefully about what your family's real requirements are, and buy only the amount of life insurance coverage you need.

One way to save is by selecting the right *type* of

life insurance policy. Broadly speaking, there are two kinds of policies: *term* policies and *whole of life* policies. For reasons that will become obvious, I strongly suggest you buy the former.

TERM LIFE INSURANCE

As the name suggests, term insurance pays a death benefit only during a specified term of coverage, which usually ranges between ten and thirty years. Term life is the cheapest and most financially efficient form of life insurance. For most young and middle-aged people, the premiums on term policies are relatively low, since the likelihood that they will die during the term of the policy is small.

Furthermore, term insurance is appropriate for most people because they can select a term that will cover them during their time of greatest financial need. Imagine a young parent with small children and a home mortgage (a typical life insurance customer). Depending on the term of the mortgage and the exact ages of the children, a fifteen-year, twenty-year, or twenty-five-year term life policy will probably carry the family right through to the time when the home is paid up and the kids are finished with university. After that, the parents' need for insurance will be much, much less; they can replace their large term policy with a small policy or none at all.

Within the general category of term life insurance there are several variations you may hear about:

- *Level term insurance* involves premiums that don't change during the term of the policy. By contrast, *escalating term insurance* charges lower premiums when you are younger, higher premiums as you get older. If you can afford it, choose a level term policy. The premium hurts a bit at first but gets easier to manage as your income rises.

- *Decreasing term insurance* involves level premiums but gradually decreasing coverage. It is sometimes sold along with a repayment mortgage so as to provide coverage for the gradually decreasing amount of debt owed on the mortgage.

- Finally, *convertible term insurance* gives you the option to convert the policy into a whole of life policy, which I'll explain below. I don't particularly recommend this.

When you buy term life insurance, make certain that your policy gives you the option of increasing your coverage when you choose (for example, if you have a second or third child). Naturally, your premiums will rise accordingly. This option will save you money, since you'll be charged premiums based on your age at the time you first bought the policy rather than at the time you expanded your coverage, and of course the premiums charged to younger people are lower.

WHOLE OF LIFE INSURANCE

Unlike term insurance, a whole of life policy pays a death benefit no matter when you die. Of course, you usually have to pay premiums for a lifetime as well. For most people, whole of life insurance provides coverage that's actually unnecessary. If you die at age eighty-five, will your widowed spouse or children really need an extra £200,000 to keep going?

Insurance salespeople will try to persuade you to buy whole of life insurance because of its investment component. A portion of your premiums goes into an investment fund which grows at a varying rate, depending on the performance of the stock market. This produces a couple of supposed benefits. For one thing, the premiums you pay may be reduced in the future if the investment fund performs well. For another, the policy gradually develops a *surrender value*—an amount you can borrow against or cash in without having to die. However, the surrender value is generally less than the amount you've paid in the form of premiums.

You can tell that I'm not enthusiastic about whole of life insurance. The investment component complicates the insurance component without producing sufficient value to be worth while. My philosophy about this is similar to what I said about endowment mortgages: I'm all for investing, but I suggest you invest on your own, and keep the insurance company out of it.

WHO OWNS THE POLICY?

When you buy a life insurance policy, in addition to choosing one or more beneficiaries to receive the proceeds when you die, you will also designate an owner for the policy. As we'll discuss in chapter ten, your estate tax situation may be complicated if you are the owner of the policy. Consider simplifying the problem by naming the beneficiary of the policy as its owner.

Whatever type of life insurance you decide to buy, shop around. Premiums for the same coverage vary surprisingly widely. Figure out how much coverage you want and get quotes from several companies, or check out a few of the many Internet sites that offer life insurance quotes. Within an hour or so you'll be able to track down a good deal and save a pretty penny.

When the flesh is weak: understanding health insurance

In my American homeland, health insurance is an expensive, complicated and politically contentious mess. As you may know, the US lacks national health care coverage (except in rudimentary form for the elderly and the very poor). Most Americans pay for medical care through a crazy quilt of employer-paid benefit plans, private insurance schemes, and the traditional fee-for-service system.

Costs keep rising, employers and private insurers keep trying to reduce coverage, and no one really understands how our non-system works.

For British citizens, the situation is much better. Most people get most of their medical care through the National Health Service (NHS). However, there are still three kinds of health-related insurance that you ought to know about. As you'll see, I strongly suggest that you take advantage of the last of the three, as described below.

The three types of health insurance to consider are:

- *Private medical insurance.* This pays for private medical treatment above and beyond what the NHS provides. If you're satisfied with your care under the NHS, there's no need to purchase private medical insurance. If you're worried about the stories of long queues for operations, you may want private insurance.

- *Critical illness insurance.* This pays a benefit to help with expenses and loss of income when you are diagnosed with a specific serious illness. Most critical illness policies cover cancer, heart disease, kidney failure, stroke and a handful of other conditions, and you won't be paid anything if you suffer from an illness that is not on the list. Premiums will vary depending on your age, sex, medical history, occupation, and health-related lifestyle practices such as smoking. In practice, critical illness insurance provides coverage that overlaps with the third type of insurance, described below.

279

- *Income protection insurance.* Also known as *long-term disability* or *permanent health insurance*, this provides income when you're too sick to work. I consider this an essential form of insurance, especially since statistics show that *most* people will in fact suffer a disability at some point in their lives. Even single people who may not need life insurance ought to consider income protection insurance.

If you're self-employed like me, income protection insurance is especially necessary. (Those with regular jobs may already have some form of disability insurance. Check at work before buying additional coverage.) An income protection policy won't make up for your entire lost income. There's usually a coverage limit of 75 percent of your normal pay. Therefore, if you want to maintain your family lifestyle despite a disabling illness, having an emergency nest egg (as I've discussed throughout this book) is important.

Unfortunately, income protection insurance is pretty costly. As with any kind of insurance, you should shop around before buying. Different companies charge widely varying premiums. One way to trim the cost is by agreeing to wait sixty to ninety days before the disability payments begin. The insurance company saves a lot of money when such a waiting period is in effect, and much of the savings are passed on to you.

Finally, give careful thought to the *definition* of disability that your policy includes. Some policies will pay you if you are unable to do your regular work. Some will pay if you are unable to do your regular work or a similar job for which you are qualified. And some will pay you only if you are unable to do any kind of work at all. The first type of policy is most costly; the third type is cheapest. You'll need to decide how willing you might be to take up a new line of work if (heaven forbid) you suffer an injury that makes your usual job impossible.

In the driver's seat: how to save on car insurance

As most drivers discover, operating a car is a risky proposition. What's worse, careless (or unlucky) drivers can easily cause harm and financial loss to other people, too. That's why the law in Britain requires car insurance.

There are three levels of car insurance you ought to know about. Here they are, together with my recommendations as to what you need and don't need:

- *Third-party only* is the minimum car insurance coverage required by law in the UK. As the name implies, it provides reimbursement for the financial losses suffered by other people as a result of your driving. So if you crush another driver's fender or run over someone's cat, the injured party can recover money from your third party only coverage. This type of bare-bones car policy does *not* cover any damage to your car caused by your own poor driving or by such unpredictable occurrences as fire or theft.

- *Third-party, fire and theft* is the next step up from third-party only insurance. I recommend that every driver buy at least this kind of policy. In addition to covering damage suffered by third parties whom you may harm, it covers fire and theft damage to your vehicle.

- *Fully comprehensive insurance* is the most thorough (and of course the most expensive) form of car insurance. In addition to the coverages provided by third-party, fire and theft, fully comprehensive insurance helps pay for the cost of repairs to your car after an accident, even if you are partly or wholly to blame. If you own a new car, or a recent model and valuable used car, fully comprehensive insurance is worth considering. However, understand that if you total the car, you can't expect to be reimbursed for what you paid for it. Because of the process known as *depreciation*, the value of your car begins to decline the moment you drive it away from the showroom, and every month you own the vehicle slices away another chunk of its value for insurance purposes.

KEEPING CAR INSURANCE COSTS UNDER CONTROL

Just as life and health insurers base their charges on your age and medical status, car insurers have developed elaborate protocols by which they judge the likelihood of costly benefit claims from specific types of drivers. These rules will determine the size of the premiums you'll have to pay. They include some points you have no control over. For example, male drivers and those under the age of twenty-five pay more than females and those over twenty-five, since statistics show they are more likely to experience serious accidents. In addition, drivers who operate their cars mainly in the suburbs or the country usually pay less than city drivers—but it's probably not worth while to pick up and move just to save a few pounds on car insurance premiums.

On the other hand, there are some risk factors you *do* control, and you can influence these so as to reduce your insurance premiums. Consider the following options:

- *Drive a cheaper car with a smaller engine.* A souped-up, sexy sports car is usually more expensive to buy and repair than a modest saloon.

- *Protect your car against break-ins.* If you lock your car in a secure garage at night and equip it with an alarm or anti-theft device, you may be able to negotiate lower insurance premiums.

- *Buy a policy with a higher excess.* The *excess* is the initial portion of an expense that you pay for before insurance coverage kicks in. Thus, if you have a policy with an excess of £100 and you incur repair charges of £350, your insurer will cover only the last £250 worth. The higher your excess, the lower your premiums. To minimise your costs, consider an excess of £500.

- *Drive safely.* Higher premiums are paid by drivers with over three points for traffic violations on their licences and by those who've been found liable for accidents in the past. Keep a clean driving history and your premiums will go down.

The best drivers are eligible for a *no-claims discount.* After six years of driving without a single insurance claim, you may be able to save up to 65 percent on your premiums—obviously a substantial saving. As soon as you file a claim, whether the accident was your fault or not, your no-claims discount goes by the boards. So keep track of your claims history and think carefully before filing a claim, especially if you're in a minor accident. You may be better off paying for repairs yourself rather than seeing your insurance premiums suddenly skyrocket.

Finally, as with all types of insurance, shop around before settling on a particular company and policy. Don't hesitate to let insurers know that you're comparison-shopping, and invite them to best one another's offers. These tactics can save you quite a lot.

Where the heart is: the ins and outs of home insurance

Most people have more money wrapped up in their homes than in anything else they own. Thus it's natural that the vast majority of homeowners have insurance policies to protect them from the financial losses they might suffer if anything happens to their homes. Furthermore, if you have a mortgage, you'll probably be required to have at least basic home insurance coverage (since the mortgage lender has a financial stake in protecting the value of your home).

There are two main types of home insurance, each with a number of variations to consider. I'll explain both and offer some suggestions about the kind of coverage you ought to have.

- *Home insurance* covers your house or flat against such dangers as fire, flood, explosions, storms, falling trees, and other forms of disaster. It also covers damages incurred when your home is broken into or attacked by vandals. Most policies will protect both the house or flat itself (walls, roof, floors, etc.) as well as attached fixtures such as baths, toilets, kitchen cupboards, and wallpaper. The typical policy is written to cover the cost of repairing or replacing what's damaged. Additional coverages can be added for an extra charge. For example, *liability coverage* pays for injuries suffered by other people in and around your home: if they trip on your front step, for example, or if a tree on your property falls on their car. Both basic home insurance and liability coverage are worth buying for most homeowners.

- *Contents insurance* covers the contents of your home against the same kinds of dangers as home insurance—fire, flood, theft, and so on. Some types of liability are also usually covered, so that (for example) if your overflowing dishwasher floods and damages the flat below yours, the costs of repairs will be covered. Coverage against accidental damage—your TV falls from the cabinet and breaks—can be

286

purchased for an extra charge.

Before deciding on whether or not to buy contents insurance, make a room-by-room survey of your home. List the things you own and estimate the replacement cost of each. Pay special attention to valuable items such as jewellery, electronic equipment, art, and antiques. If the total value of what you own would represent a significant loss you'd have trouble bearing, then consider contents insurance.

If you do buy contents insurance, take steps to make certain that everything you own is properly covered. The room-by-room survey suggested above is a good first step. Consider taking photographs of your nicest items, and if you own anything of special value (a fine work of art, for example, or a really expensive diamond ring), have a written appraisal by an expert in your files. (And keep a copy of these records in a bank deposit box or some other location *away* from your home, otherwise they won't do you much good in the event your place burns to the ground.)

As with car insurance, you can save on home insurance premiums by accepting a higher excess. You may also be eligible for a discount if you install high-quality locks on the doors and windows along with a burglar alarm or other security system.

Other kinds of insurance

In our risk-averse era, there are many other kinds of financial products touted as 'insurance'. Most of these are not worth buying. I'll conclude this chapter by briefly discussing some of the other forms of insurance you may hear about and explaining what you need to know about each.

TRAVEL INSURANCE

This heading includes all forms of insurance that are intended to protect you while you're abroad on work or holiday. It takes many forms, covering a wide range of potential risks. For most people, travel insurance is completely needless, especially since your other insurance policies are likely to cover many of the same risks. For example:

- *Car accidents when driving abroad* may be covered by your regular car insurance policy or the credit card you use to rent the car.

- *Theft of your property while you are travelling* may be covered by your home contents insurance.

- *Health care emergencies* may be covered by your private medical insurance. In addition, countries of the European Union have reciprocal health service arrangements with the UK's National Health Service, which will provide at least a basic level of care for travellers in Europe.

In each case, you'll need to consult your existing policy (and talk with a representative of your insurer if necessary) to determine exactly what is and isn't covered. If you do a lot of travelling, you may want to consider buying insurance to cover any gaps.

One type of travel insurance I definitely urge you to skip is holiday coverage. This will reimburse you for all or part of the cost of a trip that you are forced to cancel. This coverage is usually not a good deal—very few people actually have to make claims, and the policies are needlessly expensive.

EXTENDED WARRANTIES

These are offered by manufacturers of cars, appliances, cellphones, and electronic gadgets as a form of insurance against repair costs after the initial guarantee has expired. When you buy one of these items, you'll probably find that the salesperson is very eager to sell you one of these policies. That's because they're highly profitable to the manufacturers; the warranties cost a lot and are rarely used. I recommend skipping them.

LEGAL EXPENSES INSURANCE

These relatively new insurance policies will cover the cost of hiring a solicitor if you're sued or need to take action against someone else. Sometimes additional services, such as access to a free legal information hotline, are included. Most people don't need this coverage. If you are doing things that you feel are likely to provoke someone else to haul you into court, my suggestion is—stop!

9

YES, YOU *CAN* RETIRE

Planning for a prosperous old age

Beating the retirement crisis: the importance of starting young

One change I've noticed among people in the UK in recent years is a growing awareness of the need to plan for retirement. That's all to the good.

Like most of the rest of the developed world, Britain faces a future crisis in caring for its elderly citizens. As the ratio of younger workers to older pensioners gradually declines during the early decades of the twenty-first century, it'll be harder and harder for government payments to stretch sufficiently to support our retirees.

At the same time, thanks to improved medical care, most of us can look forward to longer lives in retirement than our parents or grandparents enjoyed. Not so long ago, relatively few people lived much past the retirement age of sixty-five. In the near future, active oldsters in their eighties and beyond will be quite common.

Finally, our standards and expectations have increased as well. You and I would probably define a 'comfortable retirement' in far grander terms than our counterparts a generation or two ago. We take for granted opportunities for travel, entertainment, and other leisure activities that our grandparents considered rare luxuries. Factor in the higher standards of food, clothing, housing, and medical care that we enjoy, and you can see that supporting tomorrow's retirees in the style to which they've become accustomed will be no simple task.

So retirement is now both a personal and a social responsibility. For you as an individual, the key is to start thinking about retirement as soon as possible. The earlier you start saving and investing for retirement, the less it will cost and the easier it will be.

Sadly, there are many reasons young people tend to brush aside thoughts of retirement planning. There's the age-old truth that the young simply find it hard to imagine being old. In response to that, all I can say is: if you're lucky, getting old *will* happen—and it will happen sooner than you think.

Then there's the siren song of what I call 'fake fatalism': 'What if I die early? Then all my scrimping and saving will have been for naught.' This sounds tough-minded and realistic, but at bottom it's silly. In the first place, most people today are living longer than their parents, not dying early. And anyway, so *what* if you die young? Do you really think that, in the after-life, you'll be fretting over how you managed your personal finances? The chances are good that you'll have more important things to think about—no matter which set of gates you pass through! The dead don't have regrets, but many of the living do.

A dose of reality may help you to focus on the benefits of beginning a retirement savings programme *now* rather than later. Let's start with a simple rule of thumb . . .

START SOONER IF YOU CAN . . . BUT START

IN ANY CASE

What's the moral here? It's *not* that those who, for one reason or another, have been unable to start a retirement savings programme until their forties or later have no hope of retiring. If they act quickly and decisively, they can still achieve that goal. I didn't start saving for my retirement until I was in my thirties. Today, after fifteen years of diligent effort, I'm reasonably close to my goal.

The real lesson is that every young person fresh from school, in the process of launching a career, saving for a home, and starting a family ought to devote part of his attention to retirement planning—distant though that goal may appear. So if you're a twenty-five-year-old, that's wonderful!

293

Seize the opportunity to launch your retirement programme *now*.

If you're older, then a more aggressive savings plan will be necessary. I'll shortly walk you through a process to develop a plan tailored to your specific circumstances.

Retirement planning: the three-legged stool

Think of retirement planning as a three-legged stool. Each of the three legs plays a role in making a comfortable retirement possible.

THE FIRST LEG: YOUR STATE PENSION

As everyone knows, there is a government pension to which every working British citizen is entitled. It begins to pay out when you reach state pension age, which is sixty-five for men and between sixty and sixty-five for women, depending on when they were born.

The state pension is composed of two parts. The first is known as the Basic State Pension. You're entitled to this if you've made National Insurance contributions during your working life. Its current maximum value is £67.50 per week for an individual, £107.90 per week for a couple, indexed to rise annually with inflation.

The second part is the State Earnings Related Pension Scheme (SERPS). If you're an employee (not self-employed), you have been contributing to this scheme, which pays a pension linked to your average earnings up to a maximum of £125 per week. SERPS payments are partially means-tested, so they're reduced if you've managed to save a lot on your own.

If you haven't been working—for example, if you've been a stay-at-home mum—you may be eligible for the new Stakeholder Pensions, introduced in April 2000. These allow people with no income to invest up to £3,600 per year into a pension. But you must take the initiative to participate in this new scheme.

You can find out how much state pension you will probably receive by requesting a forecast from the Retirement Pension Forecasting and Advice Service (Tel. 0191–218–7585; ask for Form BR-19).

For many retired people, Leg One, the state pension, is all they have to live on. Unfortunately, it's very hard to live comfortably in old age on less than £200 per week (less than £10,000 per year). And the cost-of-living adjustments which are made each year don't fully keep up with inflation. The result is a gradual erosion of your quality of life as time passes—a sad prospect to look forward to.

THE SECOND LEG: YOUR COMPANY PENSION

If you are employed, you are probably covered by a company pension. This is a retirement plan paid for in part or in whole by your employer. If you're required to contribute, the typical amount is 5 percent of your salary. However, you can make additional voluntary contributions (AVCs) if you wish, which will increase your pension benefits, up to a maximum contribution of 15 percent. The benefits generally include both a lump sum payable tax-free upon your retirement and additional regular payments that last as long as you live. Alternatively, if you die before retirement age, a pension is usually paid to your widow or dependants.

Most people use the lump sum paid upon retirement to purchase an *annuity*. This is an investment that pays out a specific fixed income for as long as you live. The amount you'll be paid out of your annuity varies, of course, depending on several factors, including the amount of money in your lump sum and the prevailing interest rates at the time you retire. Annuities come in several varieties and are offered by many kinds of financial firms, including banks, building societies, and insurance companies. Shop around to find the annuity whose provisions you feel most comfortable with.

Since company pensions are privately arranged, they vary widely. As you set about developing your overall retirement plan, you need to get detailed information from your firm about the nature of your plan and about the kinds of payments you can expect to receive on retirement.

Suppose you leave an employer *before* you're ready to retire? When that happens your private pension can either be *frozen* or *carried*. If frozen, your pension is held in your name by the company and continues to grow on your behalf as your invested funds earn income (although no additional contributions will be made either by the employer or by you). If carried, then the funds in the plan are turned over to you to invest as you see fit.

The tricky thing these days is that few people remain with the same employer for more than a few years. As a result many people end up owning a bunch of small, varied pension investments from several companies. These investments don't necessarily add up to a coherent plan. It's up to you to keep track of them and to make sure that the combination of investments makes sense.

To do this, I recommend that you maintain a file in which you track all your pension plans, including frozen ones. Many people lose or forget about pensions from past employers. Don't let this happen to you!

THE THIRD LEG: YOUR PERSONAL RETIREMENT PLAN

The third leg of your retirement programme—and the portion over which you have the greatest control—is your personal retirement investment plan.

Many people use so-called *personal pension plans* as part of their retirement planning. These are investment schemes specifically designed for retirement saving. They're offered by insurance companies, banks, building societies, unit trust managers, and friendly societies. You're eligible to pay into a personal pension plan if you are self-employed or if you're an employee who is not covered by an employer's pension scheme. You can get tax breaks on the money you contribute into the plan, up to (fairly generous) limits set by Inland Revenue. The timing and amount of your payments and the size of your pension benefits will vary from one plan to another and may be difficult to predict, since they'll depend in part on how your invested funds grow.

You can also save for retirement using any of the saving and investment methods I've discussed in this book, from ISAs to unit trusts to bonds to shares.

The art of retirement planning involves fitting together the retirement savings you can expect to have from all sources—including all three legs of the stool—so that they'll cover your needs in old age. Learning how to do this is so important that I'll devote the rest of the chapter to it.

Setting your retirement goal

Of course, it's impossible to make a sensible investment plan for your retirement unless you know what you're trying to achieve—that is, how much money you'll need to live the good life you dream of after retirement.

Making a financial plan for retirement is one of the trickiest money calculations you'll ever make. This is true for several reasons. For one thing, it's difficult to anticipate the lifestyle choices you'll make when you retire, especially if that time is many years in the future. If you have trouble guessing where you'll want to eat dinner this coming Saturday, how can you guess where you'll want to live when you turn sixty-five?

Another difficulty arises from the effects of

inflation. As you know, inflation forces the prices of most goods and services upwards over time. It therefore gradually reduces the value or buying power of your assets and income. Inflation rates vary from year to year, as the graph on page 136 suggests. But even in times (like the 1990s and the early months of the twenty-first century) when price inflation is low, the effects of inflation mount up over the decades. When making estimates related to something that will happen many years from now, inflation will have a real impact. Therefore, if your retirement is a decade or further in the future, you'll need to take the effects of inflation seriously.

Finally, the problem is made still more tricky by the need to determine how much money you'll need on hand in order to produce a given amount of annual income during your retirement. To do this, some assumptions must be made about the investment income you can expect—assumptions that are sure to be slightly inaccurate.

So you can see that the challenge of setting a retirement goal is a tricky one. The result should also be checked and recalculated periodically as your savings and investment plans are gradually carried out, perhaps every two or three years.

Nonetheless, it's very important to perform the calculations and set the goal! Otherwise you'll never know what you need to do to have a hope of enjoying a comfortable old age. And for most people the process of goal-setting proves to be a wake-up call.

To set your retirement goal, follow the instructions in the form on pages 301–309, entitled Your Retirement Planning Worksheet.

> **Alvin says . . .**
>
> Frankly, most people are somewhat stunned when they learn how much *more* they need to do if they want to feel prosperous in retirement. But at least they are able to take some appropriate action once they understand what's needed.

YOUR RETIREMENT PLANNING WORKSHEET

STEP ONE: *Your retirement budget*

DETAILED METHOD: To set your retirement budget, estimate your monthly living expenses after retirement in each of the expense categories listed on the next page. (These are the same categories we used in creating your current budget in chapter one.) In making these estimates, consider the following points:

☐ **Home:** Will your current mortgage be paid off? Will you remain in your current home, or move to a different one? If you move, will you rent or buy? And if you buy, will it be with a mortgage or without?

☐ **Transport:** You probably will no longer have to commute to work. But this doesn't mean you will sit at home! Don't assume that transport costs will necessarily drop.

☐ **Less-than-Monthly Expenses:** Expect the cost of medical care to increase as you age.

☐ **Discretionary Spending:** As your family constellation changes (with the birth of grandchildren, for example), your spending patterns may change—for gift-giving, for example. How much travel will you want to do after retirement? For some retirees, travel becomes a major budget item.

A. Fixed costs	Amount (£)
HOME	
TRANSPORT	
OTHER MONTHLY BILLS	
LESS-THAN-MONTHLY EXPENSES	
OTHER EXPENSES	
TOTAL FIXED COSTS:	

B. Discretionary spending	
FOOD AND DRINK	
ENTERTAINMENT	
AROUND THE HOME	
LESS-THAN-MONTHLY EXPENSES	
OTHER EXPENSES	
TOTAL DISCRETIONARY SPENDING:	

TOTAL SPENDING

QUICK-AND-DIRTY ALTERNATIVE METHOD: If you feel daunted by the Detailed Method, you can set your retirement budget more quickly (though less accurately) by assuming that you will spend about 80 percent of your pre-retirement income.

STEP TWO: *Adjusting your retirement budget for inflation*

First, make an assumption about the average annual rate of inflation during the years between now and your planned retirement date. Then locate the place in the table below where your assumed annual inflation rate intersects with the number of years until you retire. The number there is your 'inflation multiplier'. Multiply your monthly retirement budget by the inflation multiplier to obtain the inflation-adjusted amount of money you'll need each month to live as you hope.

For example, suppose you plan to retire in twenty-two years. If you assume that inflation over the next twenty-two years is likely to be around 5 percent per year, then find the place in the table where 5 percent intersects with twenty-two years. The number in that place, 2.93, is your inflation multiplier. If you decided, in Step One, that your monthly retirement budget should be £2,600, then multiply 2,600 by 2.93 to obtain your inflation-adjusted budget:

$$2,600 \times 2.93 = 7,618$$

Therefore, you'll probably need about £7,618 per month to live as you hope to in retirement twenty-two years from today.

YOUR INFLATION MULTIPLIER

Assumed Inflation Rate

Years to Retirement	2%	3%	4%	5%	6%	8%	10%
1	1.02	1.03	1.04	1.05	1.06	1.08	1.10
2	1.04	1.06	1.08	1.10	1.12	1.17	1.21
3	1.06	1.09	1.12	1.16	1.19	1.26	1.33
4	1.08	1.13	1.17	1.22	1.26	1.36	1.46
5	1.10	1.16	1.22	1.28	1.34	1.47	1.61
6	1.13	1.19	1.27	1.34	1.42	1.59	1.77
7	1.15	1.23	1.32	1.41	1.50	1.71	1.95
8	1.17	1.27	1.37	1.48	1.59	1.85	2.14
9	1.20	1.30	1.42	1.55	1.69	2.00	2.36
10	1.22	1.34	1.48	1.63	1.79	2.16	2.59
11	1.24	1.38	1.54	1.71	1.90	2.33	2.85
12	1.27	1.43	1.60	1.80	2.01	2.52	3.14
13	1.29	1.47	1.67	1.89	2.13	2.72	3.45
14	1.32	1.51	1.73	1.98	2.26	2.94	3.80
15	1.35	1.56	1.80	2.08	2.40	3.17	4.18
16	1.37	1.60	1.87	2.18	2.54	3.43	4.59
17	1.40	1.65	1.95	2.29	2.69	3.70	5.05
18	1.43	1.70	2.03	2.41	2.85	4.00	5.56
19	1.46	1.75	2.11	2.53	3.03	4.32	6.12
20	1.49	1.81	2.19	2.65	3.21	4.66	6.73
21	1.52	1.86	2.28	2.79	3.40	5.03	7.40
22	1.55	1.92	2.37	2.93	3.60	5.44	8.14
23	1.58	1.97	2.46	3.07	3.82	5.87	8.95
24	1.61	2.03	2.56	3.23	4.05	6.34	9.85
25	1.64	2.09	2.67	3.39	4.29	6.85	10.83

26	1.67	2.16	2.77	3.56	4.55	7.40	11.92
27	1.71	2.22	2.88	3.73	4.82	7.99	13.11
28	1.74	2.29	3.00	3.92	5.11	8.63	14.42
29	1.78	2.36	3.12	4.12	5.42	9.32	15.86
30	1.81	2.43	3.24	4.32	5.74	10.06	17.45
31	1.85	2.50	3.37	4.54	6.09	10.87	19.19
32	1.88	2.58	3.51	4.76	6.45	11.74	21.11
33	1.92	2.65	3.65	5.00	6.84	12.68	23.23
34	1.96	2.73	3.79	5.25	7.25	13.69	25.55
35	2.00	2.81	3.95	5.52	7.69	14.79	28.10
36	2.04	2.90	4.10	5.79	8.15	15.97	30.91
37	2.08	2.99	4.27	6.08	8.64	17.25	34.00
38	2.12	3.07	4.44	6.39	9.15	18.63	37.40
39	2.16	3.17	4.62	6.70	9.70	20.12	41.14
40	2.21	3.26	4.80	7.04	10.29	21.72	45.26

STEP THREE: *The nest egg you'll need*

Once you've determined your inflation-adjusted monthly retirement budget, you're ready to calculate how big a nest egg you'll need to produce that much income. Here's how to do it.

A. Insert here your estimated monthly retirement spending, as calculated in Steps One and Two of this worksheet:

_____

B. Now estimate how much you can expect to receive from the first two legs of your retirement plan.

As explained on page 295, you can obtain a forecast of your State Pension payments by contacting the Retirement Pension Forecasting and Advice Service. Insert the monthly forecast amount on the next line.

Leg 1: Your State Pension:

_____

If you are covered by one or more employer pensions, check with the pension administrator(s) to learn the estimated payments you'll receive on retirement. Insert the monthly amount of these payments below.

Leg 2: Your Company Pension:

_____

Now add up the payments from Leg 1 and Leg 2, and enter that figure below.

Total of Leg 1 and Leg 2:

_____

C. To determine the shortfall, subtract the Total of Leg 1 and Leg 2 (above) from your estimated monthly spending (Step B). This amount must be made up from your personal retirement plan. Enter that figure below.

Your Personal Retirement Plan:

_____

D. Now you need to calculate how much savings it will take to generate the monthly shortfall amount. You'll do this using the table on page 308, titled 'Savings Needed to Generate £1,000 Monthly Income'.

First, you must estimate how long your retirement will last. Figures are provided on the table for periods ranging from fifteen to thirty years. (Uncertain how to guess how long you'll live after retirement? Consider family longevity patterns and your own health history, and to be safe, add a few more years to your best estimate.)

Second, you must estimate the growth rate your savings and investments will earn during your retirement. It's impossible to predict this with certainty, but the table provides figures for growth rates ranging from 5.5 percent to 10 percent. Use a rate from the middle of this range if you like, or stick closer to the bottom of the range for a more conservative approach.

Third, find the pound figure in the table where your retirement time span and estimated interest rate meet. Then multiply this figure by how many *thousands of pounds* your monthly shortfall amounts to. Thus, if your monthly shortfall is £1,300, multiply the figure from the table by 1.3.

This result of this calculation will be the approximate size of the nest egg you need to accumulate in your personal retirement plan in order to generate the kind of retirement income you'd like to have.

For example, to supply a monthly shortfall of £1,300 for a time span of twenty years (covering age sixty-five to eighty-five) at an assumed growth rate of 8 percent, multiply £119,550 × 1.3. The nest egg or personal pension needed is £155, 415.

SAVINGS NEEDED TO GENERATE £1,000 MONTHLY INCOME

Assumed Growth Rate

Time Span	5.5% (£)	7% (£)	8% (£)	9% (£)	10% (£)
15 yrs	122,380	111,250	104,640	98,600	93,060
20 yrs	145,370	128,980	119,550	111,140	103,620
25 yrs	162,840	141,490	129,560	119,160	110,050
30 yrs	176,120	150,300	136,280	124,280	113,950

NOTE: the table assumes that you will spend both interest and principal during retirement, so that when you die your total nest egg will have been spent. It does *not* provide for an inheritance nest egg for your children or other heirs. If necessary, you'll need to plan for that separately.

Retirement investment choices

Now that you have an idea of your retirement savings goal, you face the next major question: where should you put your savings for retirement?

The prevailing wisdom favours equity securities—that is, shares or unit trusts that invest in shares—for retirement purposes. There's a certain logic to that. History shows that, over a long time period, shares generally grow in value faster than any other investment. (In the short run, the picture is less clear, since shares go up and down unpredictably on a day-to-day basis.) Thus, any long-term investment plan will probably enjoy the greatest success if most of the money is invested in shares.

But as with any investment decision, your personal risk tolerance must be considered. You need to assess whether you can stand to watch the value of your retirement money go up and down from time to time. If you can, then equity investments are probably the best choice. If you can't, err towards conservatism: keep at least a significant portion of your investment money in

bonds, a cash ISA, or a building society savings
account, where growth will be slower but more
predictable than in shares.

In any case, as you get older, consider reducing
your share holdings. One popular rule of thumb:
the percentage of your investment money put into
shares should equal 100 percent minus your age.
(This is the same as the Flexible Asset Allocation
model, which I discussed on page 266 in Chapter
Seven.) Thus, if you are forty years old, your
retirement investments should be 60 percent in
shares (since 100%—40 (your age) = 60). By the
time you are sixty-five, the share percentage would
be reduced to 35 percent (since 100—65 = 35). This
conservative guideline works well for the average
person. As your share investment percentage
declines, move the money into safe investments: a
savings account, a cash ISA, or bonds.

Many older people are enticed by investment
schemes that are supposedly designed to generate
high income. Some of the people who hawk these
schemes say they 'guarantee' 15 percent annual
growth. If it were real, growth at that level would
be quite attractive. It would make your retirement
nest egg throw off a lot more money to live on

while lasting longer. Unfortunately, these schemes are based on risky premises, usually involving complicated 'hybrid' securities whose real performance is unpredictable. Many people who buy into the 'guaranteed' schemes end up losing everything.

Tracking your retirement funds

Many people also make the mistake of putting money away for retirement—and then ignoring it. Your retirement investments need to be monitored at least once a year. To do this, use the form entitled Tracking Your Retirement Funds provided on page 312. On the page that follows, you can see a sample of how this form might be filled out by someone who has been investing for retirement for only a few years. As you can see, she still has quite a way to go to reach her retirement goal.

TRACKING YOUR RETIREMENT FUNDS

Investment	Date	Amount (£)	Current Value (£)	Growth (%)

TOTALS:

RETIREMENT GOAL:

HOW FAR TO GO?

TRACKING YOUR RETIREMENT FUNDS

Investment	Date	Amount (£)	Current Value (£)	Growth (%)
SHARES				
DEF Inc. shares	7/97	1,800.00	2,345.67	30
KL Co. shares	2/98	2,400.00	4,678.20	95
OP Co. shares	10/00	2,000.00	1,115.08	(44)
UNIT TRUSTS				
BC Tracker Fund	9/95	1,500.00	2,989.90	99
UV Intl. Fund	4/99	1,750.00	2,110.00	21
YZ Growth Fund	3/96	1,000.00	2,130.45	113
C Bond Fund	1/97	2,500.00	3,610.60	44
YZ Growth Fund	2/01	1,600.00	1,720.50	7
TOTALS:		12,550.00	20,700.40	68
RETIREMENT GOAL:			350,000.00	
HOW FAR TO GO?			329,300.00	

USING A SPREADSHEET TO TRACK YOUR RETIREMENT PORTFOLIO

After a few years, if your investments become more complex, you may want to create a more elaborate tracking form that captures more detail about your investments. On page 317 you can see the form my friend William uses to track his retirement portfolio. It's a form that makes use of the calculating power of a computer spreadsheet. Although it may look complicated, it only took William about an hour to set up originally, and now it takes him just ten minutes or so to update the figures each quarter.

On the form, William has listed all his retirement investments, coding each one according to type. For example, his investments in unit trusts with capital growth as their investment objective are all coded 'G', while those unit trusts that are tracker funds are coded 'T'. The coding system makes it easy for the spreadsheet to calculate automatically what percentage of William's holdings are in each type of asset or segment of the market, thereby keeping track of his asset allocation. (Refer to Chapter Seven for an explanation of asset allocation.) The totals in each area are itemised at the bottom of the table. As you can see, he currently has about 47 percent of his investments in capital growth unit trusts.

At the bottom of William's form, he has projected the future growth of his portfolio, based on the assumptions that his investments will grow until he is age sixty-five at an annual rate of 6 percent (which is quite conservative) and that he will invest an additional £5,000 each year. If these projections hold true, by the time William is sixty-five he will have accumulated a little under £700,000 in his portfolio—a pretty attractive nest egg, I must say.

The one weakness I see in William's system is that he hasn't indicated a retirement goal, a nest-egg amount he hopes to accumulate. Without this, it's hard to see how William can tell whether or not his investment plan is on track. When I asked him about this, his explanation was revealing: 'It makes me nervous to think about a goal. I'm afraid I might be too far away from reaching it! I'm a little like a poker player who doesn't want to count his chips, thinking it might bring bad luck.'

The psychology is understandable, but it's mistaken. Being *aware* of what you need for your future won't bring you bad luck. Only being *ignorant* can do that.

As for me, I review my retirement investments annually, usually on or around my birthday. (Around the same time, I have a physical exam done. It seems fitting somehow to combine the two activities.) Last year, in 2000, when I did my financial check-up, I was quite close to my retirement goal—within 15 percent. A year later, when I updated my finances in the wake of the stock market doldrums of the past year, I was fully 40 percent shy of my goal. As a result, I'm now very conscious of the need to conserve and to put more money away.

What if I'd hit my retirement goal early? Would I have retired? No, I would have gone on working. I enjoy teaching and writing about finance, and I'm too young to want to slow down. (Anyway, I loathe

315

playing golf!) But I would have had greater mental freedom, knowing that I could walk away from work any time I wanted (or needed) to do so.

It's always important to have a retirement goal in mind. After all, you never know when you may hit it!

WILLIAM'S CURRENT RETIREMENT ASSETS

Pension—Company L

		(£)
Equity Growth Fund A	G	26,518
Equity Tracker Fund C	T	28,065
Equity International Fund N	I	32,515

Pension—Company R

Gilts	B	22,092
Equity Growth Fund O	G	19,016
Bank account	C	35,000

Pension—Company J

Equity Growth Fund X	G	6,485
Equity Tracker Fund V	T	2,787
Equity Growth Fund M	G	25,194
Equity International Fund U	I	7,219

Equity Growth Fund Q	G	44,722

TOTALS

Growth unit trusts	G	121,935	47%
International unit trusts	I	39,734	15%
Tracker funds	T	33,735	13%
Bonds (Gilts)	B	21,074	8%
Cash	C	42,470	16%
Grand Total		**258,948**	

PROJECTED GROWTH
TO AGE 65
WITH 6% GROWTH
PLUS £5K/YEAR

Year	Amount
2002	279,485
2003	301,254
2004	324,329
2005	348,789
2006	374,716
2007	402,199
2008	431,331
2009	462,211
2010	494,944
2011	529,640
2012	566,419
2013	605,404
2014	646,728
2015	690,532

Home equity and the trade-down option

A common flaw in some people's retirement plans is an over-reliance on the growth in their home equity.

It's an understandable mistake. At some times and in some places, home values have risen explosively for a number of years. Hearing about such run-ups (and perhaps experiencing one yourself), you might be tempted to say, 'Maybe I don't need to invest in shares or bonds. I'll be able to retire on the value of my home!'

There are two big problems with this assumption. First, as you saw in the chapter on buying property, home values don't always rise rapidly. Sometimes they increase slowly or even fall.

Second, you have to live somewhere. So there's a practical limit to your ability to take advantage of any increase in the value of your home. Even if you sell the home, you'll need to use at least part of the proceeds to buy or rent another home, and the chances are great that the cost of *that* home will also have risen. So for the vast majority of people, it doesn't make sense to think of the home as the primary vehicle for retirement investment.

Of course, it is possible to take advantage of a portion of your home's built-up equity when you retire. The most natural way of doing this is by trading down—that is, by selling the large house you needed while raising kids (and perhaps housing parents or other relatives as well) and buying a smaller, less expensive home that's adequate for your scaled-down lifestyle after the youngsters have moved away. The difference between the amount you clear when you sell the big home and the smaller amount needed to buy the more modest home can be added to your investment nest egg.

Sensible as this approach may be, many people seem to be reluctant to trade down in their housing choices when they retire. Instead, they insist on staying in their large (often too large) houses, paying for heating and lighting them, and wasting the opportunity to realise and use the equity they've built up.

There are obvious psychological reasons for this reluctance. People develop an emotional attachment to their homes, and it can be difficult to move away from a neighbourhood and a circle of friends that have become familiar. But there are definite advantages to trading down. A smaller home is easier to care for. If you move from a house into a flat, exterior repairs, and garden chores are no longer your responsibility. Many older people feel relieved when they have fewer stairs to climb, shorter hallways to navigate and simpler kitchens to clean. And it's certainly much easier and less costly to decorate and refurbish a four-room flat than a ten-room house.

Trading down isn't necessarily for everyone, but it may be appropriate for you. Many retirees find that it gives them a new lease of life. I urge you to consider it.

A final word about retirement savings

For most people saving for retirement is a long trek, a marathon race rather than a sprint. It calls for patience and steady determination. As you've seen, it's much easier to build up a handsome retirement nest egg if you start young. But of course the younger you are, the less real the prospect of retirement appears, and the weaker your motivation is likely to feel. It's a psychological paradox, a little like the one involved in a successful weight-loss programme. You need somehow to find the strength to say 'No' to a small satisfaction today (that is, the pleasure to be enjoyed by spending an extra pound or two right now) so as to enjoy a much greater satisfaction some years in the future (that is, the pleasure of being able to say 'Farewell for ever' to the drudgery of work and the anxiety of wondering how next month's bills will be paid).

I hope you'll resist the urge to cut back on your retirement savings plan when you're tempted by an attractive spending option—a new outfit, a weekend getaway, a hot date. And resist as well the temptation to borrow against your retirement money or withdraw a slice of it for other purposes. Keep it sacrosanct and, if you can, forget that it exists—except when you sit down periodically to review how well it's been growing.

10

PASSING ON YOUR WEALTH

Estate planning for the not-so-filthy-rich

You can't take it with you: so write a will

Back in the 'greed-is-good' 1980s, there was a popular bumper sticker that satirised the obsession many yuppies seemed to have with accumulating possessions: 'He who dies with the most toys wins.' Unfortunately, no matter how many toys you own, once you die you can't play with them any more.

However, there *are* good reasons to be concerned about what happens to your toys (and all your possessions) after you die. Maybe you've been sharing them with a playmate—a spouse, a partner, or children. Maybe you know someone who needs or deserves to have them. The only way to be certain that your toys will end up in the right hands after you've met the Grim Reaper is to draw up a will.

Unfortunately, many people ignore this truth. In fact, according to some estimates, as many as two-thirds of those in the UK die *intestate*, which means without a valid will. Some neglect will-making because they prefer not to think about death, almost as if pretending it doesn't exist will protect them from it. Of course, that's not how life (or death) works.

IF YOU DIE WITHOUT A WILL

One way to appreciate fully the importance of having a will is to consider the alternative. If you die intestate, your *estate*—your savings, your investments, your home, your personal possessions—will be divvied up among your closest relatives according to the Rules of Intestacy established by the government. Though thoughtfully designed by well-meaning people, these rules are inevitably somewhat arbitrary and capricious.

Perhaps you assume that, if you're married, your estate will automatically go to your spouse when you die. Not so. In most cases, if you are a married person with children under eighteen, your spouse will inherit the first £125,000 of your estate, plus half the balance. The remainder will be held in trust and passed on to the kids when they turn eighteen. Does this make sense? Does it fit the needs of your family? Maybe, maybe not. It doesn't matter. When you make no will, the government's one-size-fits-all rules kick in.

In other circumstances, the mismatch between the rules and your actual needs and wishes may be even worse. For example, if you are unmarried but living with a partner, that person is practically invisible under the Rules of Intestacy. If you die without a will, any blood relatives you may have will receive your estate, while your life partner gets nothing. And if you die with *no* next of kin, your entire estate will go into the government's coffers. You may like the idea of turning over everything you've worked for to the Inland Revenue . . . but maybe you can think of a better alternative.

So making a will is important no matter what your circumstances. It helps ensure that those who are financially dependent on you will be cared for properly after you die. It also allows you to leave your assets and your personal belongings to family, friends, and charities in ways that will make you and the recipients happy.

YOUR WILL IS NOT A DIY PROJECT

It's smart to engage a solicitor in creating your will. Even simple estates are more complex than people realise, and a lawyer is well versed in the inheritance laws. He or she can walk you through 'if-then' scenarios you might never consider and make certain that you and your loved ones are protected even in unusual circumstances that just might happen. For example, you may want to make your spouse your heir. Fine. But supposing you and your spouse die simultaneously—on holiday, for example? What if one of you dies while the other is hospitalised and incapacitated? Will your money go into legal limbo, where it can't be used to provide needed care? Perhaps it seems morbid to raise such possibilities, but a lawyer can help you make certain you're prepared to handle them appropriately.

In drawing up a will, many people overlook some of the assets they own that ought to be accounted for in the document. The personal balance sheet that you drew up in Chapter Three will be a good start in creating your will. Bring it with you when you visit your solicitor. Other steps to follow when planning your will can be found in the checklist on page 326.

As you'll see, I suggest that at the same time you write your will you also make plans for the care of your children, the disposition of any business interests, and other final arrangements. Thoughtful planning of such things can be a real blessing to those you leave behind. When my beloved grandmother was dying at age eighty-five, she not only accepted her fate but embraced it. She planned her own funeral right down to the cars in which we'd ride to the service (which she rented in advance). For her friends and family, saying farewell to Grandma was like attending a party—all we had to do was show up.

YOUR WILL CHECKLIST

☐ **What are your assets?**

Draw up a list of everything you own in whole or in part. (The personal balance sheet you drew up in chapter three will be a helpful place to start.) Include bank accounts, investment accounts, and property, as well as personal possessions, business you own, and other assets.

☐ **Who should carry out your wishes?**

Select a trusted family member or friend to serve as the executor of your estate. This person will be responsible for carrying out the wishes expressed in your will. He or she will gather together your assets, pay any outstanding bills (including funeral expenses), and distribute the remainder of your estate to your heirs as specified in the will.

Your executor must be over eighteen years of age and should have the right personality and temperament to handle the job. He or she should be trustworthy, diligent, logical and reasonably knowledgeable about finances and the law. The executor need not be a lawyer or accountant, although some people do select a trusted professional adviser to fill this role. There's no reason why an executor may not also be one of the heirs to your estate.

It's also wise to list a back-up executor, in case your first choice is unavailable for any reason. Before listing an executor, ask to make certain the person you've selected is willing to handle the job.

☐ **Make plans for any children.**

If you have children under eighteen years of age, your will should spell out how they would be cared for in the event both parents die. You'll need to choose a personal guardian, who will be entrusted with raising the children, as well as a financial guardian, who will be in charge of handling any assets and income you provide for them. (This may or may not be the same person.) It's wise to provide for a secondary guardian in the event the first guardian is dead or incapacitated at the time your will goes into effect. As with the executor, ask beforehand to make certain that the people you name are willing to undertake the task.

☐ **Decide how to distribute your property.**

List in general how you want your assets to be distributed (your *bequests*). While you can list specific amounts, you can also indicate percentage amounts. Describe the distribution of personal possessions in general terms (e.g., 'My jewellery to my sister Elaine'). If there is a long list of specific bequests to particular people ('My diamond and ruby brooch to cousin Agnes'), consider writing up a separate list rather than incorporating this detail into the will itself. Keep this list with the will.

☐ **Write up any special wishes you may have.**

You may want to specify your preferences concerning your funeral, the disposition of your remains, and the kind of memorial service to be held in your honour. You may also want to express your wishes about the upbringing of your children, the wrapping-up of any business interests you leave behind, and the charitable purposes towards which some of your assets may have been left.

As with any detailed list of inheritance items, these wishes should probably be spelled out in a separate document kept with the will rather than in the will itself. The requests you make here will not be legally binding, but they will probably carry considerable weight with those you leave behind.

☐ **Review your will periodically.**

At least once a year, review the terms of your will and make certain they continue to reflect your wishes and your current financial status. Also update your will whenever your circumstances change. Any time there's a change in the status of a person mentioned in the will (an heir, for example) or a major change in any asset you own, you should consider whether a change in your will is required. Among the events that should trigger a review of your will:

● You get married or divorced.

- You have a child.

- One of your heirs dies.

- Your children grow up and become financially independent.

- You buy a home.

- You buy, found, or sell a business.

- You inherit a piece of property or any significant wealth.

- You retire.

☐ **Keep the will and related documents in a safe, accessible place.**

Keep your will somewhere that your spouse, partner, next-of-kin, or other concerned party will be easily able to get it when you die. A safety deposit box at your bank is *not* a good location, since such boxes are often legally sealed after the death of the owner. Instead, consider keeping one copy in a file cabinet or desk at home and a second copy at your lawyer's office. You may want to give a third copy to the executor named in the will.

Basic estate planning

In drawing up a will, you've taken the first big step towards getting your estate in order. Now it's time to consider whether some other steps might be worth considering. The answer will depend in part on how large and complicated your estate is. First, you need to understand what will happen after you die.

THE PROBATE PROCESS

When the bell tolls for you, someone will have to deal with your estate by paying debts, compiling all the assets, and distributing the estate according to the will. *Probate* refers specifically to the issuing of a legal document, generally called a *grant*, to one or more people that authorises them to handle these matters. It also refers, more generally, to the financial winding-up of your estate under the watchful eye of the government, which seeks to make certain that your wishes are obeyed, that no laws are broken, and that the government receives any tax payments that may be due.

Normally the executor named in your will receives the grant. If you have no will or name no executor, a relative will usually be given the grant, with spouses and children getting first priority. The grant is given by the nearest Probate Registry (a government office), which will ask to see the original will, a death certificate, and a list of the assets included in the estate. In turn, they'll ask the executor to fill out a set of forms and to submit to an interview at the Probate Registry to confirm the information provided.

INHERITANCE TAX (IHT)

Before a grant is issued, any inheritance tax due must be paid by the executor (or other grantee). But will IHT be due on your estate? That depends. The most important factor is the *size* of your estate.

You can estimate the size of your estate right now. Just calculate the total value of your assets. Your estate includes everything owned in your name and your portion of everything you own jointly. (Thus, if you own a house in partnership with a spouse, your estate would include half of the value of the house.)

Your estate also includes your share of any gift you've given to others from which you still receive some benefit. For example, if you've turned over ownership of a home to one of your children with the stipulation that you will continue to live there as long as you want, then a portion of the home remains a part of your estate. In the same way, any assets held in trust from which you receive some benefit (such as interest or dividend income) remain part of your estate. Finally, the proceeds on any life insurance policy you own will be counted as part of your estate. (Thus, if you own a £200,000 term life insurance policy of which your spouse is the beneficiary, you should add £200,000 to the total value of your estate.)

Note, however, that business property and agricultural property are subject to 100 percent relief from IHT. If you own buildings or property used for business or farming purposes, consult a tax lawyer for further information; the rules defining such property are fairly complicated and will be applied precisely.

For IHT purposes, your estate will be valued as of the day you die. For most assets, this is a simple matter. Savings accounts have a clearly stated value. Bonds, shares, and other securities are valued as of their closing price on the day you die. Property, however, is valued at the opinion of an expert appraiser, and valuing the assets of a private company may be quite complex.

Once all the assets have been valued, any bills you owe at the time of your death will be subtracted from your estate. So will funeral expenses, outstanding medical bills, and any other costs related to your passing. What remains is the final value of your estate.

Now a bit of maths is necessary. In the UK, the first £242,000 of your estate is completely exempt from IHT. (This is a pretty substantial amount of money. Over 96 percent of all estates have a value below this amount and therefore pay no tax at all.)

However, if you've accumulated sizeable assets over the years, you may find your net worth creeping over the £242,000 threshold. For example, if the value of your home has grown a lot, it may raise your estate over the magic number even if your savings and investments are quite modest. And once you pass the threshold, the taxes can be substantial. IHT is levied at a rate of 40 percent on the value of your estate over the threshold amount. Thus, if your estate has a total value of £600,000, IHT in the amount of £143,200 will be due. [£600,000 − £242,000 = £358,000, and then 40 percent of £358,000 = £143,200].

If you have a significant estate (or hope to have one someday), you may now be waxing indignant: 'What—those vultures from Inland Revenue won't even leave my corpse alone? After I worked hard to make all that money, I can't simply leave it to whomever I please without Her Majesty grabbing a share?'

If you feel this way, it's time to give some serious thought to estate planning. There are a number of simple steps you can take to reduce your exposure to IHT.

SHIFT INSURANCE OWNERSHIP

As I've mentioned, insurance proceeds are counted as part of your estate if *you* are listed as the owner of the policy. This can complicate your tax problems by increasing the overall size of the estate, perhaps pushing it up over the threshold.

You can avoid this problem by making the beneficiary of the policy—your spouse or your child, for example—the owner of the policy. This step does have disadvantages. For example, you can't change the beneficiary once you've done this, and if you own a whole of life policy, you will forfeit your right to any cash value the policy accumulates. Check with your insurance company or insurance agent to decide whether or not you want to make this change.

GIVE YOUR WEALTH AWAY

A very popular way of reducing IHT is by giving away a portion of your assets while you're alive. The idea, of course, is that by reducing the size of the estate you leave behind, you can reduce or eliminate the amount that is exposed to IHT.

Perhaps it occurs to you that a person suffering

from a terminal illness could escape IHT altogether by simply signing papers that transfer everything to a child or other heir—one big 'gift' in place of inheritance. Never fear, the same thought has occurred to the Inland Revenue. They've developed rules about gift-giving that are designed to prevent this. The rules are fairly complicated, so if you want to adopt gift-giving as a way of reducing IHT you should consult a financial adviser who can walk you through a detailed plan. However, the basic rule is that any gifts you give prior to seven years before your death are excluded from your estate. Gifts given later than that (that is, within the seven years before you died) are subject to IHT at a gradually increasing rate: 20 percent of the usual tax during the sixth year prior to death, 40 percent during the fifth year, and so on.

In addition, some other kinds of gifts are excluded from IHT even within the seven-year window:

- Gifts or bequests to a spouse.

- Annual gifts of up to £3,000 per year.

- Small gifts of up to £250 per year to any one person (which are counted outside the £3,000 window).

- A wedding gift of up to £5,000 to your child or to the person your child is marrying.

- Gifts or bequests to UK registered charities.

PLAN YOUR WILL

You can also reduce IHT by planning your will provisions intelligently. As I noted above, anything you give to your spouse during your lifetime or leave to your spouse on your death is excluded from IHT.

This so-called spousal exemption offers a significant savings opportunity to married couples. You can take advantage of the exemption by drafting a will that does *not* leave your entire estate to your spouse. Instead, leave a certain amount to others, such as your children, with the balance to your spouse. The potential benefit of this strategy kicks in when your spouse in turn dies.

A bit confused? Here's an example to illustrate how the strategy works. Suppose Philip and Gillian are married with two children, and they have an estate with a total value of £700,000. For simplicity's sake, we'll assume that half of this value is owned by each spouse. If Philip dies with a will leaving everything to Gillian, she will inherit £350,000 tax-free (thanks to the spousal exemption). But now suppose Gillian dies ten years later. She leaves a £700,000 estate, whose value in excess of £242,000 will be subject to tax. The total IHT due will be £183,200 [£700,000 – £242,000 = £458,000; and then 40 percent of £458,000 = £183,200].

Instead, suppose Philip's will specified that £242,000 from his estate would be left to the two children, with the balance going to Gillian. As his spouse, she will inherit £108,000 tax-free, and the children's inheritance, since it falls under the £242,000 tax exemption, will also be tax-free.

Gillian's net worth is now £458,000 [£108,000 (inherited) + £350,000 (her part of the estate)]. Now, when Gillian dies ten years later, she leaves a £458,000 estate to her children. Tax will be payable on the amount of her estate that exceeds £242,000. The total tax due will be £86,400 [£458,000 – £242,000 = £216,000; and then 40 percent of £216,000 = £86,400).

Do you see what has happened? Almost £100,000 in IHT has been saved through the redrafting of Philip's will more than ten years earlier! Of course, this strategy only works if your spouse has enough to live on even when the estate is split between her and other heirs. The advice of a lawyer is essential, as it always is when you are drafting a will. Nonetheless, this is a basic tax savings technique that many couples can take advantage of—and that too many people know nothing about.

(Note: In the example above, we specified that

Gillian died ten years after her spouse. We specified this time in order to avoid dealing with one specific complication of the IHT law. If you leave your estate to someone who then dies within five years, Quick Succession Relief reduces the IHT payable on the second death according to a declining scale, depending on how many years have passed since your death. But I'm going to stop here. Consult a tax lawyer if you really need to know more about this.)

GETTING FANCY

There are other more complicated estate-planning techniques. Some people use specially designed life insurance policies for the purpose of paying off IHT that may be due after their death, thereby leaving the full value of the estate available to their heirs. The maths of making this work properly are complicated. If you're curious, get advice from a tax lawyer or life insurance specialist.

Another popular estate-planning option among people with large estates is the use of trusts. A *trust* is a legal entity specifically created to administer assets and income on behalf of a beneficiary. By creating a carefully crafted trust to handle wealth on your behalf or on behalf of your children or other dependants, you may be able to shift some of your estate outside the probate process and thereby save time and taxes.

If you are interested in considering a trust strategy, consult a financial adviser who specialises in tax issues. Which leads nicely into my next topic: how to choose and work with a financial adviser.

11

WHO TO BELIEVE?

Choosing and using financial advisers

There's a clever advert that I've noticed printed on the side of some London taxis lately. It promotes the financial management services of a big financial firm. 'We have 280 experts,' reads the slogan, 'so you can take a back seat.'

The firm that placed the advert is a good one, and I don't mean to pick on them particularly. But the attitude they're encouraging here is, I think, exactly the *wrong* one. Too many people in the UK think that the proper role for the individual investor is sitting in the back seat, with no power and no responsibilities other than to enjoy the view. They believe they should give control of their money over to a financial adviser whose authority is not to be questioned, just as the average patient wouldn't question the advice he gets from his physician.

This is one area where American investors may have an edge on the British. In America, we believe in asking tough questions and insisting on clear answers, especially when it comes to our finances. The American investor insists on sitting in the *front* seat, at the steering wheel. (On the left side, of course.)

This is not to say that the help of a financial adviser may not be valuable. It can be, and for some tasks it's essential. But never lose sight of the fact that the money is *yours*, and that only you can determine how it should best be saved, invested, and spent.

Who needs a financial adviser?

If you've really absorbed the contents of this book, you already have a leg up on most other people. You know more about the basics of managing, saving, and investing money than the average person, and you're pretty well equipped to handle many financial issues on your own. And of course I've scattered advice throughout the book concerning where to turn for specific additional information you may need on matters such as choosing the right investment vehicles.

You're also lucky to be living in a time when sound, easy-to-understand money advice is more widely available than ever before. You can increase your knowledge about basic financial matters, current trends, new savings and investment products, and smart money strategies by using such information sources as:

- The money pages or personal finance sections in newspapers.

- Magazines that focus on financial and investment topics.

- TV and radio programmes and news coverage.

- Books on personal finance.

- Websites devoted to investment and money management.

- Financial seminars, workshops and courses.

- Government agencies.

- Trade associations and financial services firms.

Of course, not all of these sources are equally reliable. Consider the Internet, for example. Information spreads faster and easier on the Internet than anywhere else. And because no one edits or controls the content of the Internet, everyone is free to contribute ideas. Search on the Net for information on a topic such as 'mortgages' or 'share investing' and you'll find thousands of websites offering information. Unfortunately, many of these will be unhelpful. Some will contain scanty information, while others offer material that is dated, incomplete, grossly biased, or just plain wrong.

When you're trying to sort the reliable from the treacherous in today's flood of financial information, start by using the same sort of common sense and scepticism you'd apply to a television advert or a door-to-door salesman. Always consider who will benefit from any advice you read or hear. A person or company with an interest in selling a particular financial product or service has a huge incentive to slant the information they present; not necessarily by lying but by playing down or ignoring the risks and over-emphasising the potential benefits. (And there *are* firms and individuals who don't boggle at committing out-and-out fraud.)

Part of evaluating any financial information source is considering its reputation, background, and history. And weigh the ideas you get from different sources against one another. An investment strategy touted only by one or two obscure firms ought to be examined with extreme scepticism, while a strategy that's been widely reported, tested by independent journalists and industry experts, and used with success for years by many individuals may be worth considering for your own portfolio.

So there's a lot you can do to advance your own money knowledge, enabling you to make many money decisions on your own. But for many people there comes a point when soliciting professional advice is important. You may need professional financial advice if:

- You're deeply in debt or facing other serious financial problems that you don't know how to solve.

- You're in the market for life insurance, a private pension plan, a savings plan, or an annuity, and are unsure which product will best suit your needs.

- You need help in developing a savings and investment programme for goals such as retirement.

- You want to begin investing in unit trusts, shares, or bonds, and feel uncertain about how to get started.

- You already own a number of pension plans, unit trusts, annuities, or other investments and don't know whether they add up to a coherent and appropriate investment strategy.

- You are facing a major change in your life situation (marriage, divorce, retirement, selling off a business) and aren't sure how to adjust your finances accordingly.

- You've built a large estate and are concerned about reducing the inheritance tax liability your heirs will face.

If one or more of these circumstances fits you, then the time may have come when your personal finances are a bit too complicated for you to handle on your own.

Types of financial advisers

However, it's not enough to recognise that you may need financial help. It's equally important to decide what *kind* of help you need and what sort of professional is best equipped to provide it. Here's a brief rundown of the main types of financial advisers, with some guidelines as to what to expect from each.

INDEPENDENT FINANCIAL ADVISERS (IFAs)

The job of an IFA is to provide financial advice on investments and other money matters based on your personal status, current assets, and long-range goals. The IFA may be paid a flat fee or an hourly fee, or he may receive all or part of his compensation in the form of commissions from the sales of financial products he recommends to clients, for example, insurance policies, annuities, unit trusts and so on.

An IFA whose payment is fee-based can generally be counted on to provide unbiased investment suggestions (which is not to say that his suggestions will always be right). By contrast, an IFA who is paid in part or in whole from commissions is likely to offer advice that favours investment products on which greater commissions are paid (which is not to say that his suggestions will always be wrong). If you work with a commission-paid IFA, bear his or her natural bias in mind, and balance his advice against information and ideas you derive from other sources.

IFAs vary widely in their knowledge, experience, and interests. Not all are equally knowledgeable about every financial field. Be sure to select an IFA with experience working with clients like you, as well as knowledge of the specific financial topics you are keenly interested in. For example, if you are interested in getting started in the stock market, seek out an IFA with a special knowledge of shares and other securities.

TIED AGENTS

Tied agents are salespeople who represent one financial firm and its products. For example, insurance companies, banks, and building societies all employ tied agents to promote their products.

Maybe you've heard the saying, 'If the only tool you have is a hammer, everything looks like a nail.' The same limitation applies to tied agents. The tied agent who makes a living by selling insurance annuities is likely to believe that everyone needs an annuity, no matter what his or her financial status or goals.

This doesn't mean that the help of a tied agent may never be useful to you. For example, if you know from independent research and comparison-shopping that you want to buy an insurance policy offered by a particular company, a tied agent for that company can answer specific questions about the policy, help you make the purchase, submit the proper forms and so on.

SOLICITORS AND ACCOUNTANTS

Some lawyers and accountants offer financial planning as part of their professional services work. Naturally, their professional training makes them particularly well equipped to focus on specific aspects of the financial world. For example, there are solicitors who specialise in tax-saving strategies, estate-planning techniques, small-business finance, and other legal matters related to your money. The more specific you can be in describing the kind of legal or accounting guidance you need, the easier it will be for you to find just the right professional to help you.

STOCKBROKERS

At some point in your financial life, you will probably want to work with a stockbroker. A broker acts as a middleman between an individual and the investment market. A broker handles the purchase and sale of securities, keeps track of the flow of dividends and other investment income into your account, maintains financial records for you, and otherwise helps you navigate—and hopefully profit from—the investment markets. There are three main kinds of brokers.

- *Execution-only brokers* simply buy and sell shares or other securities on your behalf, for which they are paid a small commission. They offer no financial or investment advice. (As I'll explain in the next chapter, the cheapest execution-only brokers now offer service over the Internet. They're called *online brokers*.)

- *Advisory brokers* handle your trades, but they

also offer investment ideas and advice. Since your broker handles most or all of your investment transactions and maintains your financial records, he knows your portfolio well and is in a good position to suggest ways of helping it grow. After he works with you a while, he should develop a good sense of your money personality: your risk tolerance, your interests and objectives, and the kinds of investments you have confidence in.

Advisory brokers also have access to a wealth of useful investment information. Through the brokerage houses that employ them, they can get their hands on company reports, analysts' assessments of a firm's financial prospects and its quality of management, and strategic memos prepared by experts on all manner of financial topics: interest rates, foreign developments, new business sectors, economic cycles, and so on. Thus, an advisory broker can help accelerate your financial education. It's a bit more expensive to work with an advisory broker than with an execution-only broker, since the

346

commissions you pay on trades must also cover the costs of maintaining the brokerage company's research department.

If you employ an advisory broker, take full advantage of the research and advice he or she can offer. When you're curious about a particular business sector or a company's shares or other securities, ask your broker for information. He or she will probably have some research to send you: an analyst's report, a printout of company financial data, or the like. He may also be able to suggest other similar investments that are worth examining for comparison's sake. And he may have advice to offer based on the experience of other clients with these investments.

- The *portfolio manager* is the third type of broker and is generally employed only by the wealthy. In addition to executing trades requested by his clients, he actually makes investment decisions on their behalf and has discretionary authority over the account. The portfolio manager and the client may agree together on a general set of goals and investment strategies, but all the details are left up to the manager, who simply reports his results to the client periodically. Hence the alternative name for the portfolio broker, the *discretionary broker*, since you have given him the written discretionary authority to act on your behalf. He is generally paid a significant fee, sometimes based on a percentage of the total amount of money invested.

Naturally, it's not possible for a broker to act

in this capacity unless the client has given him legal authorisation to spend and invest money on his behalf. This kind of arrangement is *not* recommended for the average investor, nor indeed for anyone working with a broker in whom he has less than absolute, implicit trust.

Choosing a financial adviser

When you're considering working with a financial adviser—whether an IFA, a tied agent, a broker, or any other type of professional—be prepared for your initial meeting with a list of questions. (Your list should *not* include, 'Can you make me rich?' which is either naïve or cynical.) See the list on page 350 for a good starting point. The questions presented there can be used with any kind of financial adviser—an IFA, an insurance agent, a broker. Also go armed with a statement of your personal financial goals, which should be much more specific than 'to make money'. The more direction you can give the adviser, the better. Your conversation will be specific and detailed, enabling you to get a very clear sense as to whether or not this adviser has the right style and philosophy for you.

BE SCEPTICAL

When considering a particular adviser, don't ignore any sense of disbelief, doubt, or discomfort you may feel. Don't let yourself be swayed by an adviser's flashy accoutrements, nice office, posh accent, or shiny car. You want someone to whom you can talk straight and from whom you can receive clear, definitive answers, not necessarily someone with an impressive appearance or a silver tongue.

Take notes during your initial meeting. Then visit a couple of other advisers and compare their answers. Look for one who offers advice that is clearly tailored to you and your circumstances rather than generic advice that applies to everyone.

Some people feel shy about asking a question when they don't understand what the adviser says. They worry about being thought stupid, or about wasting the adviser's time. Just open your mouth and ask the question! Remember, the adviser should want to work for you, not vice versa. He owes you thoughtful, respectful service, just as any employee owes his employer.

TEN QUESTIONS TO ASK A FINANCIAL ADVISER

☐ **What are your charges likely to be in the first two years that we work together?**

He should enumerate all fees and other expenses and show how much his services will cost in real numbers, using concrete examples, not just percentages. Two years is a realistic time frame to ask the adviser to predict: the first year will include any initial costs, and the second year will reflect ongoing expenses. If a portion of the adviser's income is based on sales commissions, remember that this will inevitably affect the kinds of advice he offers you.

☐ **How long have you been active in your field?**

The longer the adviser's experience, the better. It's most crucial that he has been active through both bull and bear stock markets and through financial recessions and periods of inflation. This means, as of 2001, that an adviser whose experience does not date back to at least 1991 may lack certain crucial insights into market behaviour and psychology.

☐ **How successful have your clients been in following your advice?**

He should be able to show some records or reports that indicate the kind of financial results his clients have enjoyed in the past (without names, of course). It's even better if these records are *audited*—that is, bearing a mark of authenticity and accuracy from a recognised accountancy firm that has reviewed them independently.

☐ **Have you had any clients with backgrounds and goals similar to mine? How did you work with them?**

The adviser's answer will help you gain a sense as to whether or not he really understands your position and what you hope to accomplish. It will also help you gain a feeling for how fully he or she customises his advice for each client (as opposed to offering 'canned' advice that scarcely varies from one client to another).

☐ **How do you differ from other financial advisers? What makes you unique?**

Listen here as much for what the adviser *doesn't* say as for what he or she does say. Avoid an adviser who makes inflated claims, promises 'risk-free' results, or claims an 'inside track' on 'secret opportunities'. Instead, look for someone who works hard to stay on top of news and developments in the financial sphere and will take the time to work with you and for you.

☐ **Have there been any complaints from clients about you?**

If you feel the least bit doubtful on this point, check the records maintained by the Financial

Services Authority (FSA) concerning public complaints against financial advisers. Of course, one or two complaints aren't necessarily fatal, but a pattern of many complaints, or a history of charges that involve deception or incompetence, spell bad news.

☐ **What licences do you have? What professional organisations do you belong to?**

Financial advisers may belong to any of several reputable professional organisations. If in doubt, you can call to check the claimed credentials:

- The Association of Private Client Investment Managers & Stockbrokers (APCIMS). Tel: 020-7247-7080.

- The Association of Solicitor Investment Managers (ASIM), which lists solicitors' firms that provide legal and financial advice. Tel: 01892-870065.

- The Ethical Investment Research Service (EIRIS), which lists firms that specialise in ethical investments. Tel: 020-7840-5700.

- Institute of Financial Planning, which lists fee-based financial planners. Tel: 0117-9345-2470.

Call the FSA Register (0845-606-1234) if you're in any doubt as to the authenticity of an adviser's professional credentials. An unauthorised financial adviser may be committing fraud and violating the law. And if you lose money when doing business with an unauthorised adviser, you may find that you will be unable to recover your losses—a risk that is much less with a properly regulated and registered adviser.

☐ **How would my assets be held—by me, or by some other party? If the latter, how are they authorised to hold client money? What form of insurance do they have?**

You want to be certain that your shares, bonds, and other assets will be held by a responsible organisation and that their value is fully insured against loss due to the failure of the organisation.

☐ **Are you the person I will deal with on a day-to-day basis? Can I call you on the phone with questions or concerns? How often?**

Surprisingly, some advisers don't like to provide this kind of service. They seem to feel that talking with clients is a nuisance. This is a bad sign. Remember, it's your money. And if you don't know what's being done with it or why, trouble is apt to follow.

☐ **How frequently do you provide written reports to your clients? May I see a sample?**

You should receive written reports about the performance of your investments at least quarterly, preferably monthly. The sample report should be clear and easily understandable, and the adviser should be willing to explain anything on the report that is less than obvious. If the adviser shares a real client report with you, notice whether the name and identity of the client are shielded. They should be, for privacy's sake.

ASK A HYPOTHETICAL QUESTION

Here's an approach I like to follow when screening a new investment adviser. I first think about how much I might like to invest with the new adviser, based on the amount of assets I currently have in reserve. Then I give the adviser two scenarios: 'If I gave you X pounds per year to invest on my behalf, what might you do with it? And if I gave you Y pounds per year (citing a significantly larger portion of my portfolio), what might you do with it?' And I ask for the answers in writing. If the potential adviser is reluctant to provide *written* responses, that alone would make me uncomfortable.

What's the point of asking this hypothetical, two-part question? First I want to see if there's a difference between the two plans, depending on the amount of the money to be invested. Or does the broker use a formulaic approach that applies willy-nilly to everyone. And secondly I want to see how it fits into my overall financial goals.

THE QUESTIONS YOU SHOULD EXPECT TO ANSWER

Of course, the adviser must get to know you in order to provide truly customised advice. A reputable adviser will want to spend time during an initial meeting learning about your background, interests, financial knowledge, investment experience, risk tolerance, objectives, and preferences. Below, we've provided a list of the questions an adviser ought to ask you. If these topics are never broached in your first conversation with an adviser, it may be a warning sign.

SIX QUESTIONS A FINANCIAL ADVISER SHOULD ASK *YOU*

1. What are your long-term financial goals?
2. What is your tolerance for risk?
3. What are your personal assets and liabilities?
4. Have you bought shares before? If you have, what shares did you buy? How well did they perform for you?
5. What is your investment time horizon?
6. How often do you want to be involved in making your investment decisions? [The right answer is *always*.]

You should feel that the adviser has asked you for enough information to truly understand your financial circumstances. Only in this way can the adviser offer guidance that is personalised and appropriate for your needs and goals.

Maintaining a good relationship with your adviser

Once you've chosen a financial adviser, expect to invest some time and effort in making the relationship productive. Remember, you're in the front seat, helping to steer the car, not snoozing in the back. Your chance of maintaining a successful and happy relationship with your adviser will be much greater if you:

- Keep complete, accurate records of your transactions. Start a file in which you store all your financial paperwork and keep it up to date. Be prepared to review the decisions you've made and to evaluate their success or failure. This is crucial if you hope to learn from your successes and failures and gradually sharpen your financial acumen.

- Make notes of your conversations with your adviser. Be sure you capture your adviser's suggestions, advice, and warnings accurately. Otherwise, you can never be certain whether your investment gains (or losses) are occurring because of your adviser's help or in spite of it.

- Keep your adviser fully informed about your financial status, goals, needs, and wishes. Let him know how you're feeling about your money and the markets. And speak up when your objectives, your risk tolerance, or your interests change.

- Keep yourself generally informed about financial and economic trends. Read the business news, and discuss with your adviser how the latest developments may affect your personal investments and financial plans.

- Ask questions. Make sure you understand the risks and costs before you agree to any investment or other financial plan. If your adviser insists on using technical jargon and can't or won't translate it into plain, understandable English, consider changing advisers.

For his part, your adviser should always:

- Explain both the risks and the potential benefits from any financial strategy he is proposing. Remember, no investment is risk-free. Run away from any adviser who claims to offer one that is.

- Be able and willing to explain the commissions, fees, and other expenses associated with a proposed investment. Insist on clear answers, not vague ones.

- Explain how and why a proposed investment or other strategy is suitable for *your* financial goals, risk tolerance, and other personal characteristics. A one-size-fits-all approach is *never* the best.

- Tell you how long you have to change your

mind once you've signed up for an investment. Many financial products—not all!—are required to provide a cooling-off period during which a new investor may cancel and receive a full refund.

- Provide regular written reports showing the current performance of your investments as well as any investment transactions from the most recent time period. If you have any difficulty understanding every detail on these reports, he should be willing and able to explain them to you in plain English.

However, for a happy financial relationship, you *shouldn't* expect a financial adviser to:

- Make investment decisions for you, unless you specifically authorise and ask him to do so. (And as I've suggested, this is generally *not* a good idea.)

- Assume investment risk on your behalf. If the adviser informs you appropriately about the risks involved in any investment decision, then any losses you suffer as a result of those risks are simply part of the price of being an investor, not something you can blame on the adviser or expect him to repay.

- Be responsible for your making decisions that are ill-advised or inappropriate. If you insist on choosing a particular investment or strategy despite receiving reasonable notice about its disadvantages from your adviser, then you alone are to blame for the consequences.

- Remember and consider every aspect of your personal financial situation when making a financial recommendation. Be prepared, if necessary, to remind your adviser of any relevant data about yourself: 'Are you sure I ought to be moving a lot of money out of cash right now? Remember my daughter is starting university next autumn and there will be big tuition bills to pay . . .'

- Hold your hand or play psychiatrist during market swings. Managing money can be emotionally trying. If you find yourself becoming unduly anxious, fearful, confused, or angry when your investments shift, don't take out your moods on your financial adviser. Instead, consider moving your money into less risky vehicles.

WHAT IF A DISPUTE ARISES?

If you feel that your financial adviser has been giving you poor advice, neglecting you, misleading you, or even lying to you, start by bringing your complaint directly to him in writing. (Too many people register their complaints by phone call with no written follow-up. They rarely have the dispute resolved to their liking.) Be prepared to explain exactly what is troubling you and to suggest an appropriate remedy. If the problem arose from a simple misunderstanding or a minor error, a letter should suffice to correct it.

If not, you can move up the chain of command within the company that employs your adviser (unless, of course, he runs a one-person shop). Most financial service companies have well-established procedures for handling client complaints, and if your unhappiness is well grounded the firm may be willing to waive fees or reimburse small losses in order to keep you as a customer.

If you're still not satisfied with how your complaint is resolved, take it to the relevant independent complaint organisation. This will vary depending on the kind of adviser you have. Ask the adviser himself or his supervisor for the name and number of the appropriate body, or call the Financial Services Authority (FSA) for help. You may want to request the FSA's booklet *Guide to Making a Complaint*, available by phoning 0800-917-3311.

Going it alone

Some independent souls like the idea of making all their own investment decisions. If you're in that category, this section is for you. It explains two kinds of resources that many independent investors like to take advantage of: online brokers and investment clubs.

ONLINE BROKERAGE FIRMS

As I explained earlier, different types of brokers offer different levels of service and charge differing fees. Today the lowest fees are offered by the growing number of online brokerage firms, companies that handle buy-and-sell investment transactions using the Internet to save both time and money. Online brokers that are well-known and active in the UK include such firms as Comdirect, TD Waterhouse, Halifax, Selftrade, and iDealing.com.

For the do-it-yourself investor, the online broker can be a smart and economical choice. Not only are the commissions lower, but you can invest from your home or office computer any time of the day or night. (Of course, if you submit a trade during hours when the Stock Exchange is closed, the transaction will actually take place when the market opens the next morning.)

INVESTMENT CLUBS

A growing number of individual investors enjoy pooling their investment information and a portion of their financial resources with other investors in an investment club.

An investment club usually has between ten and twenty members. They may be friends, family members, neighbours, business colleagues, or simply people with a mutual interest in profitable investing. The club members meet regularly—usually once a month—to make decisions about a shared portfolio of investments. Generally the members take turns researching companies whose shares are being considered. At each meeting, one or more members will present findings about a company and a recommendation as to whether or not to invest. The final decision is based on a vote from members of the club. Other members may be assigned to track and report on economic or business trends, to read and present insights from classic books on investing, or to arrange for expert guests to speak before the club. These varied activities help make the investment club a social and educational enterprise as well as a financial one.

Each member of the club is expected to pay in a fixed amount each month to help build the investment kitty. This amount may range from as little as £20 to £100 or more. The ownership of the investment portfolio is shared by the members, along with the profits (or losses) the portfolio yields. Of course, the club uses a broker to handle investment transactions and to manage record-keeping for the portfolio.

362

Many people swear by the investment club idea. It's a fine way to learn more about share investing, since it 'forces' you to read regularly about shares and discuss their strengths and weaknesses with a bunch of like-minded friends. The investment club also helps broaden its members' financial perspective. As a club member, you may get to hear a report on retailing shares by a fellow member whose wife manages a department store, or an analysis of computer software companies by a member who works in that industry.

Furthermore, a well-managed investment club can be a lot of fun. Clubs meet in members' homes or in pubs or restaurants, and refreshments or a meal make a regular part of most meetings. Profitable investment clubs sometimes sponsor parties and outings to celebrate their successes.

The investment club movement is a worldwide phenomenon that is growing quickly in the UK. Between 1995 and 2001 the number of British investment clubs rose from around 300 to over 10,000. The UK movement is supported by ProShare, a not-for-profit organisation funded by the London Stock Exchange. It provides many kinds of information and guidance about all aspects of investment clubs, from setting up a club to conducting meetings to dissolving a club. If you're intrigued by the idea of joining or starting an investment club, visit ProShare's website at www.proshare.org.

12

ONE HOUR A WEEK

Creating and maintaining your personal money plan

If you've followed all the recommendations in this book, you can now say—perhaps for the first time in your life—that you are truly in charge of your money and the fundamental aspects of your financial world.

You know where it comes from and where it goes.

You are in control of how it is being spent, saved, and invested.

You have financial goals, both short-term and long-term, and you have realistic plans for achieving them.

Congratulations! You are far ahead of most people of *any* age or class or background. In fact, there are plenty of 'trustifarians' and nouveaux riches who need to learn how their money works, just as you've done.

This final chapter focuses on what you need to do to keep your finances flourishing for years to come. The hardest part is completed, the clearing and planting of your money garden. Now it's a question of doing what it takes to maintain its healthy growth. For most people, this is a matter of one hour a week or less—no more than you probably spend on your hair, your car, or your pet, and certainly more important and more rewarding than all three.

For convenience, we've broken down the subject into four categories: what you need to do weekly, monthly, quarterly, and annually. For each, we've provided a handy checklist of activities. You might want to copy these checklists and insert them in the proper pages in your personal activities diary or any other location where you'll be sure to spot them at the right times.

Once a week

TRACKING YOUR CASH FLOW

Have a single place at home where you put all your purchase receipts, charge slips, and cash withdrawal tickets every evening. It could be any convenient place, just so long as it's *one* place rather than a collection of random nooks and crannies throughout your home. Once a week, grab the stack of slips and add them up. Monitor the totals for each type of spending—food, entertainment, and so on—against your budgeted figures.

It doesn't matter much when you do this chore, so long as you do it consistently, the same time every week. Otherwise you're apt to put it off, and as the pile of receipts grows, the task will become so daunting that you start to avoid it and eventually forget about it altogether. Pick a time that feels right to you. I like to handle this task on Friday night while sipping a glass of Chardonnay. My co-author Karl saves it for Saturday morning. He says that getting a grip on his finances before tackling the weekly shopping at the supermarket and the mall helps him keep his cravings—and his wife's—in perspective, and in check.

This exercise forces you to relive the week from a financial point of view. Sometimes this is an unpleasant exercise, sometimes a delightful one—but it's always eye-opening. You see your own impulses at work, and you recognise the things you bought that you didn't need and perhaps didn't even really want. By matching your spending to the categories we used back in chapter one, you can see when you're saving in one area and when you're over-spending in another.

Doing this exercise weekly gives you a chance to remedy any financial troubles before they get out of hand. If you over-spent one week, you know you have to cut back the following week. This saves you from the horror of an out-of-control credit card bill or excessive use of your bank overdraft.

The weekly budget exercise can also be a way of augmenting your regular savings plan. Every time you come in under budget for a particular category for the week, move that money into savings. For example, suppose you have budgeted £120 per month for entertainment. That amounts to about £30 per week. If one week you spend only £14 on entertainment (maybe there were no good shows at the cinema last week), deposit the difference in the bank. Then you get to say, 'Oh, I saved £16 this week!' and feel pleased with yourself . . . but not so pleased that you waste the money on something else!

PAYING YOUR BILLS

The other weekly exercise is bill-paying. Why weekly? Because if you're like most people, you have a host of expenses, most often payable monthly, that come due at different times during the month: mortgage due the 1st, car loan due the 5th, phone bill due the 14th, and so on.

Here's a simple way to make sure you never lose track of what's due when. Keep all your outstanding bills in the same place. It doesn't matter where—a basket in the kitchen, a cubbyhole in your desk, a corner of your dresser drawer. As they arrive in the mail, open them and stack them in the order of their due dates. Then simply pull out the stack once a week and pay the ones that come due during the next seven days. Of course, if you know you're going to be on holiday or otherwise unavailable beyond that date, pay the next week's bills as well. This easy system will ensure that you never suffer the embarrassment of a dunning notice in the mail or a phone call from an overdue bill collector.

BALANCE YOUR CURRENT ACCOUNT

Yes, I know this is a bore. I hate it too. But it needs to be done, and it only gets worse if you put it off. Done monthly, it takes just a few minutes. Wait six months (for example), and there will inevitably be a tangle of maths errors, unexpected fees and bank charges, forgotten withdrawals and debits, misplaced cheques, and other small mistakes to rectify, which can turn this into a two- or three-hour chore. Furthermore, you'll greatly increase the chances of miscalculating your balance and writing a cheque that goes into overdraft, costing you more money in needless bank fees.

Balancing your statement is like brushing your teeth, exercising regularly, or any other beneficial habit: once you've done it half a dozen times, you'll find it easy to do, and you may even wonder, 'Why did I ever make a fuss about this?'

OTHER MONTHLY CHORES

Also once a month, pay your council taxes and any other monthly expenses.

Deposit into your savings account the extra money you've accumulated through wise saving and spending during the month. Of course, this is cash over and above the automatic savings deposits you've arranged through the bank.

Monitor your investments monthly (if curiosity

doesn't drive you to do so more often). Check the latest prices of your unit trusts or shares, and update the records in which you track how much your accounts are worth. See what business or economic news during the week has affected the value of your investments, and consider whether upcoming events are likely to drive prices higher or lower.

If any individual investment has grown a lot, consider capturing some of those gains by selling a portion of your holdings and letting the rest of your profits run.

If you are self-employed, set aside money for taxes monthly. Keep these funds in a specially dedicated savings account. And yes, make the deposits monthly, even though you only have to pay the taxes once a year. If you wait to find the money until the payments are due, the chances are good that you *won't* find it—or may end up working for months just for Inland Revenue. And really, which is easier: to save regularly for taxes, or to end up bitter and twisted over your own negligence?

Once a quarter

YOUR MORTGAGE CHECK-UP

This is a financial exercise that's a little like the regularly scheduled maintenance that gets done on your car. If you have an endowment mortgage, check the value of the endowment. Remember, this is the investment portion of the mortgage, which in theory is supposed to grow enough to pay off the balance due at the end of the mortgage term. If the endowment isn't growing fast enough, consider changing to a repayment mortgage (if possible) or making an extra contribution to the endowment.

Mortgage-holders should also take a look at current interest rates. How much have they risen or fallen since you first signed on for your mortgage? If they've fallen significantly, consider refinancing your mortgage at the new, lower rates if that option is available to you.

SCRUTINISE YOUR SAVINGS AND INVESTMENTS

Next, check the growth of your pensions and other retirement investments. Are they proceeding in line with your goals? If not, consider upping the amount you invest every month. Even an extra £10 or £20 can make a substantial difference when it's allowed to accumulate over time.

Also check whether you are saving enough for your children's education—basic school fees, college and university—and whether these invested funds are growing appropriately. Again, if the answer is No, the remedy is the same: begin to put away a little more each month.

If you happen to receive quarterly bonus cheques from your employer (as some people do), consider tucking these away in savings rather than spending them. Because this 'found money' isn't part of your regular budget, you'll never miss it.

LOOK OVER YOUR WARDROBE

Once a quarter is also a good time to plan your clothing purchases for the coming season. Survey your wardrobe and that of the kids, and decide what you really need for the next few months, whether it's for school, for work, or for play. *Planning* these purchases and budgeting for them will help you buy what you really need and want (and can afford) rather than simply snapping up whatever's on sale.

Once a year

YOUR ANNUAL FINANCIAL MAINTENANCE

For many people, it feels natural to perform their once-a-year financial check-up in late December or early January, right around the new year holiday. With so many year-end retrospective shows on the telly and stories in the newspapers, it's easy to get into the spirit of looking back and looking forward in hopes of making next year even better than last year.

On the other hand, if you find the holidays too hectic or too festive, any other time of year can work equally well. As I've mentioned, I like to do a personal financial check-up around my birthday in June. Other people like to time their annual check-up to coincide with spring cleaning or with the autumnal beginning of the school year. The important thing is to pick a date when you have a bit of time to spare and will *not* be tempted to blow off the exercise.

In any case, here are the items to consider in your annual financial check-up.

371

BOOSTING YOUR SAVING

Many people get a pay rise annually. Remember that one excellent way to start or accelerate a savings programme is to dedicate this rise entirely to savings. If this is a bit tough for you (or if you're already doing reasonably well when it comes to saving), consider this half-measure: split your rise, putting half into savings and allowing yourself to spend the other half. Also consider the same sort of fifty-fifty arrangement with any annual bonus you may receive.

PLAN MAJOR SPENDING

Once a year is a good time to plan your major spending for the coming year. This includes appliance and furniture purchases, a new (or used) car, house repairs and major home maintenance, large charitable donations, and holiday travel. Sit down with your spouse or other partner and make a plan that fits your shared priorities. Consider including your kids if they're old enough. Making such plans together provides a great opportunity to talk through your differing goals for the year ahead and to work out compromises that will leave you all reasonably satisfied: 'Well, if we *must* spend our summer holiday with your sister in Cornwall, then what about letting me trade in our nine-year-old car for a newer model?'

REBALANCE YOUR INVESTMENTS

Once a year, re-examine your investment portfolio and rebalance it as needed to maintain the proper asset allocation mix. (I described the process in chapter seven.)

Finally, look back over the *past* year and review what's changed in your life. Have you added a child (or children) via birth or adoption? Have you got married or divorced? Have you changed jobs, started a business, or retired? These and other lifestyle changes may call for alterations in your spending budget, your insurance coverages, your will(s), and your estate plans. Update them as needed.

CHECKLISTS FOR KEEPING YOUR FINANCIAL HOUSE IN ORDER

ONCE A WEEK

☐ Add up your expenses for the week by category. Compare them with your monthly budget. If you have overspent in any category, cut back during the following week. If you have saved in any category, consider banking the difference.

☐ Pay off all bills that come due in the week ahead.

ONCE A MONTH

☐ Balance your current account statement.

☐ Pay your council taxes and other monthly expenses.

☐ Deposit into your savings account the extra money you've accumulated.

☐ Monitor your investments.

☐ If you are self-employed, set aside money for taxes.

ONCE A QUARTER

☐ Do a 'mortgage check-up'. If you have an endowment mortgage, check the value of the endowment. Make sure it's growing quickly enough to pay off the balance due at the end of the mortgage term.

- ☐ Compare current interest rates to those you're paying on your mortgage. If they've fallen significantly, consider refinancing.
- ☐ Check the growth of your pensions and other retirement investments.
- ☐ Also check whether you are saving enough for your children's education—basic school fees, college, and university—and whether these invested funds are growing quickly enough.
- ☐ Plan and budget your clothing purchases for the coming season.

ONCE A YEAR

- ☐ Dedicate half or all of your annual pay rise to savings.
- ☐ Do the same with your annual bonus payment.
- ☐ Plan your major spending for the entire coming year: appliance and furniture purchases, a new (or used) car, house repairs and major maintenance, charitable donations, and holidays.
- ☐ Re-examine your investment portfolio and rebalance it as needed to maintain the proper asset allocation mix.
- ☐ Review what's changed in your life and update your spending budget, your insurance coverages, your will(s), and your estate plans as needed.

Living your new financial life each and every day

The real key to managing your money day in and day out is to keep your financial plan simple and comfortable. Your new life shouldn't feel constrained and restrictive. If you're earning a reasonable amount of money but find that you still feel financially trapped, there are three possible explanations.

One is that you may have fallen prey to an exaggerated sense of entitlement. I meet so many people who explain their excessive spending by saying, 'I work hard. Don't I *deserve* this kind of lifestyle?' If this sounds familiar, reconsider your attitude. The ability to buy things isn't a matter of what you 'deserve'. It's a matter of making choices that will benefit you in the long run. If you insist on having everything you think you deserve today, you're likely to find you lack even the basic things you *need* tomorrow.

A second possible problem is that you may attach too much importance to money or to material things. If you find that you are unable to stop obsessing over owning certain possessions, taking part in certain activities (especially shopping), or enjoying other rewards that you associate with happiness, love, or 'the good life', then take steps to figure out *why* and to learn how to control the problem. For some people, a time of self-reflection, conversations with loved ones, writing a journal, or meditation may go a long way towards helping you gain insight into the problem. For a few, counselling with a professional may be needed.

If money (or the lack of money) has become a huge obstacle to happiness for you, take whatever steps are necessary to overcome it. Remember that there are no quick, painless, magical solutions. And certainly if you are ruining your life or the lives of people you love through over-spending, debt addiction, a gambling habit, speculating on get-rich-quick schemes, or other financial illnesses, find a way to stop before you go completely over the edge.

Finally, it's also possible that you've established a money regimen that is simply a little too strict, a little too joyless. No one should be expected to live without a few well-chosen indulgences. But notice the two adjectives I've used: 'few' and 'well-chosen'! Build into your money plan an occasional reward for perseverance. For every month that you keep your spending within budget, treat yourself to a dinner out or something else that gives you real pleasure: a new pair of shoes, a round of golf, a couple of CDs. For every six months that you save according to budget, give yourself a weekend in the country or something comparable.

But remember, you get the rewards *only* if you stick to the plan (or do better)! If you bend the rules and reward yourself for 'coming close' or 'trying really hard', you are undermining your own effort to build a new set of good habits.

In addition, look for regular ways of treating yourself (and those you love) that *don't* involve spending money. There are dozens of life-enriching activities that cost little or nothing to enjoy. Why don't we think about them more often? That's easy: it's because such low-cost pleasures are rarely promoted on television, on radio, and in advertising. After all, when something is free there's little profit to be made from it, so no one has the incentive to push it.

So in a world where 'growing the economy' is a mandate for every politician as well as every business leader, the incentives for spending more and more on every possible activity are enormous. And it's all too easy to follow the crowd rather than using a bit of imagination to find our own ways of enjoying life.

Aldous Huxley's classic novel *Brave New World* is a horrific vision of life in a mindless, ultra-consumerised twenty-first century. In his imagined new world the government has imposed one simple rule for any new sport or amusement: it *must* require more, and more costly, equipment than the *most* complicated existing sport! Have we moved into Huxley's brave new world without realising it?

If you're ready to fight back against the trend of spending for spending's sake, consider rewarding yourself and your loved ones, not by spending money, but by enjoying such free or low-cost activities as:

- Playing a sport with a group of mates in the park.

- Enjoying a picnic in a nature spot you've always wanted to visit.

- Taking a drive in the country.

- Touring your local art or history museum.

- Going bird-watching or nature-walking.

- Trying your hand at drawing, painting, or photography.

- Reading poetry—and maybe writing your own.

- Attending free local talks, lectures, or concerts.

- Joining (or forming) a local singing, acting, or dancing group.

- Joining (or forming) a book club.

- Teaching yourself to cook a true gourmet dish.

- Flying a kite.

- Starting a collection.

- Tutoring local youngsters.

- Taking up a new sport.

- Learning a new language.

- Reading about a country you've dreamed of visiting.

- Volunteering to help at a service organisation.

- Making love.

I've found that the key to financial happiness isn't how much money you have—it's using the money you have in ways that bring lasting enjoyment.

Finally, get into the habit of talking every day with your partner or your family, not only about money matters but about everything that is really important to you. If you do this during the usual ups and downs of life and of a relationship, there will be a solid foundation for communication and problem-solving when things are tough. This can be a relationship-saving practice—and sometimes even a life-saving one.

✠ *Alvin says . . .*

I find that two kinds of people tend to fall into the worst financial traps: those who refuse to think about money at all, and those who think about nothing else. Give money its due. It has a major impact on your life, and it deserves to be treated with respect, consideration, and thought. But keep money in its place. The money you earn, spend, save, and invest should serve you and your life, not the other way round. If you keep money squarely in the context of what matters most to you—the people, activities and places you most deeply love—then you'll never have to choose between your money and your life. Instead, you'll be able to enjoy them both fully!